Care, Migration and Human Rights

The continuum of exploitation that has historically defined the everyday of domestic work – exclusion from employment and social security standards and precarious migration status – has frequently been neglected. It is primarily the moments of crisis, incidents of human trafficking, slavery or forced labour, that have captured the attention of human rights law. Only recently has human rights law begun to address the structured inequalities and exclusions that define the domain of domestic work.

This book addresses the specific position of domestic workers in the context of evolving human rights norms. Drawing upon a broad range of case studies, this book presents a thorough examination of key issues such as the commodification of care, the impact of the jurisprudence of the Court of Justice of the European Union and the European Court of Human Rights on 'primary care providers', as well as the effect that trends in migration law have on migrant domestic workers.

This volume will be of interest to lawyers, academics and policy makers in the fields of human rights, migration and gender studies.

Siobhán Mullally is Professor of Law and Director of the Centre for Criminal Justice and Human Rights at University College Cork, Ireland.

Routledge Research in Human Rights Law

Available titles in this series include:

The Right to Development in International Law
The Case of Pakistan
Khurshid Iqbal

Global Health and Human Rights
Legal and Philosophical Perspectives
John Harrington and Maria Stuttaford

The Right to Religious Freedom in International Law
Between group rights and individual rights
Anat Scolnicov

Emerging Areas of Human Rights in the 21st Century
The role of the Universal Declaration of Human Rights
Marco Odello and Sofia Cavandoli

The Human Right to Water and its Application in the Occupied Palestinian Territories
Amanda Cahill

International Human Rights Law and Domestic Violence
The effectiveness of international human rights law
Ronagh McQuigg

Human Rights in the Asia-Pacific Region
Towards Institution Building
Hitoshi Nasu and Ben Saul

Human Rights Monitoring Mechanisms of the Council of Europe
Gauthier de Beco

The Positive Obligations of the State under the European Convention of Human Rights
Dimitris Xenos

Vindicating Socio-Economic Rights
International Standards and Comparative Experiences
Paul O'Connell

The EU as a 'Global Player' in Human Rights?
Jan Wetzel

Regulating Corporate Human Rights Violations
Humanizing Business
Surya Deva

The UN Committee on Economic, Social and Cultural Rights
The Law, Process and Practice
Marco Odello and Francesco Seatzu

State Security Regimes and the Right to Freedom of Religion and Belief
Changes in Europe Since 2001
Karen Murphy

The European Court of Human Rights in the Post-Cold War Era
Universality in Transition
James A. Sweeney

The United Nations Human Rights Council
A Critique and Early Assessment
Rosa Freedman

Children and International Human Rights Law
The Right of the Child to be Heard
Aisling Parkes

Litigating Transnational Human Rights Obligations
Alternative Judgements
Mark Gibney and Wouter Vandenhole

Reproductive Freedom, Torture and International Human Rights
Challenging the Masculinisation of Torture
Ronli Noa Sifris

Applying an International Human Rights Framework to State Budget Allocations
Rights and Resources
Rory O'Connell, Aoife Nolan, Colin Harvey, Mira Dutschke and Eoin Rooney

Human Rights Law in Europe
The Influence, Overlaps and Contradictions of the EU and the ECHR
Kanstantsin Dzehtsiarou, Tobias Lock, Theodore Konstadinides and Noreen O'Meara

Nomadic Peoples and Human Rights
Jérémie Gilbert

Children's Lives in an Era of Children's Rights
The Progress of the Convention on the Rights of the Child in Africa
Afua Twum-Danso Imoh & Nicola Ansell

China's Human Rights Lawyers
Advocacy and Resistance
Eva Pils

The Right to Equality in European Human Rights Law
The Quest for Substance in the Jurisprudence of the European Courts
Charilaos Nikolaidis

Care, Migration and Human Rights
Law and Practice
Siobhán Mullally

Forthcoming titles in this series include:

Jurisdiction, Immunity and Transnational Human Rights Litigation
Xiaodong Yang

Business and Human Rights in South East Asia
Risk and Regulatory Turn
Mahdev Mohan & Cynthia Morel

Extraterritoriality and International Human Rights Law
The Spatial Reach of African Human Rights Treaties
Takele Soboka Bulto

Human Rights Law and Personal Identity
Jill Marshall

In Pursuit of Human Rights
NGOs, Pedagogy and Praxis in Grassroots Africa
Joanne Coysh

Indigenous Peoples, Title to Territory, Rights and Resources
The Transformative Role of Free Prior and Informed Consent
Cathal M. Doyle

The Law and Practice of the European Social Committee
Francesco Seatzu & Amaya Ubeda de Torres

Reconciling Cultural Diversity and International Human Rights Obligations
The Compatibility Approach in the Practice of International Human Rights Institutions
Michael K. Addo

Social and Economic Rights in Theory and Practice
A Critical Assessment
Helena Alviar Garcia, Karl Klare & Lucy A. Williams

The Human Rights Approach to Disability
Cases and Materials
Andreas Dimopoulos

Socio-Economic Rights in Emerging Free Markets
Comparative Insights from India and China
Surya Deva

Challenging Territoriality in Human Rights Law
Foundational Principles for a Multi Duty-Bearer Human Rights Regime
Wouter Vandenhole

Capturing Caste in Law
The Legal Regulation of Caste Discrimination
Annapurna Waughray

Care, Migration and Human Rights

Law and Practice

Edited by
Siobhán Mullally

Routledge
Taylor & Francis Group
LONDON AND NEW YORK

First published 2015
by Routledge
2 Park Square, Milton Park, Abingdon, Oxfordshire OX14 4RN

and by Routledge
711 Third Avenue, New York, NY 10017

First issued in paperback 2016

Routledge is an imprint of the Taylor & Francis Group, an informa business

British Library Cataloguing in Publication Data
A catalogue record for this book is available from the British Library

Library of Congress Cataloging-in-Publication Data
Care, migration, and human rights : law and practice / edited by Siobhán Mullally.
pages cm. – (Routledge research in human rights)
Includes index.
ISBN 978-1-138-79286-9 (hardback) – ISBN 978-1-315-76172-5 (ebk) 1. Household employees–Legal status, laws, etc. 2. Migrant labor–Legal status, laws, etc. 3. Household employees–Abuse of. 4. Migrant labor–Abuse of. 5. Human rights. I. Mullally, Siobhán.
K1841.H6C37 2015
344.01'544–dc23
2014030087

ISBN: 978-1-138-70184-7 (pbk)

ISBN: 978-1-138-79286-9 (hbk)

Typeset in 10/12 Sabon by
Servis Filmsetting Ltd, Stockport Cheshire

For Pat and my beautiful daughter Bríona

Contents

List of Contributors

Nicole Constable is Professor, Director, Asian Studies Center, University of Pittsburgh.

Siobhán Mullally is Professor of Law, Director, Centre for Criminal Justice and Human Rights, University College Cork.

Clíodhna Murphy is Lecturer, School of Law and Government, Maynooth University.

Ayesha Shahid is Lecturer, School of Law, Brunel University.

Gulnara Shahinian is Former UN Special Rapporteur on Slavery: Its Causes and Consequences (2008–2014).

Fulvia Staiano is PhD candidate, Department of Law, European University Institute, Florence.

Ann Stewart is Professor, School of Law, Warwick University.

1 Introduction

Decent Work, Domestic Work: Gendered Borders and Limits

Siobhán Mullally

Placing domestic work onto the human rights agenda has the potential to significantly challenge norms and practices on market restructuring, employment practices and, of course, immigration laws. It also raises the challenge of moving beyond individualised remedies for domestic workers, to greater scrutiny of care policies and the processes of social reproduction. As yet, it is a challenge that human rights law has not met.[1] As the return to questions of care, solidarity and social reproduction reveals, however, a question also arises as to whether the tools of human rights law, or the concept of rights itself, can adequately respond to the claims to justice and to decent work standards brought by migrant domestic workers (MDWs).

This book brings together a collection of essays that examine the limits and potential of law to vindicate the rights claims of MDWs. Drawing on the insights of leading socio-legal scholars and practitioners from several jurisdictions, it highlights the reforms introduced in recent years in response to human rights and labour rights advocacy, but also points to the continuing obstacles to reform and to the precarious, contingent nature of progressive legal change. The intersections of gender, 'race', class and migration status, as overlapping axes of discrimination, are to the fore in the analyses presented here of law's often troubled engagement with concepts of care (Chapter 3 in this volume), and in the gaps both in the letter of the laws applicable to MDWs and in the limited enforcement of such laws (Chapters 6, 7, 8).

The question explored in this book is whether the process of enacting rights is a meaningful one.[2] That is, does it hold out the potential to secure legal and policy reforms that make the world a better place to live in for MDWs (to paraphrase Hannah Arendt),[3] including, at a minimum, decent

* This research work was supported by an Irish Research Council Senior Fellowship award.

1 See, generally, Fiona Williams, 'Migration and Care: Themes, Concepts and Challenges' (2010) 9(3) *Social Policy & Society* 385; Eleonore Kofman, 'Rethinking Care through Social Reproduction: Articulating Circuits of Migration' (2012) 19(1) *Social Politics* 142.

2 Drawing on Jacques Rancière, 'Who Is the Subject of the Rights of Man?' (2004) 103(2/3) *South Atlantic Quarterly* 297–310.

3 Hannah Arendt, *Denktagebuch: 1950 bis 1973*, eds Ursula Ludz and Ingeborg Nordmann (Munich: Piper, 2002) p.105.

work standards? Or is the process of enacting rights misguided, likely only to reinforce an ideology of rights that denies the practical significance of intersecting axes of migration status, gender, 'race' and poverty?[4] Those who decry the 'crisis of legalism' in human rights argue that the legal process is shielded from both the dynamism and the unpredictability of political dialogue.[5] The process of moral and political learning necessary for any vibrant democratic society is stifled, it is argued, by legal manoeuvres. 'The laws,' as Benhabib reminds us, 'are the walls of the city, but the art and passion of politics occur within those walls.'[6] When human rights discourse and politics become confined to the pursuit of effective remedies, then it might be argued that the battle has been lost.[7] On this reading, a 'crisis of legalism' is constraining the revolutionary potential of human rights movements[8] and the cold jealous virtue of justice is proving 'too cold', (to paraphrase David Hume). Engagement with law, it is argued, creates 'only the most marginal opportunities for engaged political contestation',[9] with rights discourse keeping pressing social problems at arm's length, not only distorting the parameters of debate, but also reducing the transformative potential of political movements for reform.[10] However, while the 'protective distance' that rights discourse can provide may seem 'abstract and alienated' to some, for others it can be a welcome reprieve from ties that bind, or from pervasive societal discrimination, scrutiny and complicity/culpability.[11] Such a reprieve may be particularly important in the context of gendered expectations of the inevitable 'lot' of domestic workers.

Despite pessimism as to the impact of human rights law and the proliferation of human rights instruments, activists continue to frame their demands for change in the language and practice of rights. The significance of this collective organising to secure legal reforms cannot be overlooked. According to International Labour Organisation (ILO) statistics, at least 52.6 million women and men over the age of 15 are engaged in domestic work as their main occupation. Women comprise 83 per cent of the total domestic workers worldwide.[12] Due to the largely unregulated and

4 See Catherine Dauvergne and Sarah Marsden, 'The Ideology of Temporary Labour Migration in the Post-Global Era' (2014) 18(2) *Citizenship Studies* 224–242.

5 See Conor Gearty, *Can Human Rights Survive?* (Cambridge: Cambridge University Press, 2006), pp. 60–98.

6 Seyla Benhabib, *The Claims of Culture: Equality and Diversity in the Global Era* (Princeton, NJ: Princeton University Press, 2002), p. 130.

7 Illan rua Wall, *Human Rights and Constituent Power: Without Model or Warranty* (New York: Routledge, 2012), pp. 1–4.

8 See Gearty (2006) *supra* n.5, pp. 60–98.

9 D Kennedy, *Of War and Law* (Princeton, NJ: Princeton University Press, 2006), p. 25.

10 See, generally, Frances Olsen, 'Statutory Rape: A Feminist Critique of Rights Analysis' (1984) 63(3) *Texas Law Review* 387.

11 P Williams, 'Alchemical Notes: Reconstructing Ideals from Deconstructed Rights' (1987) 22(2) *Harvard Civil Rights – Civil Liberties Law Review* 401, at 409.

12 International Labour Organisation, *Domestic Work Policy Brief 5: Coverage of domestic*

hidden nature of domestic work, the number of domestic workers may be in the region of 100 million, significantly higher than the ILO figures.[13] The 'decent work deficit' that has characterised domestic work includes low wages, unpredictable working hours, limited access to social security and an ambiguous employment status.[14] More extreme types of exploitation and abuse to which domestic workers may be subjected include forced labour, human trafficking and other forms of gender-based violence.

The United Nations (UN) Committee on the Elimination of All Forms of Discrimination Against Women (CEDAW) has noted that 'gendered notions of appropriate work for women' lead to job opportunities that reflect the traditional 'familial and service functions ascribed to women', and are concentrated in the informal sector of precarious work, in particular, domestic work.[15] Human rights law has somewhat belatedly begun to address the structured inequalities and exclusions that define the domain of domestic work. Recent standard-setting initiatives have attempted to address this gap and have included the adoption of the landmark 2011 ILO Convention Concerning Decent Work for Domestic Workers,[16] a General Recommendation from CEDAW on Women Migrant Workers[17] and a General Comment from the UN Committee on Migrant Workers and their Families on Migrant Domestic Workers.[18] Against the background of this 'justice cascade',[19] however, migration laws continue to limit the transforma-

workers by key working conditions laws, available at www.ilo.org/travail/whatwedo/publications/WCMS_157509/lang--en/index.htm, accessed 27 November 2013 (hereafter ILO Policy Brief 5).

13 Margaret Visser, 'Sweeping Changes? Organising and Bargaining for the Realisation of the Rights of Domestic Workers', Domestic Workers Research Project, Social Law Project, University of the Western Cape 1, available at www.dwrp.org.za/index.php/research/by-title-and-abstract/article/77-sweeping-changes, accessed 16 December 2013.

14 Manuela Tomei, 'Decent Work for Domestic Workers: Reflections on Recent Approaches to Tackle Informality' (2011) 23 *Canadian Journal of Women & Law* 186, at 187. See also Asha Da'Souza, 'Moving Towards Decent Work for Domestic Workers: An Overview of the ILO's Work', Working Paper 2/2010 (Geneva: ILO, 2010), p. 19.

15 Committee for the Elimination of All Forms of Discrimination Against Women, General Recommendation No. 26 on Women Migrant Workers, 5 December 2008, CEDAW/C/2009/WP.1/R (2008) (hereafter, CEDAW Committee General Recommendation on Women Migrant Workers) at para. 13. Within the domestic work sector, gendered divisions can also be found with male workers employed primarily in the more lucrative sectors of gardening, security or driving.

16 ILO, Convention Concerning Decent Work for Domestic Workers (100th session of the International Labour Conference), Geneva, 16 June 2011 (hereafter Convention Concerning Decent Work for Domestic Workers).

17 CEDAW Committee General Recommendation on Women Migrant Workers.

18 UN Committee on the Protection of the Rights of All Migrant Workers and Members of Their Families, General Comment No. 1 on Migrant Domestic Workers, 23 February 2011, CMW/C/GC/1 (2011) (hereafter UN Committee on Migrant Workers, General Comment No. 1).

19 This term is borrowed from Kathryn Sikkink, *The Justice Cascade: How Human Rights Prosecutions Are Changing World Politics* (New York: WW Norton & Co., 2011).

tive promise of human rights law. Although migration status is recognised as adding yet another axis of discrimination to the status of domestic workers, states remain reluctant to acknowledge this role or to remedy the 'dissensus' that arises between 'border norms' and human rights law.[20]

In addition to migration status, there is the wider problem of the gendered division of labour that defines the realm of domestic work, and the continuing absence of state or wider societal supports for such work. Domestic work and the realm of the domestic has been a central concern for feminism and feminist legal theory. As Joan Tronto reminds us, 'Care is not a parochial concern of women, a type of secondary moral question, or the work of the least well off in society.'[21] It is a 'central concern of human life', one that is founded, as Fineman argues, in the inevitable vulnerability of the human condition.[22] Feminist critiques of human rights law and rights discourse have often pointed to its failure to attend to the everyday, and to the relationships of interdependence in which the human self is embedded. The case law of the Court of Justice of the European Union (CJEU) on 'primary care providers' and the effective enjoyment of fundamental rights by dependent European Union (EU) citizens, point to the possible links between care and the discourse of human rights. Yet the recognition of such links comes with limits, reflected in the cautious jurisprudence of the CJEU and the wider limits of the European integration project.

The right to give and to receive care may also be considered as a fundamental element of human dignity, and as central to citizenship as paid labour. Recognising the centrality of care requires fundamentally rethinking the gendered divisions between the public and the private that persist in domestic, European and international law structures. A key question that arises is, if care is recognised as an expression of interpersonal solidarity and valorised in human rights discourse (for example, through the jurisprudence of Article 8 of the European Convention on Human Rights), how might this valorisation progress the claims of care workers – including MDWs – to decent work standards?

The significance of 'race' and class must also be recognised. The demand for MDWs in a context where citizens and/or long-term residents could compete in the market force for such work raises complex issues of 'race', gender and class. As Anderson has noted, the 'racial othering' that takes place in the context of the employment of MDWs presents the gendered, racialised and classed hierarchies of domestic work as the inevitable

20 Linda Bosniak, *The Citizen and the Alien: Dilemmas of Contemporary Membership* (Princeton, NJ: Princeton University Press, 2006).

21 Joan C Tronto, *Moral Boundaries: A Political Argument for an Ethic of Care* (New York: Routledge, 1993), p. 180.

22 See, generally, Martha Fineman, 'The Vulnerable Subject: Anchoring Equality in the Human Condition' (2008) 20(1) *Yale Journal of Law and Feminism* 1.

consequences of differing employment patterns and choices.[23] The angst that might otherwise be felt by employers relying on domestic workers to discharge demanding caring roles is partly displaced by such 'othering' processes. The complex intersections of 'race' and gender are evident in each of the chapters in this collection, manifesting themselves in varying wages and terms and conditions of work for MDWs, and in the prevalence of a paternalistic discourse on migration, underpinning sponsorship mechanisms such as the *kafala* (sponsorship) system in Lebanon.

In the angst and anxieties played out in feminist commentary on domestic work and advocacy for decent work standards, questions remain as to whether domestic work can move beyond its legacies of slavery, exploitation and abuse. Can law reform initiatives and expanding human rights norms produce transformative remedies or is the search for decent work standards misguided? Adelle Blackett and others have pointed to the potential of decent work standards to provide 'an important corrective to abstract articulations (and applications) of rights' that have frequently overlooked the realm of the household.[24] Recent standard-setting developments and evolving human rights jurisprudence on forced labour, slavery and servitude have sought to address the decent work deficit that has characterised domestic work to date. Yet this expansion of rights has been accompanied by a push-back from states and an enactment of limits. The *jurisgenerative* processes of standard setting, evident at the ILO, in the work of UN human rights treaty bodies and in courts, offer some resistance to the sovereigntist impulses of states and the push to permit or accept more precarious working conditions. At the same time, 'de-juridification' processes enacting exemptions and limitations to decent work standards bring into question how transformative the apparent expansion of rights can be.[25]

Advocacy for reform in relation to MDWs' rights has focused on a key demand, that domestic work is recognised as 'real work' – that is, work in relation to which full employment rights and social protections apply, including rights to the minimum wage, sickness and maternity pay as well as pension rights.[26] It is precisely this recognition that has been lacking and that has served to legitimate the continued exclusion of domestic work from core labour and social security standards. For temporary or irregular MDWs, the rights afforded by such standards, even where applicable, are often illusory

23 Bridget Anderson, 'A Very Private Business: Exploring the Demand for Migrant Domestic Workers' (2007) 14(3) *European Journal of Women's Studies* 247.

24 Adelle Blackett, 'Introduction: Regulating Decent Work for Domestic Workers' (2011) 23 *Canadian Journal of Women & Law* 1, at 44, citing Adelle Blackett, 'Situated Reflections on International Labour Law, Capabilities, and Decent Work: The Case of Centre Maraîcher Eugène Guinois' (2007) hors série, *Revue québécoise de droit international* 223, at 242.

25 See Seyla Benhabib, *Dignity in Adversity: Human Rights in Troubled Times* (Cambridge, MA: Polity Press: 2011).

26 See, for example, the *Parliamentary Assembly of the Council of Europe Recommendation 1663* (2004), adopted on 22 June 2004, para. 6 (ii)(a).

in practice.[27] The ILO has argued that the expansion of a decent work framework to the sphere of domestic work would signal a transition from the 'paternalistic conception of the "good employer" acting out of a sense of *noblesse oblige*, to one that is founded on respect for domestic workers' labour rights'.[28] This trajectory, one that has been characterised in other contexts as a movement from 'status to contract', is a familiar one. It is also a progress narrative that is often disputed, however.

This book seeks to explore the limits and potential of international human rights law and domestic law, in vindicating the rights claims of MDWs. The adoption of ILO Convention no. 189 on Decent Work for Domestic Workers followed more than a decade of sustained political activism by domestic workers worldwide, and has rightly been described as a landmark moment in the campaign for decent work standards. Yet the Convention itself offers little to MDWs. The Convention is unusual in human rights law in defining its scope with reference to a particular sector of workers who, in turn, are defined primarily by their place of work – the household. The significance of place for domestic workers is, of course, key to determining whether or not legal protections apply.[29] This reification (and exclusion) of the household was one of the key issues that emerged in debates leading up to the adoption of the Convention. The Convention seeks to extend core labour rights concerning fair terms of employment and decent working conditions to the realm of domestic work. States are required to ensure that domestic workers enjoy equality with other workers regarding working time,[30] entitlements to minimum wage,[31] healthy and safe working conditions[32] and social security protection (including maternity).[33] It also requires states to introduce measures providing for the regulation of employment agencies[34] and for effective and accessible dispute resolution mechanisms for domestic workers.[35] Despite the commitment to addressing disadvantage within the domestic work sector, however, the Convention's scope is deliberately limited.

Allowing for the possibilities of opting out, of excluding certain categories of domestic workers, was a concession to states and to employers' organisations, many of whom were opposed to the proposal to adopt a

27 *Hounga v. Allen* [2012] EWCA Civ 609 and, on appeal, *Hounga (Appellant) v Allen and another (Respondents)* [2014] UKSC 47 (discussed *infra* by Murphy in Chapter 6).

28 ILO, *Decent Work for Domestic Workers, Report IV(1)* (99th session of the International Labour Conference) Geneva, 2010, p. 46 (hereafter ILO Report IV(1)).

29 Convention Concerning Decent Work for Domestic Workers, Article 1(a), which provides that for the purposes of the Convention 'the term "domestic work" means work performed in or for a household or households'.

30 Ibid., Article 10.

31 Ibid., Article 11.

32 Ibid., Article 13.

33 Ibid., Article 14.

34 Ibid., Article 15(a).

35 Ibid., Article 16.

legally binding instrument.[36] This flexibility is found in Article 2 of the Convention, which allows for a sweeping measure of disentitlement with respect to 'limited categories of workers in respect of which special problems of a substantial nature arise'.[37] These special problems are not specified. A requirement of consultation with employers/employees (and, where they exist, domestic workers' organisations) is intended to provide a check on the process of 'opting-out'. During the drafting process, the Office of the High Commissioner for Human Rights had specifically expressed concern at the wide discretion allowed by Article 2.[38] Despite its concerns, the provision remained in the final text, however, and is a significant concession to the pursuit of greater flexibility (for employers and states) in defining the content of rights enjoyed by domestic workers.

This flexibility is found elsewhere, with repeated reference throughout the Convention text to the 'special characteristics of domestic work'. Only limited recognition is given to the unequal bargaining positions in which employers and domestic workers are placed. Article 7 of the Convention, for example, requires that domestic workers are informed of the terms and conditions of their employment, but further specification of those terms and conditions is not given.[39] Article 9 requires Members to ensure that domestic workers are 'free to negotiate with the employer whether to reside in the household'.[40] Such freedoms remain illusory, however, where immigration laws limit access to public funds or welfare supports (such as affordable or social housing programmes), and where minimum wage protections are not applicable or enforced. Article 13 sets out the obligations of Members to take 'effective measures' to ensure the occupational safety and health of domestic workers and to safeguard the right to a safe and healthy working environment. This requirement is tempered, however, by the caveat that due regard must be had for the 'specific characteristics of domestic work'. The obligation to take effective measures is one that can be realised progressively, an over-reaching concession and one that, as critics note, potentially turns the clock back on decades of labour rights activism on health and safety at work. The obligation of progressive realisation is limited further by the requirement that due regard must be given to domestic work's 'specific characteristics',[41] a claw-back provision that is repeated in the provisions relating to social security protections.[42] On labour inspection and enforcement mechanisms, an additional requirement of 'due respect for privacy' reinforces the Convention limits.[43]

36 ILO Report IV(1) at para. 15.
37 Convention Concerning Decent Work for Domestic Workers, Article 2(2)(b).
38 ILO, *Decent Work for Domestic Workers*, Report IV(2A), 100th session of the International Labour Conference, Geneva, 2011, at 21.
39 Ibid., Article 7.
40 Ibid., Article 9(a).
41 Convention Concerning Decent Work for Domestic Workers, Article 13(1).
42 Ibid., Article 14(1).
43 Ibid., Article 17.

The only specific provision in the Domestic Work Convention relating directly to migration is found in Article 8, which provides that written job offers or contracts of employment are to be provided to domestic workers pre-departure from the country of origin,[44] along with information on repatriation arrangements following expiry or termination of the contract of employment.[45] This requirement, while important, is relatively weak, however. It requires only that such terms and conditions be specified, but does nothing to address the inequalities of bargaining power between worker and employer that will ultimately define the terms and conditions agreed. The proposed model contract of employment for domestic workers, noted in the accompanying Recommendation, seeks to overcome the minimal approach taken in the Convention itself concerning the terms and conditions of employment.[46] Its inclusion in the non-binding text of the Recommendation, however, reflects again the reluctance of states to take concrete steps to realise the aspirations of a shift 'from status to contract' for domestic workers, or to accept positive obligations, particularly when addressing the rights claims of migrant workers. The limits of law, and of human rights law in particular, is a recurring theme in the essays presented in this collection. Both international and European standards have failed to significantly transform the regulation of domestic work.

Ann Stewart (Chapter 2) examines care work in the context of contemporary forms of globalisation and the changing nature of relationships between the employer and domestic worker. The analysis of global care chains, she notes, needs to take account of the international gendered division of socially reproductive labour, and not limit itself to the emerging discourses of fundamental labour and human rights. While the rights claims of care givers and care receivers must be vindicated, what is at issue, she notes, is the need for solidarity and an interrogation of forms of globalisation that fail to address deficiencies in state support for care work. Fulvia Staiano (Chapter 3) takes on the jurisprudence of the Court of Justice of the European Union (CJEU), and the limited engagement with the value of care work in the European Court of Human Rights Article 8 case law. She points to the *jurisgenerative* potential of continuing dialogue between both courts, and highlights the ground-breaking nature of claims brought by MDWs under the European Convention of Human Rights, Article 4. While the judgments handed down have focused on the need for states to pursue effective criminal prosecutions for the crimes of servitude and forced labour, Staiano argues that the boundaries of Article 4 jurisprudence can be expanded. The recognition of care work in the CJEU's case law, she

44 Convention Concerning Decent Work for Domestic Workers, Article 8(1).

45 Ibid., Article 8(4).

46 ILO, Recommendation Concerning Decent Work for Domestic Workers (ILO Recommendation No. 201) Geneva, 16 June 2011, para. 6(3) (hereafter ILO, Recommendation Concerning Decent Work for Domestic Workers).

suggests, albeit in the context of giving practical effect to the fundamental rights of EU citizens, can provide support for such expansion, through an innovative process of judicial dialogue between both Courts.

Clíodhna Murphy (Chapter 6) returns us to domestic laws, and to the obstacles faced by irregular MDWs, in particular, in accessing legal redress for breaches of employment law. Citing the work of Bridget Anderson, she notes that MDWs are caught 'between the excesses of immigration regulation on the one hand and employment on the other'.[47] Through an examination of case law and legislative exemptions, Murphy explores the limitations of contract law remedies, grounded as they are in assumptions of capacity, consent and equal bargaining power. Such inequalities are exacerbated of course by the 'deportability' of the alien, and the precarious migration status of many MDWs. The impact of migration status on vulnerability to abuse is also addressed by Gulnara Shahinian (Chapter 7), former UN Special Rapporteur on Slavery, who takes us through the operation of the *kafala* mechanism in Gulf states, and in Lebanon. Shahinian provides us with a snapshot of the abuses of MDWs encountered through the work of her mandate and highlights the transformation of the cultural practice of *kafala* into a highly exploitative migration management tool. Again, in this chapter, as in Shahid's case study of MDWs in Pakistan (Chapter 8), the role of diplomacy and of diplomatic protection plays a critical role in securing incremental reforms. Such bilateral moves, combined with the imposition of travel restrictions – themselves potentially contravening prohibitions of gender discrimination – do not, however, address the deep-rooted structural problems that construct and enforce the vulnerability of MDWs.

Nicole Constable (Chapter 5) examines the status of MDWs in Hong Kong, and the laws and policies that have underpinned its reputation as a model destination for migrant workers. As she notes, however, the rights enjoyed 'on paper' by MDWs are 'hard to claim' and 'difficult to enforce'. The guarantees of contract are illusory for those whose migration status is highly temporary, and who do not have the resources, time or networks to pursue their claims. Hong Kong, she argues, has developed 'a system of governmentality' in which migrant workers are constituted as 'neoliberal exceptions' to the rights that are enjoyed by citizens or permanent residents.

The many exceptions and limits imposed on the labour and human rights of domestic workers are examined by Mullally and Murphy (Chapter 4) in the context of reforms to the Overseas Domestic Worker visa regime in the UK. These reforms, it is argued, reflect a resistance to the 'cascade' of human rights standards that have sought to overcome the limits of migration status as a prerequisite to the exercise of rights.[48] A series of cases before

47 Anderson, p.176, see n.23.

48 See, for example, Inter-American Court of Human Rights Advisory Opinion on the 'Juridical Condition and Rights of the Undocumented Migrants' (Advisory Opinion OC-18/03, 17 September 2003, Inter-Am. Ct. H.R. (Ser. A) No. 18 (2003)). See also the

the European Court of Human Rights[49] has highlighted the nexus between migration status and heightened risks of exploitation, as has the work of the UN CEDAW and Migrant Workers Committees. Limited access to secure migration status, however, remains the norm for many domestic workers. As the changes in the UK Overseas Domestic Worker visa regime reveal, states continue to invoke the 'deportability' of migrant workers.[50]

The move by the UK Government to introduce a highly precarious temporary status for MDWs and wider policy discourse on circular migration mark a resistance to the expansion of human rights norms to the realm of domestic work and to migrants.[51] This resistance is accompanied by appeals to protective norms that have shaped law's engagement with migrant women, and is reflected in the imposition of travel restrictions, the closing off of migration pathways and sponsorship mechanisms that, in practice, have been shown to limit rather than enhance the effective enjoyment of women's human rights. Added to the precarious migration status imposed on MDWs, the transformative potential of rights is further limited by a deeply gendered division between the public and the private spheres and a presumption that the tests of decent work that normally apply within the public sphere, do not extend to domestic work or to the domestic sphere. The obstacles placed in the way of securing decent work standards and recognition of domestic work as 'work like no other' are similar to those that delayed, until recently, the progressive development of human rights standards on domestic violence and on gendered traditional harms.

This book examines the expansion of human rights and labour rights standards at international level, and the difficulties faced by MDWs in claiming those rights in practice. The activism of MDWs, and their appeal to human rights law, can be understood as a process of enacting rights, of claiming equality and of making visible the 'dissensus' between the lived reality of domestic work and the promise of human rights law. As the essays here reveal, however, this process of enacting rights, and of realising human rights law's promise, requires overcoming many obstacles.

work of the Global Forum on Migration and Development: Background Paper, 'Protecting Migrant Domestic Workers – Enhancing Their Development Potential' (Prepared for Mauritius GFMD 2012, available at www.gfmd.org/docs/mauritius-2012), and 'Checklist to Support and Protect Domestic Workers', Mauritius GFMD 2012, available at http://www.unwomen.org/~/media/headquarters/attachments/sections/library/publications/2012/domestic-workers-checklist%20pdf.pdf

49 *Siliadin v France* (2006) 43 EHRR 16; *Rantsev v Cyprus and Russia*, Application No. 25965/04, Judgment of 7 January 2010; *C.N. and V. v France*, Application No. 67724/09, Judgment of 11 October 2012; *C.N. v The United Kingdom*, Application No. 4239/08, Judgment of 13 November 2012.

50 On the 'deportable alien', see Kesby, *The Right to Have Rights: Citizenship, Humanity, and International Law* (Oxford: Oxford University Press, 2012), p. 111 *et seq.*

51 C Dauvergne and S Marsden, 'The Ideology of Temporary Labour Migration in the Post-Global Era', in Shachar and Brahm Levey (eds) *Citizenship in a Globalized World: Perspectives from the Immigrant Democracies, Citizenship Studies*, 2014, 18(2); 224–242.

2 Care or Work? The Tyranny of Categories

Ann Stewart

Introduction

Ela Bhat, reflecting on four decades of organising with the Self Employed Women's Association in India, argues that:

> [...] the tyranny of having to belong to a well defined 'category' has condemned women to having no identity. The livelihoods of millions of people are ... not perceived as work, and, therefore, remain uncounted, unrecorded, unprotected, unaddressed by the nation, conveniently 'invisible' to policy makers, statisticians and theoreticians. ... If you ever come to official attention, it is only as an obstacle.[1]

This chapter considers the extent to which and in what ways the approach adopted by the International Labour Organisation (ILO) to protecting the interests of domestic workers contributes to the reproduction of this tyranny by categorisation. The Domestic Workers Convention 2011 (No. 189) (henceforth Convention) and Recommendation 2011 (No. 201), (henceforth Recommendation)[2] undoubtedly represent much-needed international recognition of the importance of improving the lives of such workers. The Convention addresses the key issues which domestic workers face: its Articles and the Recommendations provide a comprehensive package of measures which are mindful of the particular socio-economic context in which such work is carried out, whether this is within the worker's home or host country. It is also the case that care has been taken to embed the Convention within the more recent 'soft law' approaches adopted by the ILO including the Decent Work initiative which addresses the limits to adoption and enforcement of 'hard law' Conventions by member States.

1 Ela Bhat, 'Looking Back on Four Decades of Organizing. The Experience of SEWA' in Naila Kabeer and others (eds) *Organizing Women Workers in the Informal Economy* (Zed Press 2013) 3

2 The texts of Convention No. 189 and Recommendation No. 201 can be found at www.ilo.org/ilolex/english/index.htm

The ILO framework as a whole can in many ways be seen as tackling head-on the problems identified by Ela Bhatt. It firmly establishes domestic labour as work which must be counted, recorded, protected and addressed by nation states. The ILO and the many domestic worker campaigners can claim that coming to official attention is a solution rather than an obstacle.

However, the ILO also argues that domestic work is both 'work like any other, work like no other'.[3] This is perhaps the first iteration of the problem identified by Ela Bhatt. The problem of categorisation remains. This chapter argues that the relationship under consideration, which involves activities carried out within or for a household, is most commonly discussed within conceptual frameworks based upon binaries: production/social reproduction; public/private; formal/informal; work/care; labour/human rights; free/forced and so on. It will suggest that it is preferable to place such labour within frameworks that favour analysis based upon relationships, both personal and structural, and which seek to dissipate these binaries.

The ILO Convention for a variety of cogent reasons defined domestic work narrowly.[4] It is paid work carried out in a domestic context. The focus is on how to extend labour law protections to these workers and by so doing bring them within the domain of the formal labour market. The aim is first to separate this work from association with relationships of care. Yet the rise in the demand for such labour in recent years is directly linked to the lack of recognition of the way in which social reproduction, which encompasses nurturing and caring, underpins productive activities. Who is responsible for caring and broader social reproduction, and how is it to be provided, when the economic imperative seems to be that all adults must be gainfully incorporated into the global market? The increasing number of domestic workers in the last two decades is one response, set within a wider marketisation and commodification of caring relations which has led to the rise in body work (work involving intimate contact with others' bodies such as assessment, diagnosis, handling or manipulation) more generally.[5] It is important therefore to understand caring work, wherever located, as part of these processes and consider the ways in which it addresses the perceived crises in social reproduction.[6] Arguably, the ILO approach, which seeks to establish a framework to enable policy makers to count, record and protect domestic work, is essential for its incorporation within the dominant neo-liberal global economy. It is less able to address the lack of political will to

3 International Labour Conference, 99th Session, *Decent Work for Domestic Workers: Report IV(1)* (International Labour Organisation 2009) 12

4 International Labour Organisation, *Domestic Workers Across the World: Global and regional statistics and the extent of legal protection* (ILO 2013); Recommendation

5 Carol Wolkowitz, *Bodies at Work* (Sage 2006); Carol Wolkowitz and others, *Body/Sex/Work: Intimate, embodied and sexualized labour* (Palgrave Macmillan 2013)

6 Catherine Hoskyns and Shirin M Rai, 'Recasting the International Political Economy; Counting Women's Unpaid Work' (2007) *New Political Economy* 12 (3) 297; Shirin M Rai and others, 'Depletion' (2013) *International Feminist Journal of Politics* 1

tackle the consequences for individuals and communities of the loss of social reproductive capacity that accompanies commodification.

Secondly and relatedly, the ILO objective is to separate this type of work from other forms of informal working including sex work. Yet it shares important characteristics and continuities. Such work is often associated with shame and stigma, undertaken by marginalised groups including internal and international migrants, and is understood as a livelihood or survival strategy. Economically, these services are difficult to 'scale up' and therefore do not easily attract mainstream investment to improve productivity. They are more likely to be associated with exploitation and criminality. Seeking to extend a framework originally designed to protect organised, predominately male, workers making things in factories may miss the lessons to be learned from how informal workers perceive their needs and organise their demands to achieve them. There is much to learn by recognising the role played by informality in contemporary socio-economic contexts and to consider the way in which informal workers seek recognition as citizens as well as workers.

The chapter will go on to focus more specifically on the way in which these new international measures relating to domestic workers 'fit' into the categories associated with global labour governance. Here the focus is on binaries such as: State or market (rights or trade); human or labour rights; 'hard law' labour rights or 'soft law' standards; rights or voluntary corporate social responsibility. While the ILO has promulgated a 'hard law' Convention to provide rights to domestic workers, the new orthodoxy is to rely more on 'soft law' measures, which some would argue can amount to 'reflexive labour law'.[7] Global governance debates, while recognising the way in which globalisation has produced informalisation, flexibility and precarious working, tend to focus more on commodity rather than service production. These processes, which underpin the way in which a commodity moves through its life cycle from inception to disposal, attract scholarly and policy analysis and civil society activism. The focus, particularly within a development framework, is on global value chains (GVC) or networks to highlight the way in which each stage in the process adds value.[8]

Different analytical frames of reference, primarily migration studies, tend to be used when it is a 'factor of production', a person who is to provide a service, that is passed along the chain or within the network rather than a commodity, although trade economists understand migration in this way.[9] Feminists have characterised these processes as global care chains (GCC)

7 Ralf Rogowski, *Reflexive Labour Law in The World Society* (Edward Elgar 2013)

8 P Gibbon, J Blair and S Ponte, 'Governing Global Value Chains: An Introduction' (2008) *Economy and Society* 37 (3) 315

9 Alan Hyde, 'Legal Responsibility for Labour Conditions Down the Production Chain' in Judy Fudge, Shae McCrystal and Kamala Sankaran (eds) *Challenging the Legal Boundaries of Work Regulation* (Hart Publishing 2012)

and established analogies with GVC.[10] We increasingly 'see' the distant workers, large numbers of whom are women, involved in the production of commodities for export partly because of high-profile events such as the death of textile workers in Bangladesh but also because of sustained campaigns such as those relating to the conditions of workers in agribusinesses in Africa and Latin and Central America. Pressure from alliances of global north consumers, non-governmental organisations (NGOs), activists, policy makers and trade unions has contributed to the development of a raft of measures aimed at ensuring basic rights for workers. Such ethically inspired interventions are increasingly being understood as smart business where they result in a more productive workforce.

We do not 'see' so easily the proximate women involved in GCC. To what extent do global labour governance measures including the ILO approach to domestic worker protection extend to these chains? Such an assessment reveals the real challenges to effective protection for domestic workers whose labour is being used in many respects to avoid the essential political debate on how to ensure that communities are able to socially reproduce themselves in ways that do not involve profound inequalities and injustices. In this respect Ela Bhatt is right – the obstacle is a policy and law reform focus that isolates domestic work from broader public consideration of responsibilities for caring.

International Labour Organisation approach: context and content

The ILO reports that:

> [...] at least 52.6 million persons above the age of 15 worldwide engage in domestic work as their principal job; and 83 per cent of them are women. Domestic work is a truly global phenomenon ... and on the rise everywhere. It accounts for 3.6 per cent of wage employment worldwide, representing 0.9 per cent of wage employment in industrialized countries, almost 12 per cent of wage employment in Latin America and the Caribbean, 8 per cent in the Middle East, and about 5 and 3.5 per cent in Africa and Asia, respectively.[11]

10 Ann Stewart, *Gender, Law and Justice in a Global Market* (Cambridge University Press 2011); Nicola Yeates 'Global Care Chains: A State-of-the-Art Review and Future Directions in Care Transnationalization Research' (2012) *Global Networks* 12 (2) 1470

11 International Labour Organisation Governing Body 312th Session, Geneva, November (2011). Third Item on the Agenda, Matters arising out of the work of the 100th Session (2011) of the International Labour Conference. Follow-up to the adoption of the resolution concerning efforts to make decent work a reality for domestic workers worldwide, www.ilo.org/global/topics/domestic-workers/WCMS_210411/lang--en/index.htm 1

Work like any other

The ILO adopted Convention and Recommendation at its 100th Session in 2011. These new measures lay down basic principles and minimum labour standards for domestic work and make it clear that 'domestic workers, like other workers, are entitled to fundamental rights at work and to minimum labour and social protection. [They are] grounded on the principle of no-less favourable treatment between domestic workers and workers generally'.[12] The ILO's approach is made very clear:

> [l]egislation and regulatory policy are ... essential tools for eliminating the negative aspects of informality in the domestic work sector ... Extending the reach of labour law to domestic workers is an important means of bringing them within the formal economy ... Bringing domestic workers ... under the protection of labour legislation is a matter of gender equality and equal protection under the law: a question of human rights.[13]

The Convention defines domestic work narrowly as work performed in or for a household or households and a domestic worker as any person engaged in domestic work within an employment relationship.[14] The definition distinguishes this work from that undertaken within the wider care economy. The ILO decided not to

> rely on a listing of the specific tasks or services performed by domestic workers, which vary from country to country and may change over time ... [but to use] a general formulation that draws on the common feature of domestic workers that they work for private households.[15]

In so doing, it enables them to be identified and counted using the International Standard Industrial Classification, a recognised industry-based approach.[16] The ILO uses this classification for its research on domestic work.

The Convention seeks to treat domestic work like other work by promoting and protecting the human rights of workers through incorporation of the ILO Declaration on Fundamental Principles and Rights at Work 1998 (see below).[17] The Convention limits the employment of children.[18] It pro-

12 ILO n 4 2
13 International Labour Organisation, *Effective Protection For Domestic Workers: A guide to designing labour laws* (ILO 2012) 2–3
14 Article 1 (a) and (b)
15 ILO (n 4) 8
16 Ibid 8
17 Articles 3, 4 and 11
18 Article 4: States are required to set a minimum age and to extend extra protections to workers between the ages of 15 and 18

tects against all forms of abuse, harassment and violence.[19] Domestic workers, like other workers, are entitled to fair terms of employment and decent working conditions.[20] Importantly, they must be informed of their terms and conditions of employment, ideally through a written contract.[21] They have a right to a safe and healthy working environment[22] and to similar social security protections as other workers, including maternity benefits.[23] It requires States to provide accessible and effective dispute settlement processes including access to courts or tribunals and to ensure compliance with the national laws enacted to protect domestic workers through such measures as labour inspections.[24]

Work like no other

However, it also addresses the issues that tend to mark such work out from other forms of work. Thus Article 10 requires States to take measures to ensure that domestic workers are treated the same as other workers with respect to normal hours of work, overtime compensation, periods of rest, 'standby' time and annual leave. The Recommendation is obliged to provide very detailed guidance on this area in order to address the difficulties associated with establishing clearly demarcated working time due to the nature of the activities undertaken and the complex power relationships which underpin much of such work.[25] Equally, ensuring equality of pay with other workers is not straightforward given the difficulties associated with turning what is often seen as an uneven power relationship into a time-bound and economically valued activity.[26] The Convention recognises the particular issues relating to 'live-in' workers and seeks to set minimum standards in relation to decent living conditions that respect the workers' privacy;[27] the freedom to decide on whether to reside in the household[28] and to leave the premises during periods of rest and leave;[29] and the right to keep identity and travel documents.[30] However, in any dispute the workers' right to

19 Article 5
20 Article 6
21 Article 7
22 Article 13
23 Article 14
24 Article 17
25 Guy Mundlak, 'ReCommodifying Time: Working Hours of "Live-in" Domestic Workers' in Joanne Conaghan and Kerry Rittich (eds) *Labour Law, Work, and Family: Critical and Comparative Perspectives* (Oxford University Press 2005)
26 Article 11 requires workers to be paid the applicable minimum wage while Article 12 addresses issues such as payment in kind (limited and not including uniforms or protective clothing).
27 Article 6
28 Article 9
29 Article 9
30 Article 9

protection must be balanced against the right to privacy of household members.[31] Again the Recommendations seek to provide detailed guidance on how to achieve these goals.

Given that a very significant proportion of domestic work is undertaken by migrant workers, in some countries almost exclusively,[32] the Convention addresses their particular vulnerabilities. It requires States to ensure that workers receive a written contract that is enforceable in the country of employment, or a written job offer, prior to travelling to the country of employment and that there are clear conditions under which workers are entitled to repatriation at the end of their employment.[33] Because such migration is often orchestrated by private employment agencies, Article 15 requires States to ensure that domestic workers are protected from abusive practices; that such agencies are regulated and that the fees charged are not deducted from their pay. Article 8 promotes co-operation between sending and receiving countries to ensure the effective application of these provisions including considering the use of bilateral, regional or multilateral agreements.

Albin argues that the legal situation of domestic workers will remain precarious 'as long as special attention is not given to the[ir] sectoral disadvantage. Their work has to be treated as "work like no other" for the rules to be effective.'[34] She defines sectoral disadvantage 'as a situation in which the *rules* of a specific sector – its structure and culture – impact on workers in the direction of disadvantage'.[35] She considers that the 'Convention and recommendations have generally adopted such a focus, but there remains a tension in the instruments'.[36] What comparators are going to be used? Is sleeping in the employer's house a loss or a gain? Are deductions for accommodation and food appropriate even if the worker agrees to them? 'Each and every rule should be thought of in light of the particular disadvantaged state of domestics and the primary causes of the distinction between them and other workers.'[37]

While this approach highlights the challenges that legislators and policy makers face in translating the aspirations contained in the Convention and Recommendation into substantive equality for domestic workers, it identifies the location of the work, reinforced through rules (or lack of them) as

31 Article 17

32 For instance, there are 750,000 domestic workers in the United Arab Emirates, comprising 20 per cent of the total migrant workforce. They outnumber family members in almost a quarter of households.

33 Article 8

34 Einat Albin, 'From "Domestic Servant" to "Domestic Worker"' in Fudge et al (n 9) 231, 248.

35 Ibid 231. She points to the long history of subjecting such work in the UK to a particular legal regime.

36 Ibid 248–249

37 Ibid 249

the key source of disadvantage while others would point to continuities with other forms of caring work and with work undertaken in informal settings more generally. We will return to these points below.

Implementation in a soft law era

This is the 189th ILO Convention. The Convention and the accompanying Regulations represent the 'traditional' ILO approach to global labour rights whereby Member States are encouraged to ratify and then ensure compliance with the content of the Convention through the implementation and enforcement of national level legal and policy measures. To this end, the ILO is pushing hard to encourage ratification in the crucial initial period after promulgation. To date,[38] there have been 12 ratifications: 7 in South and Central America; 2 in Europe (Germany and Italy);[39] 2 in Africa (South Africa and Mauritius); 1 in Asia/Pacific (Philippines). In recent times, support for this 'top down' approach to the setting of global labour standards has waned, leading to fewer new Conventions.[40] There are a number of reasons why this has occurred. First, given the history of geopolitical power relations, there has been very uneven ratification by States generally and some key States such as the USA and China have ratified very few. Second, national implementation is very patchy and the ILO, like many other international institutions, has weak enforcement mechanisms.[41]

On a more general level, this method of international labour standard setting has its origins in a different economic era, one in which an industrial relations framework based upon formal employment was assumed to be the norm or to be the 'direction of travel'. The tripartite structure, involving employers' organisations and trade unions as well as representatives of States were in effect protecting domestic labour rights in capitalist welfare states against competition from States that did not abide by these standards. Power has shifted significantly with the liberalisation of trade and the expansion of multinational enterprises (MNE). The incorporation of lower-income countries into the world capitalist economy has been accompanied by changed economic relations including far more informalisation and commercialisation of labour.[42] The boundaries between formal and informal sectors dissolved, along with distinctions between free and unfree labour. Nationally focused instruments such as labour law and collective bargaining do not fit easily with increasingly fluid cross-border movements of business,

38 1 March 2014

39 The UK abstained on the vote to adopt the Convention and is therefore very unlikely to ratify.

40 Philip Alston, 'Labour Rights as Human Rights: The Not so Happy State of the Art' in Philip Alston (ed.) *Labour Rights as Human Rights* (Oxford University Press 2005); B A Hepple, *Labour Law and Global Trade* (Hart Publishing 2005)

41 Ibid

42 Judy Fudge, 'Blurring Legal Boundaries: Regulating for Decent Work' in Fudge et al n 9

labour and services. Both were weakened further by the reforms, designed to enhance international competitiveness, promulgated in one form or another from the late 1970s onwards by the international financial institutions.

As a result the ILO has adapted its methods of working to respond to demands for employer flexibility and regulatory experimentation.[43] It has increasingly resorted to the discursive power of human rights to establish a core set of universally recognised labour principles, although historically labour rights have been recognised as a combination of measures that protect workers' substantive workplace rights and those that protect human beings from State-backed forms of coercion. The 1998 Declaration on the Fundamental Principles commits ILO Member States to respect and promote a number of core principles and rights, whether or not they have ratified the relevant Conventions upon which these are based[44] (freedom of association and recognition of the right to collective bargaining; the elimination of forced and compulsory labour; the abolition of child labour; and the elimination of discrimination in respect of employment and occupation). These core principles feature not only in ILO Conventions but also in the International Bill of Rights, which has been ratified by most States, and therefore are a response to critics who argue that the expansion of international rights dissipates their value.[45]

The ILO has incorporated the Principles within its third Declaration on Social Justice for a Fair Globalisation 2008[46] and translated these principles into policy through its Decent Work strategy. It uses an extended concept of work to include all who work or seek work, which covers informal workers. It links work to poverty reduction and recognises the need for social protection, particularly for vulnerable groups. The Decent Work agenda promotes work that is 'productive and delivers a fair income, security in the workplace and social protection for families' as well as 'better prospects for personal development and social integration'. It reasserts that workers are not mere factors of production in a global marketplace.[47] In the Decent Work country programmes, the ILO extends beyond its usual tripartism to use 'social dialogue' with wider constituencies to support implementation in individual States.

The ILO has sought co-operation with a range of institutions including those associated with international business and finance. The 1998 Declaration principles provide a 'ready-made' package which is able to

43 Alston n 40; now incorporated into the ILO Declaration on Social Justice for a Fair Globalisation adopted by ILO at its 97th Session, Geneva, 10 June 2008, www.ilo.org/global/about-the-ilo/mission-and-objectives/WCMS_099766/lang--en/index.htm

44 ILO 2000, www.ilo.org/global/about-the-ilo/newsroom/news/WCMS_007913/lang--en/index.htm

45 Susan Marks 'Four Human Rights Myths' (LSE Legal Studies, Working Paper No. 10/2012)

46 Above n 43

47 ILO, www.ilo.org/global/topics/decent-work/lang--en/index.htm

be incorporated as soft law into a wide range of settings including its own ILO's Tripartite Declaration on Multinational Enterprises,[48] the OECD Guidelines on Multinational Enterprises,[49] the United Nations' Global Compact with business and the Guiding Principles on Business and Human Rights (Ruggie Principles)[50] and the European Union's Generalised System of Preferences (GSP) and GSP+.[51] They are embedded within private standard setting initiatives, such as codes of conduct, adopted by Multinational Enterprises, which have accompanied the development of the liberal market, such as Global Framework Agreements and the multi-stakeholder Ethical Trading Initiative.[52]

A State-focused institutional and normative framework of international labour law has not been conducive to the development of 'modern' global labour law.[53] A key question that labour lawyers pose, therefore, is whether international labour law can realign itself towards the shared task of 'mitigating the distributional consequences of globalisation and transnational flexible production'.[54] Historically, structural inequalities have been tackled through the recognition of the need for resources, won through labour market collective bargaining and employment protection legislation. States have also been direct providers of services via social security benefits, access to health and education services. Welfare states not only provide social protection but also a guarantee of the right to collective action. Thus labour rights have been used to make claims on States as well as employers to provide work and economic security and to recognise the collective interests of workers. With the rise of a social enterprise culture, with its critique of collective consumption and solidarity, social resources become claimed as juridical rights, more akin to civil and political rather than social and economic rights.[55] Market discourses of contract, competitiveness and efficiency have entered labour and social welfare law. The fear is that individualised claims to resources will be used to undermine still further the principal institutions of the welfare State and be associated with the levelling down of rights and, while collective bargaining and freedom of

48 First produced in 1977; most recently revised in 2006 which invites MNEs to observe its principles.

49 First produced in 1976; most recently revised in 2000.

50 Office of the High Commissioner 'Guiding Principles on Business and Human Rights: Implementing the United Nations Protect, Respect and Remedy Framework' (United Nations Human Rights: Office of the High Commissioner New York and Geneva HR/Pub/11/04, 2011)

51 Hugh Collins, with Keith Ewing and Aileen McColgan, *Labour Law* (Cambridge University Press 2012) 55–56

52 Ann Stewart, 'Engendering Responsibility in Global Markets: Valuing the Women in Kenya's Agricultural Sector' in Amanda Perry-Kessaris (ed.) *Law in the Pursuit of Development: Principles into Practice* (Routledge 2010) 39–40

53 Collins et al n 51

54 Collins et al n 51 87–90

55 Simon Deakin, 'Social Rights in a Globalized Economy' in Alston n 40

association are broadly recognised rights, they have proven very difficult to enforce within a culture of liberal individualism. These developments further undermine the already limited international labour rights of trade unions to operate outside their national borders to protect workers within a global marketplace.

The failure to impose a social clause within World Trade Organisation (WTO) proceedings in order to utilise its more developed enforcement procedures has led to separate institutional responsibilities between WTO (trade) and ILO (labour) and the 'softer' co-operative rather than the coercive approach described above.[56] These initiatives are part of the general attempt to ensure that social justice is not lost in the processes of globalisation and to find ways of attaching human rights values to economic actors. They are often treated with considerable scepticism by progressive labour and human rights lawyers who view them as recasting labour rights as a subset of universal human rights and marginalising the progressive re-distributional aspects of labour rights within international human rights laws.[57] The fear is that labour rights become just one more consideration to be taken into account in shaping the values underpinning the liberalised global economy.[58] Being 'human rights compliant' becomes smart business.

Application to domestic work strategy

The processes that led to the adoption of the Convention and which now underpin the attempts to implement it are a product of the ILO's changed positioning. Such work did not fit the former model. The ILO recognises that protecting domestic work through a formal labour rights framework requires much more than a 'hard law' Convention. As indicated in an earlier section, an effective legal and policy framework needs to recognise that such work is heavily associated with its private, familial/household location. It must overcome the difficulties of: establishing legal relations given the varied arrangements in which workers are employed; the differing legal regimes and socio-economic circumstances of Member States; and the socio-economic disadvantage and vulnerability of the workers (associated with being from marginalised communities, internal or international migrants and being young and 'living in'). The usual tripartite institutional building blocks are very weak:

56 The USA rather curiously given its general position on ratification of labour rights includes a social clause in its bilateral agreements; see Collins et al n 51, 54.

57 H W Arthurs, 'Private Ordering and Workers' Rights in the Global Economy: Corporate Codes of Conduct as a Regime of Labour Market Regulation' in Joanne Conaghan and others (eds) *Labour Law in an Era of Globalization Transformative Practices and Possibilities* (Oxford University Press 2002)

58 Alston n 40; Hepple n 40

> [...] most domestic workers typically have little contact with other workers and often are either unorganized or organized in volatile, understaffed and unequipped associations. Isolated, and without voice and organization, they would be in a weak position to claim their rights. Employers of domestic workers are equally hardly organized, and both groups have little or no experience in collective bargaining or in dealing with authorities on labour laws and social security.[59]

To tackle these complex issues, the ILO has produced detailed guidance, incorporating numerous, specific examples, on how to implement every aspect of the Convention. It seeks to raise awareness and encourage attitudinal change through its applied research programme which provides a comprehensive profile of the local and regional contexts and a survey of existing legislative coverage.[60] This information also provides a baseline for action by States. However, while promoting the implementation of State legislative measures via the ratification of the Convention, the ILO nevertheless stresses the Convention's flexibility and the importance of social dialogue as a key principle in the implementation process. It roots domestic work within its Decent Work campaign and provides support to countries that are willing to improve the protection and working conditions of domestic workers, without the necessity of ratification.[61] It acknowledges the difficulties associated with ensuring an effective institutional framework to produce legislative reform and offers support to build institutions at country level and to facilitate the organisation and representation of domestic workers and their employers. The ILO recognises the value of a combined human and labour rights approach. The 1998 fundamental principles are incorporated into Convention no. 189 and their importance is stressed within the Recommendation and guidance.

Arguably, this approach fits the experiences of women and offers a more inclusive way of protecting women workers. More expansive concepts of work go some way towards softening the informal/formal dichotomy. The critiques of collaborative approaches based on social dialogue, discussed above, reflect a perspective predicated upon a decline in collective organisational capacity and challenges to the labour and social protections achieved by formal workers. As is now recognised, this is rarely the starting point for women. Their work has not attracted labour law protections and while, in welfare states, they have been able to access some universal social protections (often health and education) as citizens, access to other benefits has been derived from their relationship with men. The shift in approach towards more rootedness in 'social dialogue' and 'global governance' than in State government may enable more focus on process and the institution

59 ILO n 11
60 ILO n 4
61 ILO n 11

building that is essential if informal work is to attract the protections associated with the formal labour market.[62]

It has become policy orthodoxy that access to paid work is empowering for women as well as making good business sense – smart economics, to use the World Bank phraseology.[63] However, as Kabeer and others point out, while formal working has been found to empower individuals, increasing self-worth and control over activities, it has had limited effect on enhancing women's overall status as citizens and workers more generally.[64] Women's access to the labour market has not promoted the wider organisational capacity to struggle for the recognition and realisation of rights that would increase broader economic security and political inclusion.[65] In any case, the industrial model which has trade unionism as its dominant form of labour organisation extended only as far as import substitution industries in the developing world. As such it covered only a tiny proportion of the working population and very few women. Trade unions have often been unwilling or unable to embrace informal workers, particularly women. They are unlikely members because of: the nature of the activities they undertake – 'casual, dispersed, isolated, part-time, irregular and often home-based'; their lack of an obvious employer; their 'direct competition with each other... for work, for orders for their products, for space to sell their goods and services'.[66] Equally importantly, they undertake stigmatised and marginalising activities, which are dirty or symbolically shaming – while often being drawn from groups which experience intersectional inequalities based on class, ethnicity, caste or legal status. Women who are heavily dependent on the goodwill of dominant family and community members and who are culturally not expected to challenge authority will struggle to identify with the dominant public organisational strategies.[67] Women informal workers therefore face multiple injustices which, in Fraser's terminology, must be addressed through measures involving a combination of redistribution, recognition and representation.[68]

To organise collectively, informal workers often rely upon sustained external support from (middle class) activist organisations, not trade

62 Guglielmo Meardi and Paul Marginson, 'Global Labour Governance: Potential and Limits of an Emerging Perspective' Paper for the 2013 Work, Employment and Society Conference, Warwick University, Sept 3–5

63 World Bank, *World Development Report 2012: Gender Equality and Development* (World Bank 2011)

64 Naila Kabeer, Kirsty Milward and Ratna Sudarshan, 'Introduction' in Naila Kabeer, Ratna Sudarshan and Kirsty Milward (eds) *Organizing Women Workers in the Informal Economy: Beyond the Weapons of the Weak* (Zed Press 2013) 1, 2

65 Ibid

66 Ibid 5–6

67 Ibid 6

68 Nancy Fraser, *Justice Interruptus: Critical Reflections on the 'Postsocialist' Condition* (Psychology Press 1997)

unions, to enable them to develop their own strategies.[69] Their primary goal is often to tackle the stigma or indignity attached to the activity which they see as a means to survive or to secure a livelihood rather than 'work'. The initial organising factor may be violence experienced as a particular group of migrants, rather than grievances relating to their work. Women re-value their activities: from rummaging on waste tips to providing a recycling service; from prostituting themselves to being entrepreneurs; from natural feminine dexterity to skilled and valued horticultural or fisheries work and, in so doing, develop a group identity.

The organisational focus will often involve in the first instance claims on the State for inclusion in social protection schemes. In these contexts the discourse of human rights, pursuing claims to be treated as citizens, can have significant rhetorical power. Some groups use the power associated with the law more broadly to pursue claims using mechanisms such as arbitration rather than 'spontaneous, largely ineffectual' strike action.[70] As a result of these strategies, an organisational framework emerges which reflects a re-valued identity such as claiming the Convention rights as a worker rather than being 'part of a family' – and which can then be used to pursue re-distributional issues. However, while the workers may establish a new trade union or link with an established one, they may use alternative forms of organisation – a self-employed union (such as the Self Employed Women's Association) or an NGO which focuses more on everyday needs such as the provision of child care, toilets or small scale loans.

Those working with such precarious workers recognise that

> access to some form of social protection may be a necessary precondition for taking the risks associated with strategies for longer-term change. In addition, for those whose work, and status as workers, had been largely overlooked by the State, the struggle for social security can also be, to some extent, a struggle to gain recognition of their status as citizens.[71]

The struggle to make care visible through social security rights unites women along the formal/informal continuum and across borders, a point increasingly recognised by trade unions and international campaigners. Thus the 'same processes of globalization that promoted the pursuit of flexible labour and the expansion of the informal economy have also opened up new possibilities for organization among sections of the working poor' and for the organisation of 'informal workers at the global level'.[72] One such is the International Domestic Workers' Network (2011). As we shall see below,

69 Kabeer and others n 64
70 Ibid 23
71 Ibid 27
72 Ibid 37

this is not an easy task and it is important 'not to overstate the significance of such embryonic and small scale organisations'.[73]

As Kabeer notes, 'the struggle against capital appears to have less relevance for these workers than the struggle for rights'. This can be interpreted 'as conceding defeat on the larger more important issues' or 'as reflecting the priorities that begin to surface when some of the most marginalized sections of the working classes ... become actively engaged around the politics of redistribution, recognition and representation'.[74]

Caring economies?

The importance of social protection for women informal workers reflects the growing recognition that there may be what some call a crisis in social reproduction[75] and others a process of social depletion.[76] Feminists highlight the artificial dichotomy between 'productive' paid labour carried out in the market and 'reproductive' unpaid labour carried out in the household and community that nurtures and cares but also maintains and transfers social norms and values to next generations.[77] Failing to recognise the importance of these activities produces a partial and biased picture of the economy as well as of society.[78] Fraser, adapting Polanyi's concepts, suggests, however, that it is less a matter of recognition and more an attempt by neo-liberalism to 'dis-embed' markets from the restraints of society: to free them from the extra-economic controls which would value a 'just price' and a 'fair wage', to be 'self-regulating'. However, Polanyi argues that markets can never be fully dis-embedded and such attempts always ultimately fail. Markets operate 'within cultural understandings and solidarity relations'. A process in which land, labour and money are factors of production destroys the fabric of society and provokes opposition from a range of actors, seeking to protect in one way or another their vision of 'society'. 'Far from enhancing social cooperation, then, the project of dis-embedding markets inevitably triggers social crisis' and leads to demands for the social regulation of markets.[79]

73 Ibid 37

74 Ibid 45

75 Nancy Fraser, 'Between Marketization and Social Protection: Resolving the Feminist Ambivalence' in *Fortunes of Feminism: From State-Managed Capitalism to Neoliberal Crisis* (Verso 2013) 227; Stewart n 10 chapter 1; Ann Stewart, 'Gender, Justice and Law in a Global Market' in Margaret Davies and Vanessa E Munro (eds) *The Ashgate Research Companion to Feminist Legal Theory* (Ashgate 2013)

76 Hoskyns and Rai n 6; Rai and others n 6

77 Diane Elson, 'Gender at the Macroeconomic Level' in Joanne Cook and others (eds) *Towards a Gendered Political Economy* (Macmillan Press 2000) 80

78 Paula England and Nancy Folbre, 'Contracting for Care' in Marianne A Ferber and Julie A Nelson (eds) *Feminist Economics Today: Beyond Economic Man* (University of Chicago Press 2003)

79 Nancy Fraser, 'Between Marketization and Social Protection: Resolving the Feminist Ambivalence' in Nancy Fraser, *Fortunes of Feminism* (Verso 2013) 230–231

Political economists argue that in order to dis-embed care from being a field of life, it needs to be marketised and commodified.[80] The former process turns caring, whether taking place in private households or through publicly provided services, into a market product while the latter fundamentally changes the understanding of caring. To become a commodity, care has to acquire value – to be 'really' subsumed within capitalism[81] – a process that involves the simplification, subdivision and rationalisation of tasks. An economic or market logic must develop to enable care to be competitively exchanged. Informal care is priced so that social providers can contract for services. Governments contribute to this process by creating ways of measuring and evaluating care and supporting the development of differentially skilled care workers catering for different market sectors. Within an 'enterprise' society, individuals and families are expected to take responsibility for anticipating and meeting their care needs. A logic of choice based upon transactions in which fluid things become fixed replaces a logic of care as understood by care ethicists,[82] which involves interactions between active participants.

A variety of care economies are developing rapidly, involving differing degrees and forms of marketisation and commodification.[83] Within the UK we see commodification in the way in which adult social care, particularly for the elderly, is now provided. Government creates understandings of need through policy criteria.[84] Local authority commissioners turn these criteria into tasks, priced by the minutes needed to undertake them. Suppliers bid against tender specifications to provide a set number of these specific tasks. Care workers are closely monitored to ensure that they undertake and are paid for the precise amount of time involved in completing each task.

These developments raise the question: to what extent can care be commodified? Human relationships are complex, and caring is complicated, highly culturally specific and involves often physically and emotionally

80 Tiina Vaittinen and Hanna-Kaisa Hoppania, 'The Governance of Care through the Body: A (Bio)political Reading of Commodification' Paper for Corporeal Capitalism: Body Matters in International Political Economy seminar, Birmingham University, 2013

81 Nancy Fraser, 'The Wages of Care: Reproductive Labor as Fictitious Commodity' lecture, University of Cambridge, 19 March 2011.

82 Rianne Mahon and Fiona Robinson, 'Introduction' in Rianne Mahon and Fiona Robinson (eds) *Feminist Ethics and Social Policy: Towards a New Global Political Economy of Care* (University of British Columbia Press 2011). Modern liberal theorists place the detached, neutral objective subject centre stage while ethics of care scholarship argues that subjectivity is rooted in the interdependency of human beings. We all need care to be truly human and caring is part of all our lives whether or not we recognise it.

83 Ibid

84 Support for a social enterprise culture in the UK can be seen clearly in the recently enacted Care Act 2014; see also Fiona Williams, 'Claiming and Framing in the Making of Care Policies: The Recognition and the Redistribution of Care' (United National Research Institute for Social Development 2010); Ann Stewart, 'Legal Constructions of Body Work' in Carol Wolkowitz and others (eds) *Body/Sex/Work: Intimate, embodied and sexualized labour* (Palgrave Macmillan 2013)

intensive, time-consuming body work.[85] In economic terms, without lowering standards, the productivity of caring cannot be raised through mass production. Arms and legs cannot be washed separately in mass showers in different locations. Measures of high productivity are indices of low-quality care.[86] There is considerable evidence in the UK that the market model for the provision of adult social care is failing and is in crisis. High-profile businesses, such as residential care providers Southern Cross, have collapsed.[87] The present model is built around a low-skilled, low-paid, marginalised workforce. Many work informally, attracting few labour protections, or are classified as self-employed. The intensive, gruelling conditions of work result in a very high turnover. There is clearly a major lack of investment in the sector as a whole, in part due to reliance on highly rationed public funding, but more generally because there is no agreement on how the costs of such care should be distributed between the individual and society more generally. It comes therefore as no surprise that the sector is heavily reliant on migrant, predominately female labour.[88] Such workers are usually better educated and deemed 'more willing' and 'empathetic' than their local counterparts.[89] Their undervalued labour hides the costs of care.

There is huge public concern over the often appalling quality of care provided, highlighted in high-profile exposés of abuse by care workers. These developments have led to a range of demands for greater public regulation to protect the interests of vulnerable care recipients and to the blaming of individual workers, resulting in increasing monitoring and surveillance as well as criminal prosecutions. As such, workers are seen as potentially dangerous factors of production.

Is this a specific crisis therefore – a product of commodification within the particular UK context? Or has the increasing entanglement of women within global economic processes resulted in a general crisis? In many parts of the world, there has been a rapid drop in fertility levels and family size which eases women's burdens considerably, although there has also been a reduction in extended family networks and the nuclearisation of families at a time when the population is ageing.[90] In the global south, there has been a general improvement in access to primary education, and to

85 Wolkowitz n 5

86 Susan Himmelweit, 'Policy on Care: A Help or Hindrance to Gender Inequality?' in Jacqueline Scott and others (eds) *Women and Employment: Changing Lives and New Challenges* (Edward Elgar 2008) 347

87 Ann Stewart, 'From Family to Personal Responsibility: The Challenges for Care of the Elderly in England' *Journal of Social Welfare and Family Law* 34 (2) 179–196

88 Sixty per cent of care workers working in institutional care in London are foreign-born workers of whom 28 per cent are estimated to be UK citizens, Isabel Shutes 'Social Care for Older People and Migrant Workers' (Migrant Observatory 2011) http://migrationobservatory.ox.ac.uk/policy-primers/social-care-older-people-and-demand-migrant-workers

89 Stewart n 10 chapter 6

90 Lourdes Benaria, 'Globalization, Women's Work, and Care Needs: The Urgency of Reconciliation Policies' (2010) *North Carolina Law Review* 5

health services,[91] thereby shifting some responsibility from women to other institutions. There have also been improvements in basic infrastructure, such as water supply and roads, that ease women's burdens.[92] These developments enable more women to undertake paid work but have not changed the enduring gendered assumptions relating to women's responsibility for socially reproductive activities.

Geo-historical contexts of care differ: particular institutional contexts, including State economic and social policies and specific political economies of livelihoods produce different care practices.[93] For instance, in India these take the form of stratified familialism whereby the State deals with family and community networks, not with citizens with individual rights. In elite and middle-class homes there is 'good' care including activities associated with investment in children's future, while in poor and labouring households, where women undertake paid work in or away from the home, there are few resources for care and so practices appear as poor care – as a care deficit. Public provision of formal care is scarce and not available to the bulk of informal workers; workplace provision is lacking, even for formal workers. Elite and middle-class families in any case prefer privately hired, individualised services. Their ability to replace and supplement familial care through services in this way reinforces the idea of familialism and women's central role in maintaining it.[94]

Local care chains are stratified according to the range of kin and unpaid care available and the extent to which it can be drawn upon. Care work is pooled within families across urban and rural locations, classes, regions and castes. The most successful are large households and those living near kin, consisting of non-migrant, middle- and upper-class households and rural households, which can maintain relationships and reciprocity, and therefore are able to call on kin who are available to assist. The urban poor and migrants are not in this position and poor labouring households all have to earn. Their poverty ensures that they cannot provide much assistance to others which undermines long-term reciprocity within kinship networks.[95]

Changing needs and understandings of care in India are met primarily through informal arrangements. Wealthier, urban families supplement these with paid domestic workers and nannies either recruited locally or through placement agencies, which supply internally migrant workers. Different contexts result in differently constructed needs and ways of meeting them. In other Asia-Pacific countries, such as Thailand, Singapore and Malaysia,

91 World Bank n 63

92 Ibid

93 Shahra Razavi, 'Rethinking Care in a Development Context: An Introduction' in Shahra Razavi (ed.) *Seen, Heard, Counted: Rethinking Care in a Development Context* (Wiley 2012)

94 Rajni Palriwala and N Neetha, 'Stratified Familialism: The Care Regime in India through the Lens of Childcare' in Shahra Razavi n 93

95 Ibid

and in a number of Latin America countries there is far more reliance on domestic workers who migrate within the region. As we have seen, the ILO records significant rises in the number of domestic workers over the last 20 years, accounting for almost 8 per cent and 12 per cent of all women in paid employment in these two regions.[96] They attribute this rise to high levels of income inequality within and between States as well as to women's increased labour force participation. Wealth accounts for the exceptionally high levels of domestic workers in the Middle East where there are very low levels of female employment.

In contrast there is very low reliance on domestic workers in Nordic and Eastern European countries with different histories. Both regions have given higher priority to supplementing informal care with social forms of provision. Households in European welfare states more generally rely less on domestic workers (although migrant workers are used in Spain, France and Italy). Similar work is undertaken by 'social' rather than 'domestic' care workers although the work can take place in domestic as well as institutional settings.

Women who have gained access to formal work can utilise its associated labour and social protections to help manage their care responsibilities. The extent of these social protections and linked rights will depend on economic positioning within global markets but they are more extensive in global north welfare states than in the global south. European reconciliation policies, in particular, seek to address the 'balance' between work and family responsibilities. There is little or no appetite within States with emerging economies to substantiate further the rights of their formal workers or to extend these forms of entitlements to the many more informal workers. Informed by feminism, development campaigners are increasingly constructing a care crisis for women living in extreme poverty as a barrier to social and economic inclusion.[97] As we saw in relation to informal workers' campaigns, they focus on rights to social protection. Women's still huge burden of unpaid care constitutes a violation of their rights as citizens: to education, political participation, leisure and to decent work as well as to gender equality. They therefore seek to recast existing measures within Convention on the Elimination of all forms of Discrimination Against Women (CEDAW) and other human rights treaties as rights to be relieved of care. They call for more quality public services including basic infrastructure, social protection, early child care and health services to be financed through more 'progressive domestic resource mobilisation' (taxation).[98] Women who are incorporated at the margins of globalisation

96 ILO n 4

97 Action Aid, *Making Care Visible: Women's unpaid care work in Nepal, Nigeria, Uganda and Kenya* (Action Aid 2013)

98 Ibid

or who are decoupled from such processes tend to view their activities as meeting their socially reproductive responsibilities, as a survival strategy.

International policy makers tend to see the problem in economic terms, as impeding efficiency and productivity: not 'smart economics'.[99] The international financial institutions have seen the social damage caused by their earlier rampant free-market policies with minimal 'safety nets' and now recognise the need for social expenditure if their liberalisation agenda is to continue.[100] There is support for a social enterprise model which values more participation, greater community solidarity, more care-focused services and some basic social protection measures, one form popular in Latin America and now in some parts of Africa being (conditional) cash transfer programmes.[101]

Care is becoming a political issue as a variety of constituencies make it visible in order to tackle a range of 'crises' in relation to social reproduction. The increasing reliance on predominately migrant women workers to undertake care in a wide variety of institutional contexts, because they are often unable otherwise to survive and to meet their own socially reproductive responsibilities, raises the question as to whether this phenomenon itself constitutes a crisis and, if so, for whom, and whether the ILO approach based on valuing 'domestic' workers addresses it adequately.

Domestic workers, as defined by the ILO, at present 'fit' into less commodified local care economies. Nonetheless, their caring labour serves similar purposes in terms both of the activities undertaken and of hiding the social costs of care within familial structures. The ILO strategy to make domestic work valuable facilitates marketisation and commodification – it makes it more like social care. It can facilitate the further development of a stratified global care service industry. The logic of choice rather than care will be strengthened. While the express aim of the Decent Work agenda is to avoid labour being seen as purely a factor of production, the formalisation of a work relationship may work against this objective. If, however, the strategy is successful, domestic workers will be more visible and valued but also potentially more costly.

Who will bear this more visible cost of care? Hugely wealthy households will have no difficulty – but for the rest? Is it appropriate for individual households in societies where there are very few state-provided social welfare rights or facilities to bear more commodified costs? Will individual (female) employers be blamed for non-compliance? Making domestic work visible facilitates the development of a stratified global care service industry. To what extent will such workers, the majority of whom are migrants, be able to realise the potential protections and an improved market position when caring itself remains economically and socially un/undervalued?

99 World Bank n 63
100 Shahra Razavi n 93, 1
101 Ibid

Global value chains, global care chains and the international division of reproductive labour[102]

As we have seen, the ILO has adapted its approach to international labour standards in order to embed within the global governance framework workers' claims to be more than factors of production. This strategy is part of a more general shift to tame trade through soft law and voluntarily adopted measures. Labour rights are reconstructed as fundamental human (and labour) principles; public rights are transposed into pre-packaged private standards. MNEs 'care' for more than their shareholders through the adoption of corporate social responsibility measures such as social labelling.[103]

Global value chain or network analysis reveals the impact on labour of the complexity, fragmentation and geographical distribution of contemporary production processes.[104] By considering each and every stage in the development, production, distribution, consumption and disposal of a commodity, it is possible to see where and through which processes value is added. Both macro and micro governance measures play their part. Thus the extensive macro context (for example, the WTO multilateral trading framework, the Organisation for Economic Co-operation and Development's (OECD's) corporate governance measures, the US and EU Generalised Systems of Preferences, bilateral and regional agreements such as the North American Free Trade Agreement (NATFA) and EU Economic Partnership Agreements) contributes to the corporate governance processes that regulate the supply chains.

This frame of analysis enables a wide variety of stakeholders including global south States, development practitioners, civil society organisations, trade unions and consumer activists to seek to capture more value for those who are involved at the 'end' of the chain including workers.[105] High-profile disasters such as the death of over a thousand (mainly) women workers when the Rana Plaza building containing five textile factories collapsed in Bangladesh, and the threat of mass suicide by (mainly) women workers at FoxConn, an Apple manufacturing partner in China, provoke (often short-term) public debate on the human cost of a tee shirt or an iPhone and also put pressure on companies with reputations to protect to ensure that workers are treated better. Generally there is a growing policy consensus that it is not 'smart economics' for those involved in GVCs to 'race to the bottom' or assume a country gains a competitive advantage by offering

102 Rhacel Salazar Parrenas, 'The Reproductive Labour of Migrant Workers' (2012) *Global Networks* 12 (2) 269

103 Stewart n 10 for detailed discussion.

104 Gibbon et al n 8

105 Capturing the Gains: Economic and Social Upgrading in Global Production Networks and Trade www.capturingthegains.org/about; Cornelia Staritz and Jose Guilherme Reis (eds) *Global Value Chains, Economic Upgrading, and Gender: Case Studies of the Horticulture, Tourism, and Call Center Industries* (World Bank 2013)

the cheapest labour force.[106] The argument is that in the medium to long run there is more value to be added in home States through upgrading strategies including boosting capacity to comply with company, State and international standards and regulations. This involves States investing to strengthen watchdog organisations such as trade unions and civil society groups and co-operating with lead firms and suppliers to ensure compliance.

While some may argue that what is being created here is a form of reflexive law which will ensure compliance,[107] there are many problems with this approach,[108] not least of which is that these types of measures only extend to or can be enforced within first-tier production. They cover factory workers but not those working for subcontractors, more informally or at home. Private standards only apply to those who are able to join the global production process and unless they are generalised through public legal and policy measures protect only the most advantaged. Unless the companies are subject to pressure from their consumers and/or are operating in a sector with a strong trade union presence there is little or no incentive to develop these measures or capacity to monitor implementation.[109]

Because the main aim is to protect the supply chain, the regulations tend to focus on product quality and safety and may extend only to the core labour principles. Some, such as the multi-stakeholder Ethical Trading Initiative, go further to require that signatories provide 'living' wages; do not require 'excessive' working hours; and ensure safe and hygienic working conditions.[110] Because most use compliance with home-State legal rights as the benchmark for compliance, the process rights – freedom of association and collective bargaining – are compromised in States that restrict these, particularly in Economic Process Zones. Very few such initiatives address gender issues such as harassment at work, sex discrimination and the need for social protections and, because State labour protections are at best provided to employees, few women are able to rely on them even when they are used as the benchmark.[111]

Despite the many limitations, the development of global governance mechanisms has facilitated international campaigns to highlight the position of women workers. Alliances of stakeholders, not restricted to trade unions, have been able to use social dialogue to think creatively about women's needs and how to meet them, including through use of the Decent Work

106 UNCTAD, *Global Value Chains: Investment and Trade for Development, World Investment Report 2013* (United Nations 2013)

107 Rogowski n 7

108 Alston n 40; Deakin n 55; Collins et al n 51; Hepple n 40

109 Jimmy Donaghey and others, 'From Employment Relations to Consumption Relations: Balancing Labor Governance in Global Supply Chains' (2014) *Human Resource Management* 53 (2) 229–252

110 Ethical Trading Base Codes available at www.ethicaltrade.org/sites/default/files/resources/ETI%20Base%20Code%20-%20English_0.pdf

111 See Stewart note 10

framework.[112] As a result, women workers in global value chains are more visible, partly because their position can be fitted within emerging global governance regimes.

Here we are primarily concerned with workers (not commodities) who move to provide caring services. Recent iterations of GCC analysis have been enriched by drawing upon the GVC conceptual framework to provide a 'materialist relational approach' to this form of migration.[113] GCC now encompasses those who migrate to undertake public caring such as nurses[114] and to include sex work within a body work framework.[115] It uses globalist, ethical and policy analysis to identify the relations of interdependence within the chains and the ways in which vulnerability is created. It asks who benefits, who bears the risks, how are costs distributed and who is exploited. It recognises the important part played by global governance structures.[116]

Generally services play a significant and growing part in national economies worldwide.[117] Does the trade-related global governance framework extend to protect those who provide such services? Global services providers such as G4S have embraced this framework. It has signed up to the Global Compact, adopted the Ruggie Principles and is developing a code of conduct for the security sector.[118] The market in care services is not generally constituted by multinational service providers although there are large players such as BUPA.

We have seen that the way in which caring is undertaken depends heavily on local contexts. The demand for migrant care workers comes from State, social or private service providers or from households. These markets are mediated through recruitment agencies or through informal networks which work within the political economy of migration. As the relative lack of support for the WTO General Agreement on Trade in Services (GATS) process demonstrates, establishing a robust multilateral trade in services framework has proven difficult. In particular, little progress has been made in developing mode 4 which potentially facilitates the movement of natural persons.[119] This process, if based upon easily available mode 4 visas for

112 Stephanie Barrientos, 'Gender and Ethical Trade: Can Vulnerable Women Workers Benefit?' in Sylvia Chant (ed.) *The International Handbook of Gender and Poverty* (Edward Elgar 2010) 440

113 Yeates n 10

114 Ibid

115 Stewart n 10

116 Stewart ibid; Yeates n 10

117 Jane Kelsey, *Serving Whose Interests? The Political Economy of Trade in Services Agreements* (Routledge 2008)

118 Ethical Performance http://ethicalperformance.com/reports/view/790

119 Article 1.2 General Agreement on Trade in Services mode 4: the presence of a natural person (that is not a legal entity) when the service provider is established (temporarily) in a different country – eg an intra-company transfer of IT workers between India and the UK; Stewart n 10 195–197

those providing care services, could facilitate the development of a transparent visible market. However, there is little political support for a free trade discourse, most particularly if it involves low-skilled workers (although free movement is a founding EU principle). Instead, States impose immigration controls. Because care labour is not politically or socially valued, it is seen as a problem, while economically it is sought after because it keeps wage, and therefore care, costs down.[120] As a result, recruitment agencies often operate on the margins of legality, while those outside the boundaries are constructed as traffickers or smugglers and attract international criminal sanctions. While some States seek to regulate agencies, this is not conducive territory for embedding fundamental human rights and labour principles.

In the absence of a functioning multilateral framework, States enter into bilateral agreements to address particular care service demands.[121] Here there are opportunities to ensure that workers are protected via the incorporation of the core principles and adoption of the Decent Work agenda. However, much depends on the relative power relations between the particular States.[122]

It is also difficult to replicate in these segmented but often highly familiarised informal markets the conditions that have given rise to the wider corporate social responsibility initiative associated with GVC. Large private service providers have reputations to protect and are more likely to respond to ethics-based campaigning. Social providers, such as charities or public authorities, may also be responsive. For instance within the UK, the NHS has an ethical recruitment policy which guarantees that internationally recruited staff enjoy the same rights as locals while restricting recruitment from countries with high healthcare needs.[123] UNISON, a public sector trade union, has produced an ethical care charter directed at commissioners of home care services.[124]

However, small providers employing few staff, and households, even less, are not in the same position as Apple, Walmart or Zara. Not only are the difficulties with providing an institutional framework to support domestic workers identified by the ILO replicated in the global governance context,

120 Shereen Hussein and others, *International Social Care Workers in England: Profile, Motivations, Experiences and Expectations* Social Care Workforce Unit (King's College London 2010), www.kcl.ac.uk/sspp/kpi/scwru/pubs/2010/husseinetal2010internationalfinalreport.pdf

121 For example, the Japanese–Philippines Economic Partnership Agreement allows Filipino nurses and care workers to work in Japan, www.wipo.int/wipolex/en/other_treaties/text.jsp?file_id=225225

122 For example, Ethiopia has less bargaining power than the Philippines which in turn has far less bargaining power than the USA or the EU.

123 NHS Code of Practice for International Recruitment 18 March 2014 www.nhsemployers.org/your-workforce/recruit/employer-led-recruitment/international-recruitment/uk-code-of-practice-for-international-recruitment

124 UNISON's ethical care charter (UNISON 2012) www.unison.org.uk/news/unison-welcomes-sign-up-to-ethical-care-charter

but, as we have seen in relation to organising informal workers, transnational multi-stakeholder alliances focused around the production process are unlikely to emerge. These difficulties are all the more pronounced in familial care settings where employers are also recipient and consumers of care.

Conclusion

On one level, the recent ILO measures relating to domestic work suggest that it is possible for women to come to official attention without being seen as an obstacle to policy makers. The ILO brings domestic work into the public sphere and fits it within the wider Decent Work framework. This framework reflects an understanding that present forms of globalisation have changed the relationship between employers and workers. Solidaristic means of achieving labour and social rights through collective bargaining and State social provision are being replaced by social dialogue and greater reliance on the discourse of fundamental human and labour rights. Within this framework, informal working including domestic work is not, in principle, an obstacle to protection. It reflects the necessity of recognising that women are entitled to be treated as citizens, irrespective of their migrant status, with claims to social protections and freed from unequal care responsibilities, as well as workers, when undertaking often socially ostracised and undervalued work.

The concerns of labour activists that such developments in global labour governance undermine solidarity and do little to tackle profound disparities in wealth are valid. Reliance on a consumption-based politics involving alliances of multinational stakeholders to nudge or shame State policy makers and employers into the provision of better rights may have positive effects in some sectors of production, but this form of politics does not fit easily with service provision. Care economies are very context specific. As the rising numbers of domestic workers indicate, they are often based upon models of familialism.

Problems associated with the provision of care are becoming more politically visible. The focus for the anxiety varies. In the UK, the focus is very much on the rights violations of the care recipient by care workers, not the lack of social investment in care, being cast as the problem – very much a case of workers coming to public attention as an obstacle. Development campaigners highlight the plight of women socially and economically excluded by the burden of their caring responsibilities. Activism around domestic work highlights the violations of rights of workers, not consumers/care recipients who, due to huge inequalities in wealth, are not seen to be of concern.

GCC analysis must therefore take account of feminist analysis of the international division of socially reproductive labour. As Parrenas argues, such an approach allows us to factor in the women who employ workers and the ways in which they seek to manage their socially reproductive and work roles in any given context. It avoids individualising conflicts and culpabilities while not missing the hierarchies that exist.[125] The present ILO conceptualisation of domestic workers does not fit their work into this wider framework, which would focus on the creation of segmented global markets in care and how domestic work fits within these segmented markets. Care workers are vulnerable in part because care is difficult to trade. Care is not recognised as valuable yet it is costly to provide in the marketplace. The costs of the failure to develop a regulated global market are borne, often invisibly, by migrant care workers. It is essential to ensure that the rights of all those involved – care workers and care recipients – are recognised, and to relieve women of the need to do too much caring, the real challenge is ensure that there is public recognition of the value of the social reproductive relationships which support each and every person and community.

125 Parrenas n 102

3 Care Work in the European Court of Human Rights' Case Law: Beyond Servitude and Forced Labour?

Fulvia Staiano

Introduction

In 2011, the Preamble of International Labour Organization Convention no. 189 Concerning Decent Work for Domestic Workers (hereafter Domestic Workers Convention)[1] pinpointed the current situation of domestic workers worldwide by highlighting the contrast between the socioeconomic importance of this type of work and its devaluation. On the one hand, indeed, the International Labour Organization (ILO) recognized the significant contribution of domestic workers to the global economy, which includes increasing paid job opportunities for women and men workers with family responsibilities, greater scope for caring for ageing populations, children and person with a disability, and substantial income transfers within and between countries.[2]

On the other hand, however, the Preamble also underlined that

> domestic work continues to be undervalued and invisible and is mainly carried out by women and girls, many of whom are migrants or members of disadvantaged communities and who are particularly vulnerable to discrimination in respect of conditions of employment and of work, and to other abuses of human rights.[3]

The contradiction between the effects and the assigned value of domestic work is not only reflected but also reinforced by law. The provision of special legal regimes regulating domestic work and often envisaging weaker protections and lower standards in comparison with the general discipline of employment, the exclusion from general social security schemes and the precarious migration status entailed by national immigration laws applicable to migrant domestic workers are among the most common examples

1 ILO Convention C189: Convention Concerning Decent Work for Domestic Workers (100th International Labour Conference Session, Geneva, 16 June 2011).

2 Ibid Preamble.

3 Ibid.

of this phenomenon.[4] As a consequence, domestic workers today continue to experience serious decent work deficits as well as a general condition of disempowerment due to the lack of recognition of their work as a ground to access rights and entitlements.

Arguably, human rights law has shown increasing attention to this matter. The key development constituted by the Domestic Workers Convention is not indeed an isolated display of interest in this field. Within the United Nations (UN), the Committee on the Elimination of Discrimination Against Women and the Committee on the Protection of the Rights of all Migrant Workers and Members of Their Families have not only criticized the exclusion of domestic workers from labour laws and protections, but have also emphasized the need to recognize the high social and economic value of domestic work – and they have done so from the specific angle of human and fundamental rights. In particular, the Committee on the Elimination of Discrimination against Women (CEDAW) has expressed the view that States' obligations under human rights treaties "must be undertaken in recognition of the social and economic contributions of women migrant workers to their own countries and countries of destination, including through caregiving and domestic work",[5] while the Migrant Workers Committee has observed that "States should take all the necessary measures to promote a shift in public perceptions so that domestic work becomes widely recognized as work and domestic workers as workers with fundamental rights, including labour rights".[6]

The recognition of the actual value of domestic work is not merely a matter of principle. Analyzing the notions of domestic work adopted by human rights law and the value attached to such activities, indeed, provides us with invaluable insights on the degree to which work performed within private households is accepted as a valid ground to access rights and entitlements. In other words, it reveals whether and to what extent domestic

4 With respect to the exclusion of domestic workers from labour protections, see, for instance, International Labour Organization, *Domestic Workers Across the World: Global and Regional Statistics and the Extent of Legal Protection*, Geneva 9 January 2013, 46. In relation to the vulnerability generated by national immigration laws applicable to migrant domestic workers, the Committee on the Protection of the Rights of All Migrant Workers and Members of Their Families has rightly observed that "even for workers with a documented or regular migration status, ... vulnerabilities arise where immigration laws tie their status to the continued sponsorship of specific employers" and that "consequently, migrant domestic workers may risk deportation if they try to escape an abusive employment relationship or seek legal remedies against their employers" (UN Committee on the Protection of the Rights of All Migrant Workers and Members of Their Families, "General Comment No. 1", 23 February 2011, UN Doc CMW/C/GC/1 para 21).

5 UN Committee on the Elimination of Discrimination against Women, "General Recommendation No. 26", 5 December 2008, CEDAW/C/2009/WP.1/R para 3.

6 UN Committee on the Protection of the Rights of All Migrant Workers and Members of Their Families, "General Comment No. 1 on migrant domestic workers", 23 February 2011, UN Doc CMW/C/GC/1 (4) para 39.

workers are able to access and enjoy rights and entitlements on the grounds of their work in the context of human rights law.

Arguably, such an analysis is significantly easier and more meaningful when it concerns the judicial enforcement of human rights sources in individual cases initiated by or concerning household workers. It is precisely in its everyday application, indeed, that human rights law reveals its true potential and new perspectives are opened by individual claims pushing the boundaries of the literal meaning of conventions and treaties in this field.

It is therefore regrettable that none of the above-mentioned sources recognizing the high socioeconomic value of domestic work are assisted by a supranational court in charge of their implementation and enforcement in national legal orders. ILO Conventions in general, despite their character of hard-law sources, have been deemed to be weak instruments vis-à-vis their implementation, since

> not all countries that have ratified ILO conventions have given effect to their provisions, and unfortunately the ILO appears helpless in ensuring compliance [and] many member countries just pay lip service to the ideals of the body by ratifying conventions they do not intend to implement.[7]

Moreover, it has been noted that "ILO Conventions ... lack the clarity of discrete court enforcement mechanisms where distinct legal remedies may be available to a state and/or individual litigant".[8] Similarly, both the UN Committee on the Elimination of Discrimination against Women and the UN Committee on the Protection of the Rights of All Migrant Workers (respectively in charge of monitoring the implementation of the Convention on the Elimination of All Forms of Discrimination against Women[9] – CEDAW – and the International Convention on the Protection of the Rights of All Migrant Workers and Members of their Families[10]) do not have the power to issue binding judicial decisions, despite the possibility to assess individual complaints on claims of violation of the rights enshrined in their respective Conventions.

Conversely, at regional level and more specifically in the European context, human and fundamental rights are gradually but increasingly providing a legal framework in the judicial analysis of carers' claims of access to

7 F Adewumi, "The Global Economy, Trade Unions and the Protection of Workers' Rights in Nigeria" (2012) 15 *Working USA: The Journal of Labor & Society* 529, 535.

8 T Buck and A Nicholson, "Constructing the International Legal Framework", in G Craig (ed.) *Child Slavery Now: A Contemporary Reader* (The Policy Press 2010), 54.

9 Convention on the Elimination of All Forms of Discrimination against Women (adopted on 18 December 1979, entered into force on 3 September 1981) 1249 UNTS 13.

10 International Convention on the Protection of the Rights of All Migrant Workers and Members of Their Families (adopted on 18 December 1990, entered into force on 1 July 2003) 2220 UNTS 3.

rights and entitlements on the grounds of their (paid or unpaid) care work. This process is observable both before the European Court of Justice (CJEU) and before the European Court of Human Rights (ECtHR). On the one hand, on multiple occasions[11] the CJEU has granted third-country national women with residence rights in their host countries on the grounds of the unpaid reproductive and care work performed by them to the benefit of Union citizens, observing that such care was indispensable for the latter's enjoyment of their fundamental rights and freedoms. On the other hand, the ECtHR is currently building an interesting body of case law with respect to violations of the right to be free from slavery, servitude and forced labour of third-country national women who had been forced to perform unpaid domestic work against their will in private households. Since the landmark *Siliadin* judgment of 2005,[12] concerning a Togolese minor forced to perform unpaid domestic work in France, the Court has issued three other judgments recognizing the responsibility of host States for breaches of the right to be free from slavery, servitude and forced labour, due to the lack of domestic legislation affording effective protection to the victims and to the consequent failure of the national authorities to effectively investigate allegations of trafficking, forced labour and servitude.[13] Two of these judgments, in particular, concerned forms of labour exploitation within the scope of article 4: *C.N. v. the United Kingdom*[14] – initiated by a young Ugandan woman held in domestic servitude – and *C.N. and V. v. France*[15] – concerning two minor sisters from Burundi brought to France by their uncle and aunt, who had subjected the older sister to servitude and forced labour within their household. While the judgments of *Siliadin* and *C.N. and V.* concerned provisions of the French Criminal Code which had in the meantime been reformed,[16] it is possible to observe how the *C.N.* judgment directly encouraged the United Kingdom to improve its normative framework in order to adjust it to the standards established by the Court and to comply with its

11 Case C-60/00 *Mary Carpenter v Secretary of State for the Home Department* [2002] ECR-I 6305; Case C-413/99 *Baumbast and R v Secretary of State for the Home Department* [2002] ECR I-07091; Case C-200/02 *Kunqian Catherine Zhu and Man Lavette Chen v Secretary of State for the Home Department* [2004] ECR I-9951. In relation to this case law, see also Case C-34/09 *Gerardo Ruiz Zambrano v Office national de l'emploi (ONEm)* [2011] ECR I-01177; Case C-434/09 *Shirley McCarthy v Secretary of State for the Home Department* [2011] ECR I-03375; Case C-256/11 *Murat Dereci and Others v Bundesministerium für Inneres* [2011] ECR I-11315; Joined Cases C-356/11 and C-357/11 *O. and S. v Maahanmuuttovirasto and Maahanmuuttovirasto v L.* [2012] OJ C 26/11; Case C-86/12 *Adzo Domenyo Alokpa and Others v Ministre du Travail, de l'Emploi et de l'Immigration* [2013] OJ C 344/13.

12 *Siliadin v. France* ECtHR 2005-VII 289.

13 *Rantsev v. Cyprus and Russia* ECtHR 2010 6; *C.N. v. the United Kingdom* App no 4239/08 (ECtHR, 13 November 2012); *C.N. and V. v. France* App no 67724/09 (ECtHR, 11 October 2012).

14 *C.N.* (n 13).

15 *C.N. and V.* (n 13).

16 *Code Pénal articles* 225-13; 225-14; 225-15.

positive obligations of protection of victims of slavery, servitude and forced labour. These normative changes[17] have also led the Court to strike off its lists two other cases concerning allegations of article 4 violations, raised by third-country national women obliged to perform unpaid domestic work.[18] In any case, the specific developments concerning the United Kingdom do not undermine the importance of such case law nor its possibilities of future expansion and growth.

A comparison between the jurisprudence of the CJEU and that of the ECtHR, however, reveals a fundamental difference in their respective approaches to the problem of the value of care and domestic work. In particular, it is crucial to stress that the Court of Justice has so far granted carers access to rights and entitlements on the grounds of their work within the household, only as long as such work was functional to Union citizens' enjoyment of their fundamental rights and freedoms. This constant feature was already observable in the *Carpenter* judgment, concerning a Philippine woman married to a United Kingdom national who had overstayed her leave and had been issued with a deportation order by the national authorities. Here, the Court of Justice observed that the decision to deport Mrs Carpenter (who looked after Mr Carpenter's children from his first marriage, facilitating his business travels in other Member States) would be disproportionally "detrimental to their family life and, therefore, to the conditions under which Mr Carpenter exercises a fundamental freedom [i.e., his freedom to provide services within the Union]".[19] Such an approach, therefore, brought the CJEU to examine whether the presence of the involved third-country nationals was so essential that their expulsion would force the Union citizens to leave the Union or to renounce the exercise of their fundamental freedoms.[20] Unsurprisingly, a similar scrutiny worked to the advantage of third-country nationals who cared for minor children, while relationships with adult Union citizens[21] were not considered as involving a sufficient degree of dependence to justify the granting of residence rights.

The ECtHR's approach to date, on the other hand, appears to bear the potential to offer a wider scope of recognition and protection of domestic workers' rights. So far, indeed, the protection offered by the Court to the applicants in the mentioned judgments based on violations of article 4 of the Convention on Human Rights (ECHR) has been granted regardless of the "usefulness" of their care work for other individuals. At the same time, this feature has also meant that the inherent value of such work has remained relatively unexplored by the Court. Understanding its position

17 Coroners and Justice Act 2009. In this context, further progress is also expected to come from the currently pending Draft Modern Slavery Bill 2014.

18 *Kawogo v. the United Kingdom* App no 56921/09 (ECtHR, 3 September 2013); *O.G.O. v. the United Kingdom* App no 13950/12 (ECtHR, 18 February 2014).

19 *Carpenter* (n 11) para 39.

20 See, for instance, *Zambrano* (n 11) paras 42–44.

21 *McCarthy* (n 11); *Dereci* (n 11).

on this specific matter is crucial to disclose whether and to what extent the Court will be able in the future to move beyond the perspective of servitude and forced labour towards a more extensive protection of domestic workers' rights. With that in mind, this chapter will use the Court's case law on article 4 ECHR as a starting point to explore the notion(s) of care work adopted by the Court itself in selected key judgments, while reasoning on their significance vis-à-vis the level of acceptance of this type of work as a gateway to access rights and entitlements. While I am aware of the manifold gendered implications underlying this matter, in this specific context I will not adopt a gender perspective since this inquiry would require an entire additional chapter.

Furthermore, it is important to clarify that, although domestic work entails a variety of chores (care labour but also household activities such as cleaning and cooking), this chapter will focus on a notion of domestic work as also or mainly entailing the provision of care to other individuals – such as children, elderly people, persons with disabilities and so forth. The ultimate aim of this critical review will be to explore future possibilities for the protection and the empowerment of domestic workers before the ECtHR and more broadly in a human rights framework beyond the valuable but narrow perspective of servitude and forced labour.

Domestic workers' labour rights before the ECtHR

Notwithstanding the pivotal importance of the mentioned ECtHR judgments, two main shortcomings emerge from this under-construction case-law on domestic workers. Both are due to the fact that domestic work has been so far discussed by the Court exclusively in relation to possible violations of article 4 of the Convention.

First, the focus of the Court's analysis has inevitably been fixed on the most severe forms of abuse and exploitation encountered by domestic workers, such as trafficking, servitude and forced labour. On the other hand, the everyday and most subtle forms of exploitation endured by this category, and more broadly their claims in terms of labour rights and work standards, have so far remained unaddressed by the Court.

Second, analyzing domestic work under the lens of slavery and forced labour has directed the Court's attention towards a notion of care work based on lack of choice, vulnerability and extremely degrading working and living conditions. While this constituted an unavoidable and actually logical result of the fact that the claims submitted by the applicants concerned violations of article 4 of the Convention, it is also true that as a consequence the Court has so far exclusively considered domestic workers in a perspective of victimization. Thus, the Court has yet to analyze a key question for domestic workers in the European legal space: that is, whether the professional provision of care – as a freely chosen occupation – can constitute a sufficient ground to access rights and entitlements through the human rights framework enshrined in the Convention. Against this background, in order to assess whether and to what extent the ECtHR will be able to effectively protect domestic workers' rights and respond to their decent work claims, it is necessary to consider whether the Court will be able to move beyond the described shortcomings.

From the outset, it must be noted that an assessment of the Court's capability to offer effective protection to domestic workers' labour rights beyond extreme forms of exploitation (such as forced labour and domestic servitude) would require a degree of development of the Court's case law which is yet to be reached. It is indeed well known that the absolutely primary – if not exclusive – role played by civil and political rights in the ECHR gave rise to severe doubts that the ECtHR could offer any protection at all to economic and social rights, including labour rights. In recent years, this view has been partly contested by scholars who have observed how the ECtHR is in fact progressively expanding the scope of the Convention by also offering protection to social and economic rights. An integrated approach has been identified whereby "certain social and labour components are essential elements of the Convention, and should therefore be protected as such".[22] This view has been mainly inspired by the observation that in several judgments the Court "took cognisance of social and labour rights materials of other international bodies that illuminated the scope of the Convention".[23] In particular, it has been noted that while "the focus so far has been mainly, if not exclusively, on negative obligations and non-discrimination obligations",[24] positive obligations are being identified by the Court in relation to the right to work and – more importantly for our purposes – with respect to working conditions. In particular, the case of *Siliadin* has been pointed out as an example of the newly found capability of the Court to establish positive state obligations with respect to decent work under the Convention, since in this case "the Court held that lack of criminalisation of extremely harsh working conditions … amounted to a breach of Article 4".[25]

However, it must not be overlooked that the *Siliadin* judgment, as I stressed with respect to the first shortcoming of the ECtHR's case law on domestic work, did not originate from "ordinary" decent work claims, but

22 V Mantouvalou, "Labour Rights in the European Convention on Human Rights: An Intellectual Justification for an Integrated Approach to Interpretation" (2013) 13 *Human Rights Law Review* 529, 536. According to Mantouvalou, the concept of integrated approach was introduced by M Scheinin, "Economic and Social Rights as Legal Rights", in A Eide, C Krause, A Rosas (eds) *Economic, Social and Cultural Rights: A Textbook* (Martinus Nijhoff 2001).

23 Mantouvalou, "Labour Rights" (n 22) 536.

24 R O'Connell, "The Right to Work in the European Convention on Human Rights" (2012) 2 *European Human Rights Law Review* 176, 189.

25 Mantouvalou, "Labour Rights" (n 22) 536–537. See also O'Connell, "The Right to Work" (n 24) 189.

rather concerned a foreign young woman in a position of extreme vulnerability who had been subjected to labour exploitation of such gravity that it fell under the scope of article 4 of the Convention. While the judgments of *Siliadin*, *C.N.* and *C.N. and V.* have clearly drawn the Court's analysis closer to elaborating a state obligation to ensure decent working conditions for all, caution is mandated before concluding that such cases constitute a definite proof of its capability to establish judicial guarantees for workers' rights. From this point of view, it is regrettable that the *Kawogo* case was not examined by the Court on its merits. This case indeed could have marked a further step forward in this respect, because the situation of "domestic forced labour"[26] described by the applicant directly stemmed from an initial violation of her rights as a domestic worker. Differently from the other applicants in the Court's judgments on labour exploitation under article 4, Ms. Kawogo had entered the United Kingdom with a domestic worker visa which recognized her with a right to "proper employment conditions"[27] and, of course, with a right to receive remuneration for work done. She was then forced to breach the terms of her visa, having been left by her employer in the United Kingdom with another family while the visa only allowed her to work for her employer and imposed her to return to Tanzania with the latter. As a consequence, she became liable to expulsion and thus vulnerable to exploitation. If the Court had considered the alleged violation of article 4 ECHR as a possibly direct result of the violation of the applicant's labour rights, the resulting judgment may have constituted a landmark decision. Instead, the everyday exploitation of domestic workers, that is, of professional providers of care in private households, currently remains unaddressed by the Court.

These observations direct us to the second main shortcoming observed in relation to the Court's judgments on labour exploitation as a violation of article 4 of the Convention, that is, their focus on care work as forced labour. This limitation is indeed equally due to the Court's inevitable focus on extreme forms of labour exploitation against individuals forced to perform domestic work against their will, and to the consequent lack of claims brought by applicants choosing to perform domestic work as a profession. As a result of this focus, domestic and care work in the Court's judicial analysis has only been considered in its worst possible version – as an undesired, exploitative, unpaid activity. As such, a profession commonly performed by disproportionally disenfranchised individuals, such as third-country national migrants (especially women), has not yet been considered by the Court as a gateway to access rights and entitlements on the grounds of its social and economic importance (a perspective that is increasingly being adopted and promoted by key international human rights law sources). An analysis of the prospective capability of the human rights

26 *Kawogo* App no 56921/09.
27 Ibid para 1.

framework provided by the European Convention to tackle this challenge – and live up to the standards established, among other sources, by the 2011 Domestic Workers Convention – raises questions concerning the intrinsic value assigned by the Court to care work *per se*. Such questions include the Court's attitude towards the existence of a right to provide care, towards care work as a freely chosen occupation – paid or unpaid – as well as the degree to which the highly personal relationships established through the provision of care may imply a recognition of rights and entitlements for carers.

With respect to these questions, interesting cues may be extracted from a different case law than the one currently under construction concerning article 4 ECHR. More specifically, in the following section I will critically review a selection of judgments by the ECtHR concerning claims of violations of the right to private and family life, protected in article 8 of the Convention, brought by or strictly related to unpaid carers within private households. A comparison between individuals providing unpaid care to their own family members and professional carers may seem weak. However, I am of the view that these judgments offer precious cues concerning the Court's perception of the inherent value of domestic and care work within households, which transcend the unpaid work realm. In this case law, indeed, the Court was repeatedly presented with the question of whether the care and domestic work provided by the applicants was a sufficiently valuable and necessary activity to legally justify and support their access to key rights and entitlements, such as residence rights or the right to access social security benefits. The following section will be devoted to exploring these points.

Care Labour: article 8 and the ECtHR

Unpaid care work within the household or towards family members has been addressed – more or less directly – on multiple occasions by the ECtHR under the right to private and family life enshrined in article 8 of the Convention. However, in cases where care labour constituted the main or a major ground for the applicants' claims, it has rarely (if ever) been recognized as an expression of interpersonal solidarity. Rather, in multiple cases the Court has revealed a quite negative attitude towards carers' responsibilities and importance within their families, conveying a devalued notion of unpaid care work. This section will focus on two main aspects of the Court's assessment of carers' claims, that is, the framing of care work as not amounting to "actual work" (i.e., to productive paid work) and the consideration of carers as interchangeable (with other workers or other family members) rather than as essential to the functioning and well-being of their families.

"She preferred to care":[28] *care labour as a choice not to work*

In 1986, a Swedish couple (Mr A. and Mrs K.) submitted an application to the European Commission of Human Rights lamenting a violation of their right to respect of their family life due to the national authorities' refusal to grant them social welfare benefits in the form of financial help.[29] In fact, the couple had been granted a social assistance benefit: they were given priority for placing their children at a day home care centre. However, such a benefit was incompatible with the family arrangement established by the applicants, whereby Mrs K. would carry out unpaid care work within the household while Mr A. would take up employment. This division of productive and reproductive work stemmed from the couple's consideration of what they believed to be the best interest of their children. After judicial controversies before lower courts, the Swedish Supreme Court applied a principle established in its previous case law, whereby "an applicant for assistance, who without a valid reason refuses to take up employment, can be refused assistance",[30] and held that the couple had no right to choose the forms of social benefits granted to them because Mrs K. did not have "any other reason for her failure to apply for employment other than her own wish to take care of the children".[31]

In its judgment *Andersson v. Sweden*,[32] the European Commission of Human Rights upheld the Supreme Court's decision. It indeed refused to recognize a breach of article 8. The Commission indeed noted that according to Swedish law "the applicants [had] decided that one of the parents should stay at home and take care of the children",[33] that "such decisions involved, for all couples, a financial burden"[34] and that in any case "the facts of the present case [did] not suggest that the authorities [had] in any way disrespected the applicants' decision to take care of their children themselves".[35] The Commission concluded on these grounds that

> it [was] true that under Swedish law the applicants [were] entitled to public assistance in order to obtain a reasonable standard of living, and that they were granted such assistance in the form of day home places but refused financial assistance, but this [could not] be interpreted as a failure to respect their family life.[36]

28 *Haydarie v. the Netherlands* App no 8876/04 (ECtHR, 20 October 2005).
29 *Andersson v. Sweden* (1986) 46 DR 251.
30 Ibid.
31 Ibid.
32 Ibid.
33 Ibid.
34 Ibid.
35 Ibid.
36 Ibid.

In support of its reasoning, the Commission stated that such a decision had to "be seen in the context of the general development in society which is characterised by a larger degree of equality between sexes and an increased number of women seeking employment on the labour market".[37] Thus, because Mrs K. had deviated from this norm, her reproductive and care work within the household was not recognized by the Commission as a sufficient ground to access social assistance benefits.

It is interesting to note in this respect that, in a subsequent judgment concerning the effects of an exactly opposite "norm" on a Swiss woman's enjoyment of her right to social security benefits, the ECtHR was ready to quash the domestic courts' decisions due to their discriminatory character. In particular, in the case of *Schuler-Zgraggen v. Switzerland*,[38] a woman (Mrs Schuler-Zgraggen) who had been receiving an invalidity pension for a pulmonary illness that made her completely unfit to work and 60–70 per cent capable of carrying out household work was subsequently denied the benefit by the Swiss authorities. The main justification for this change was that "her family circumstances had radically changed with the birth of her child"[39] and that "it could not be discounted that even if [she] had been fit, she would have been content with looking after her home once her child had been born".[40] Thus, the applicant "was in a position to be more active if she really wished to work despite her new family circumstances".[41] The stereotype presumption that the applicant would have chosen to perform reproductive and care work instead of productive work was also reinforced by the domestic judicial authorities. The Federal Insurance Court, indeed, observed that in relation to the applicant's pension claim it was necessary to consider "the fact that many married women go out to work until their first child is born, but give up their jobs for as long as the children need full-time care and upbringing" and that "on the balance of probabilities ... the applicant, even if her health had not been impaired, would have been occupied only as a housewife and mother".[42] Thus, Mrs Schuler-Zgraggen turned to the ECtHR, claiming a violation of her right to a fair trial pursuant to article 6 of the Convention and – most importantly for our purposes – that "the assumption made by [the Federal Insurance Court], that she would have given up working even if she had not had health problems, amounted to discrimination on the grounds of sex".[43] In this case, the Court recognized a violation of the applicant's right to non-discrimination in conjunction with the right to a fair trial (pursuant to article 14 and 6 of the Convention). This conclusion was strongly based on the principle of equality between

37 Ibid.
38 *Schuler-Zgraggen v. Switzerland* (1993) Series A no 263.
39 Ibid para 15.
40 Ibid para 20.
41 Ibid.
42 Ibid para 30.
43 Ibid para 39.

sexes, and on the view that the gendered assumptions drawn by the national authorities constituted the sole basis for their decisions and introduced an unjustified difference of treatment on the grounds of sex.

Despite their dated character, the *Andersson* and *Schuler-Zgraggen* judgments constitute an important reference for our purposes because they aptly epitomize how the legal and judicial framing of care work as a choice negatively affects carers' access to their rights and entitlements. In *Schuler-Zgraggen*, the negative effects of considering the applicant's situation as a result of an alleged choice to stay at home and take care of her child rather than resuming paid employment were promptly quashed by the Court. In the *Andersson* case, a similar framing was instead shared by the European Commission itself. At this point, I would argue that if the Court had framed the care work performed by Mrs K. not as a choice to remain outside the labour market but rather as a way of carrying out necessary activities within the household – and thus as actual work, unpaid but with its own social and economic value – its conclusions may have been different. This view is reinforced by the fact that, at a domestic level, a similar framing had been adopted by lower courts and had led them to recognize the couple's right to receive social assistance benefits in a form that they could actually benefit from. In this respect, the judicial reasoning of the Jönköping Administrative Court of Appeal appears particularly significant in its observation that "the children [were] so small that the care of them and the home must be regarded as a full-time employment"[44] and that in any case Mrs K. did "not have any training or professional experience which [made] her attractive on the labour market".[45]

The framing of care work as a choice not to perform actual work rather than as unpaid labour carried out to fulfil family responsibilities and obligations, or as an equally valuable way of contributing to the family management and economy as paid employment, has not exclusively characterized carers' right to access social assistance or social security benefits on the grounds of their work. Such discourses have also affected migrant carers' access to residence rights and family reunification. The *Haydarie v. the Netherlands*[46] judgment appears particularly interesting in this respect. It constitutes a fitting and contemporary example of judicial framing of unpaid care work as a choice to stay inactive and thus as a lesser occupation in comparison with paid employment, and is an example of how such framing worked against the carer's claim to family reunification.

The applicant, an Afghan woman (Mrs Haydarie) who had been residing in the Netherlands with one of her children and her disabled sister, having been granted asylum was denied the right to family reunification for her three other minor children. The justification given for this denial was that

44 Ibid.
45 Ibid.
46 *Haydarie* (n 28).

the applicant did not satisfy the minimum income requirements established by domestic law since her sole income consisted in welfare benefits. Under domestic law, the minimum income threshold was not to be enforced upon persons who could demonstrate that they had made "during a period of three years, serious but unsuccessful efforts to find gainful employment".[47] These serious efforts consisted in

> actively looking for and accepting work even where a job would not correspond to her education or professional experience, registering at an employment office ... and interim employment agencies indicating to be willing to accept any kind of work, reacting to vacancy announcements, intensive writing of (un)solicited job applications, and undertaking labour-market oriented studies.[48]

The Dutch Minister of Foreign Affairs assessed that Mrs Haydarie had failed to make such efforts, that "it was not excluded that the ... applicant would be able to comply with the income requirement within a reasonable time",[49] as well as that "for the time being, it could not be said that it was impossible for [her] ever to comply with the requirements for family reunion".[50] Therefore, her application for family reunification, to sponsor her minor children to join her in the Netherlands, was denied.

However, even if Mrs Haydarie was not participating in the national labour market, she could hardly be qualified as an inactive individual. Indeed, she submitted that her main occupation consisted in carrying out unpaid care work within her house. More specifically, "she had to care for her wheel-chair bound sister who refused aid from strangers and ... she did not wish to leave her sister alone in the house fearing that she might cause a fire".[51] Notwithstanding this, the Minister assessed that "it was the first applicant's own choice to care for her sister and ... she could appeal to aid providing bodies".[52] In other words, the applicant was penalized in her possibility to access family reunification and enjoy family life in her host country with her children because of a system clearly privileging a breadwinner model, constructed around the primacy of paid employment as a ground for accessing rights and entitlements. Unpaid care work, on the other hand, was not granted with such dignity and worth and was considered by the national authorities not only as synonymous with inactivity and passiveness, but also as a mere choice to personally carry out tasks which could well be outsourced to aid-providing bodies. The Regional Court confirmed this view by arguing that the applicant had "taken on the care

47 Ibid.
48 Ibid.
49 Ibid.
50 Ibid.
51 Ibid.
52 Ibid.

for her disabled sister, which *choice* [emphasis added] apparently entailed that she distanced herself from the labour market and thereby indirectly from her [three] children on account of failing to comply with the income requirement".[53]

Mrs Haydarie and the children therefore turned to the ECtHR lamenting a violation of their right to respect for their family life, as protected by article 8 of the Convention. Among other arguments, one of the main complaints of Mrs Haydarie was that "the Netherlands authorities had given insufficient weight to her moral responsibility and unpaid care labour in respect of her sister".[54]

Against this background, the Court observed that its main aim in this case was to establish "whether it could be expected from [Mrs Haydarie] to comply with the income requirement under the domestic immigration rules".[55] This framing of the *Haydarie* case raised key questions with respect to the worth given to care labour. Most importantly, it provided the Court with a precious occasion to establish whether care labour could indeed constitute a ground to access key rights for carers – such as, in this case, the right to family reunification – as an equally valid alternative to paid employment. Unfortunately, the Court entirely upheld the national authorities' characterization of care work within the household as a free choice not to perform actual work. In particular, the Court considered that imposing a minimum income requirement was reasonable not only in principle but also in the specific case at issue, because it considered that instead of pursuing paid employment Mrs Haydarie had "preferred to care for her wheel-chair bound sister at home".[56] Furthermore, the Court went so far as to argue that "it [had] not been demonstrated that it would have been impossible for the first applicant to call in and entrust the care for her sister to an agency providing care for handicapped persons".[57] By doing so, the Court not only framed the applicant's exclusion from residence rights as a situation of her own making, but it also deemed the care work provided by her as equivalent to that performed by commercial service providers notwithstanding the applicant's statement that her sister "refused aid from strangers"[58] and that personally caring for her sister was perceived by her as "her moral responsibility".[59]

The qualification of carers as willingly inactive individuals, and as such unworthy of accessing rights and entitlements reserved to those devoted to "actual" work – that is, paid employment – is clearly observable in the

53 Ibid.
54 Ibid.
55 Ibid.
56 Ibid.
57 Ibid.
58 Ibid.
59 Ibid.

Andersson[60] and *Haydarie*[61] cases. The de-valuation of care work by the Court as an alternative to actual work is discouraging for future possibilities of progressing domestic workers' rights. As Bridget Anderson rightly observed, "the notion that domestic work is unproductive downgrades its social and economic contribution and excused its invisibility".[62] In fact, the discussed cases may even be considered as a confirmation of the view that rights-based approaches *per se* are ill-equipped to effectively capture the reality of mutual interdependence and thus of addressing the needs of all workers – not only women workers but "all persons living in networks of care and responsibility".[63]

Nonetheless, I would argue that the Court's lack of recognition of the worth of unpaid care work should not prompt a pessimistic view concerning the possibilities of judicial recognition of domestic workers' claims. This conclusion stems from the observation that the problematic hierarchy of paid employment over unpaid care work in the Court's judicial analysis arises from its reliance on a classic productive/reproductive work dichotomy. The Court failed to see unpaid care work as actual work merely because such an activity is not performed in exchange for a salary. Domestic workers, on the other hand, may not be affected by this dichotomy to the same extent, because they comply with the model of "active" individual enforced in the described judgments. Therefore, while indirectly limiting the value accorded to care work, this construction does not completely rule out the possibility of domestic workers obtaining recognition of their labour rights in the human rights framework of the ECHR.

In fact, the productive/reproductive work dichotomy suggests that future applications by domestic workers concerning violations of their labour rights may prompt positive results not only for this category but for unpaid carers as well. Domestic work constitutes an interesting variable in this discourse because of its potential to blur the boundaries between paid employment and unpaid care labour. Domestic work can indeed be inscribed with certainty in the category of paid employment, but at the same time it is much more than a mere provision of services in exchange for a salary because this profession inevitably entails a certain degree of intimacy and often even of emotional investment, which draws it closer to the unpaid care work provided by family members.

As a form of paid employment consisting in the provision of care, domestic work brought to the Court's attention as a core element in a human rights claim may support greater recognition of unpaid care labour by sparking a judicial discourse on the worth of care work beyond a merely

60 *Andersson* (n 29).

61 *Haydarie* (n 28).

62 B Anderson, *Doing the Dirty Work? The Global Politics of Domestic Labour* (Palgrave-Macmillan 2000).

63 S Sevenhuijsen, "Caring in the Third Way: The Relation between Obligation, Responsibility and Care in Third Way Discourse" (2000) 20 *Critical Social Policy* 5, 29.

economic perspective. Thanks to the hybrid character of this profession, a judicial analysis of domestic workers' rights claims would necessarily be based not merely on the economic worth of this activity but also on its emotional and logistical importance for the employer's family life. Thus, domestic workers' claims may actually prompt the Court to move beyond the productive/reproductive work dichotomy. For this reason, the relevance of the judgments analyzed here does not so much rest in their meaning and importance for future recognition of domestic workers' claims, but rather lies in the fact that they constitute a further argument in favour of bringing such claims to the Court's attention – by revealing a serious shortcoming in its capacity to value forms of labour beyond paid employment.

It has been rightly argued that the low pay widely characterizing domestic work is strictly related to the "assumption that this work somehow flows naturally from women's genetic endowments rather than knowledge and skills acquired through education, training or experience".[64] The de-valuation of care work therefore generates decent work deficits and exclusion from labour rights for those who perform this activity in a professional capacity – making the analysis of domestic workers' claims by the ECtHR an even more desirable development for paid and unpaid carers equally.

Carers as interchangeable figures in the ECtHR case law on residence rights

A second group of judgments of the ECtHR concerns claims of violation of the right to family life submitted by third-country national migrant men carrying out unpaid care work within their families. More specifically, in these cases irregularly staying migrants pursued access to residence rights in their host country, on the grounds of the care they provided to family members and their household work. The Court's responses to such claims are fascinating in their effort to assess whether the applicant men played such an important role in their families that their expulsion would constitute a disproportionate interference with the rights protected by article 8 of the Convention.

Beyond the realm of the right to family life, the Court's answers to this question relate to the importance of care work itself for the recipients of care, and even more so to the eventually indispensable character of carers in the family realm. Such questions may equally be applied to domestic workers, because of the highly personalized relationships created between employer and employee in this field. Thus, the judicial assessment of the

64 S Razaavi and S Staab, "Underpaid and Overworked: A Cross-National Perspective on Care Workers" (2010) 149 *International Labour Review* 407, 412. For a thorough analysis of this critique and its factual confirmation, see P England, "Emerging Theories of Care Work" (2005) 31 *Annual Review of Sociology* 381.

indispensability of a specific carer within the family is of particular importance in determining whether and to what extent domestic work may be considered by the Court as a gateway to rights.

An early case where the ECtHR was presented with these questions was that of *Khan v. the United Kingdom.*[65] Here, a man of Pakistani origin had appealed at domestic level against an expulsion order issued against him on the grounds of his criminal convictions, arguing that "his mother and his siblings were all in poor health and he was the main person who kept the house clean".[66] The national authorities, on the other hand, assessed that the applicant's family life "did not go beyond the natural ties of affection"[67] and that "the family had managed to cope without the applicant while he was in prison"[68] and upheld the expulsion order against him.

Before the ECtHR, the applicant reproduced the same arguments, by stating that the care he had provided to his mother and brothers "created a relationship of dependency"[69] between him and them. Moreover, he submitted that – contrary to what had been maintained at domestic level – his care was essential for his family members' well-being because his mother had fallen ill while he was in prison. In particular, he contested the Asylum and Immigration Tribunal's view that his family had coped well while he was in prison as "completely unfounded",[70] arguing that "his mother in fact suffered a mild heart attack and he was concerned that his deportation would exacerbate her heart condition". In the end, the Court held that the applicant had suffered from a violation of his right to family life, but not because of the care provided by him to his family members.[71] The Court in its analysis divided the care work carried out by the applicant into his cohabitation with family members on the one hand, and family members' illnesses on the other. Because these two components of his care role were not causally linked, it became impossible to recognize the indispensable role that he played within the family. In particular, the Court

> [did] not accept that the fact that the applicant was living with his mother and brothers, or the fact that the entire family suffered from different health complaints, [constituted] a sufficient degree of dependence to result in the existence of family life.[72]

65 *A.W. Khan v. the United Kingdom* App no 47486/06 (ECtHR, 12 January 2010).
66 Ibid para 9.
67 Ibid para 10.
68 Ibid.
69 Ibid para 25.
70 Ibid.
71 The decisive element for a recognition of a violation of article 8 of the Convention in the *Khan* judgment was rather the fact that pending the proceeding the applicant had had a daughter from his British long-term girlfriend – see *Khan* (n 65) paras 33–36.
72 *Khan* (n 65) para 32.

What is more, the Court held that the presence of the applicant's "three married sisters" in the United Kingdom was evidence that he was not "necessarily the sole carer for his mother and brothers".[73]

Only one month after the *Khan* judgment, the Court adopted an opposite stance in the case of *Zakayev and Safanova v. Russia.*[74] This case concerned a migrant couple (Mr Zakayev and Mrs Safanova) who had established their family life in Russia, and who complained that the expulsion order issued by the Russian authorities against Mr Zakayev (on the grounds of a breach of registration rules applicable to foreign nationals) violated their right to respect for their family life. The applicants argued that Mr Zakayev "had played a particularly important role in the upbringing of the couple's three elder children, since it was [Mrs Safanova] who had worked following their move to Moscow".[75] The key role played by Mr Zakayev when performing unpaid care work within the family emerged clearly also from his wife's statement before the Court stating that the expulsion of her husband had negatively affected the family economy and management because "she had been unable to work for a while, since she had no one to look after the children"[76] and had subsequently been able to secure only "casual work".[77]

This time, the Court was receptive to the indispensable role of Mr Zakayev within the household because of the unpaid care work performed by him. In its judgment it recognized a violation of the applicants' right to family life precisely on the grounds of Mr Zakayev's dedication to reproductive and care work within the family, which had meant that his expulsion had "seriously affected the situation of the children and [Mrs Safanova]".[78] Nonetheless, I would argue that the more positive attitude of the Court in this case did not depend on its willingness to recognize the irreplaceable character of Mr Zakayev as the main carer of his children. Rather, the Court's decision stemmed from a consideration of the specific family situation, and in particular that of the children. The Court considered that the trauma experienced by the applicants' children because of the expulsion of their father was exacerbated by the family's experience of forced migration arising from the conflict in Chechnya. In this light, the Court on the one hand observed that the interference with the applicants' right to family life constituted by Mr Zakayev's expulsion pursued legitimate aims, "such as the economic well-being of the country and the prevention of disorder and crime".[79] Nonetheless, because of the special situation of the applicants, the Court concluded that "in the particular circumstances of the ... case ...

73 Ibid.
74 *Zakayev and Safanova v. Russia* App no 11870/03 (ECtHR, 11 February 2010).
75 Ibid para 45.
76 Ibid para 29.
77 Ibid.
78 Ibid para 45.
79 Ibid para 40.

the economic well-being of the country and the prevention of disorder and crime did not outweigh the applicants' rights under Article 8".[80]

The special character of the *Zakayev and Safanova* case is confirmed by subsequent cases where the Court did not show an equally receptive attitude to the irreplaceable character of individual carers. Instead, it returned to the view previously expressed in the *Khan* judgment, denying access to residence rights to migrant carers on the ground that their presence on the national territory was not indispensable because their care work could be easily resumed by others. In the following judgments of *Antwi v. Norway*[81] and *Akbulut v. the United Kingdom*,[82] other prospective carers were identified within the family. In the already mentioned case of *Haydarie*,[83] the Court even suggested that the care work provided by the applicant could be "outsourced". In all three cases, the Court's tendency to consider individual carers as interchangeable undermined the latter's claims for recognition of their right to reside in the host country together with their family members. In the case of *Antwi*, a Ghanaian man (Mr Antwi) opposing an expulsion order – issued against him together with a five-year entry ban due to his repeated violations of national immigration rules – argued that this measure was disproportionate because "since he had lost his work permit ... [he] had assumed the role as [his daughter's] main caretaker within the family",[84] playing "the main role in following up the home work of [his daughter] ... and in assuming the contacts between the family and school",[85] while his wife was "the family's main breadwinner".[86] In other words, he argued that his "important role in attending to [his daughter's] care, education and sporting activities [and] the strong emotional bonds between them"[87] suggested that his expulsion "would constitute a disproportionate measure vis-à-vis her in particular".[88] The Court, however, dismissed this argument, stating that "it [did] not emerge that [the daughter] had any special care needs or that her mother would be unable to provide satisfactory care on her own".[89] Similarly, in the *Akbulut* judgment the Court rejected the argument of the applicant, a Turkish national, that his expulsion from the United Kingdom (following his criminal conviction) would constitute a disproportionate interference with his right to family life. In particular, he argued that his wife would not be able to follow him to Turkey due to her care responsibilities towards her elderly parents. Nonetheless, the Court

80 Ibid para 48.
81 *Antwi and Others v. Norway* App no 26940/10 (ECtHR, 14 February 2012).
82 *Akbulut v. the United Kingdom* App no 53586/08 (ECtHR, 10 April 2012).
83 *Haydarie* (n 28).
84 *Antwi* (n 81) para 72.
85 Ibid.
86 Ibid.
87 Ibid para 73.
88 Ibid.
89 Ibid para 99.

held that the unpaid care work performed by the applicant's wife did not make her indispensable to her parents because "she [had] several siblings in the United Kingdom who also [assisted] in caring for their parents"[90] and therefore "there were no insurmountable obstacles to the applicant's wife relocating to Turkey and maintaining her family life with the applicant in this manner".[91]

In the cases discussed, and in particular in the *Antwi* and *Haydarie* judgments, the carers had submitted before the Court that the unpaid care labour provided to their family members had made them irreplaceable – or at least difficult to replace – not only from the point of view of the person being cared for but also for the well-being of their whole families. Thus, the applicants' arguments (echoing those submitted in the *Carpenter* case before the CJEU, which were in fact upheld by the Court itself)[92] raised important points about the crucial character of unpaid care work performed within private households which may be applicable to paid care work also. In the case of *Antwi*, Mr Antwi's inability to continue carrying out care labour within the household made it extremely difficult for his wife to balance work and family life. This claim could easily be raised by a domestic worker as well. The decisive role played by domestic workers with respect to their employers' efficient family life/work balance, or their employers' (especially female employers') participation in the labour market, has been widely commented on by scholars.[93] Therefore, just like the applicant father in *Antwi*, domestic workers could pursue access to core rights (such as labour rights or, in the case of migrant domestic workers, residence rights) on the grounds of the primary importance of their work for ensuring the emotional, organizational and economic stability of their employer's family. It is therefore quite disappointing that, except in the case of *Zakayev and Safanova*,[94] the ECtHR failed to recognize the indispensable role of the carers involved in the mentioned judgments. It has indeed been rightly observed that the recognition of the emotional bonds created through domestic work goes hand in hand with an acknowledgment of its worth.[95]

90 *Akbulut* (n 82) para 22.

91 Ibid.

92 *Carpenter* (n 11).

93 See, for instance, E Gutiérrez-Rodríguez, *Migration, Domestic Work and Affect: A Decolonial Approach on Value and the Feminization of Labor* (Routledge 2010) 68 ff. See also R Salazar Parreñas, *Servants of Globalization: Women, Migration and Domestic Work* (Stanford University Press 2001) 71, and H Lutz, "Migrant Domestic Workers in Europe", in H Lutz (ed.) *Migration and Domestic Work: A European Perspective on a Global Theme* (Ashgate 2008), 1.

94 *Zakavey and Safanova* (n 74).

95 This view has been expressed by Gutiérrez Rodríguez with reference to political recognition but it can aptly be referred to the matter of the legal recognition of domestic workers' rights in a human rights framework. In particular, the author has highlighted "[the] reproductive value of care work as a contributor to the upbringing and emotional growth of a human being", arguing that "[care] work needs to be considered … as a socially significant

Concluding remarks

In the judgments examined in this chapter, individuals providing unpaid care work to their family members raised arguments that could potentially be borrowed by domestic workers in order to support their claims before the ECtHR. Only the observation of future developments of the Court's case law will unveil whether or not domestic workers will succeed in turning the risky discourse of being considered as "just like one of the family"[96] into a positive force to support recognition of their rights claims. I would argue that the pursuit of claims by domestic workers (beyond the already explored perspectives of servitude and forced labour) are not bound to fail, despite the Court's limited recognition of the value of care work to date.

First, the increasing dialogue and mutual exchange between the ECtHR and the CJEU may lead to greater recognition of care work. Admittedly, the CJEU's case law recognizing third-country national carers' right to reside in the territory of the Union has been limited to the context of supporting Union citizens' enjoyment of their fundamental rights and freedoms. Moreover, there is no guarantee that the principles established by the CJEU with respect to individuals providing unpaid care labour within their own households for the benefit of the members of their families would be extended to domestic workers. However, throughout this chapter I have argued that judicial recognition of the worth of care work *per se* constitutes an important clue to a court's readiness and capability to effectively protect domestic workers' rights. In this sense, and with the mentioned limitations, the CJEU case law might constitute a positive influence for the ECtHR.

Second, and most importantly, the constantly evolving character of the ECtHR's jurisprudence should encourage domestic workers to formulate claims before this judicial organ. The very case law on article 4 violations stemmed from claims of severely exploited carers who pushed the boundaries of the prohibition of slavery and forced labour established by this provision in order to obtain redress from the ECtHR. Before *Siliadin*,[97] claims of violation of the prohibition of slavery, servitude and forced labour (beyond contexts of trafficking) had been consistently rejected by the Court.[98] Nonetheless, the *Siliadin* judgment clearly disclosed a path for

moment in the reproduction of life, which is made invisible when we negate the affective bonds of care and domestic work" (E Gutiérrez Rodríguez, "The 'Hidden Side' of the New Economy: On Transnational Migration, Domestic Work, and Unprecedented Intimacy" (2007) 28 *Frontiers: A Journal of Women Studies* 60, 70.

96 B Anderson, *Doing the Dirty Work? The Global Politics of Domestic Labour* (Palgrave-Macmillan 2000).

97 *Siliadin* (n 12).

98 Previously, the Court had either declared inadmissible or had found no violations of article 4 in cases initiated by professionals, such as lawyers or doctors, complaining about having provided certain services without receiving any remuneration – see, for instance, *Van Der Mussele v. Belgium* (1983) Series A no 70, subsequently confirmed by *Steindel v. Germany* App no 29878/07 (ECtHR, 14 September 2010), *Bucha v. Slovakia* App no 43259/07

all domestic workers who suffer from extreme forms of exploitation, being forced to work in private households against their will. The capability of the Court to respond to new challenges and to uphold unprecedented argumentations – which in my view has clearly been shown in the case law initiated by the *Siliadin* judgment – should encourage domestic workers to push the boundaries of its so far restrictive interpretation of the right to private and family life *ex* article 8 with respect to carers' rights. By doing so, this category may be finally able to extract rights and entitlements both as workers and as human beings. One can only hope that this result will be achieved, so that the detrimental trope of domestic workers being "just like one of the family" may finally generate protection and empowerment for this category of workers by highlighting their importance for entire families' economic, social and legal self-fulfilment.

(ECtHR, 20 September 2011), *Graziani-Weiss v. Austria* App no 31950/06 (ECtHR, 18 October 2011) – or by detainees required to perform unpaid work during detention – see, for instance, *De Wilde, Ooms and Versyp v. Belgium* (1971) Series A no 12, and *Van Droogenbroeck v. Belgium* (1982) Series A no 50, subsequently confirmed by *Stummer v. Austria* ECtHR 2011 93, *Zhelyazkov v. Bulgaria* App no 11332/04 (ECtHR, 9 October 2012), and *Floroiu v. Romania* App no 15303/10 (ECtHR, 12 March 2013).

4 Migrant Domestic Workers in the UK: Enacting Exclusions, Exemptions and Rights

Siobhán Mullally and Clíodhna Murphy

Introduction

Domestic work, the provision of caring work in the intimate, domestic sphere, is work that continues to be undertaken primarily by women and increasingly by migrant women.[1] The expected reduction in demand for paid domestic workers has not materialised, leading some to ask whether the emergence of 'global care chains' should be assessed as a major defeat for feminist movements or as 'unfinished business'.[2] Combined with the movement of women into paid employment, the retreat from welfare state supports in Western Europe has produced care economies that are increasingly reliant on the outsourcing of intimate, reproductive labour.[3] A range of factors has contributed to the demand for paid domestic labour, including population ageing, changing household structures, increasing female participation in the labour market, difficulties in reconciling paid employment and caring for dependants, and the availability of a flexible, low-cost, female (and mainly migrant) work force.[4]

Human rights law has somewhat belatedly begun to address the structured inequalities and exclusions that define the domain of domestic work. As in other areas of international law, it is primarily the moments of crisis that have captured the attention of human rights law. The 'everyday' of

* This chapter was first published in (2014) 36 (2) *Human Rights Quarterly* pp. 397–427.

1 Lutz, 'At your Service Madam! The Globalization of Domestic Service' (2002) 70 *Feminist Review* 89. See also Galotti, 'The Gender Dimension of Domestic Work in Western Europe', No. 96 *International Migration Papers* (International Labour Office, Geneva, 2009), in particular 9–13.

2 Lutz, 'Gender in the Migratory Process' (2010) 36(10) *Journal of Ethnic and Migration Studies* 1647, 1652. See also Fudge, 'Global Care Chains: Transnational Migrant Care Workers' (2012) 28(1) *International Journal of Comparative Labour Law and Industrial Relations* 63.

3 Lutz, ibid., 1654; Anderson, *Doing the Dirty Work? The Global Politics of Domestic Labour* (Zed Books, 2000).

4 For a detailed analysis of global care chains in the context of globalisation and North–South inequalities, see Stewart, *Gender Law and Justice in a Global Market* (Cambridge University Press, 2011).

work-place exploitation, exclusion from the protections of employment law, social security and precarious migration status have attracted less attention to date. Recent standard-setting initiatives have attempted to address this gap and have included the adoption of the landmark 2011 International Labour Organisation (ILO) Convention Concerning Decent Work for Domestic Workers,[5] a General Recommendation from the United Nations (UN) Committee on the Elimination of All Forms of Discrimination Against Women (CEDAW) on Women Migrant Workers[6] and a General Comment from the UN Committee on Migrant Workers and their Families on Migrant Domestic Workers.[7] Against the background of this 'justice cascade',[8] however, migration laws continue to function as limits to the transformative promise of such initiatives. Migration status adds yet another axis of discrimination to the intersections of gender, race and class, and contributes further to the constructed vulnerability of domestic workers.[9] States remain reluctant, however, to recognise the 'dissensus' that arises between 'border norms' and evolving human rights standards.[10]

The UN Special Rapporteur on Contemporary Forms of Slavery has identified a 'net of dependency factors' that prevent domestic workers from leaving situations of exploitation, many of which include constructed vulnerabilities linked to migration status.[11] The exploitation of migrant domestic workers is often presented by states as the action of an aberrant and abusive individual employer. The role played by migration law in creating the conditions within which such exploitation occurs, and often goes unchecked, is not acknowledged. As Anderson notes, however, migration law not only reinforces the unequal power relations between migrant domestic workers and their employers, it also provides unscrupulous employers with mechanisms of control they might not otherwise have.[12]

This chapter examines the reforms introduced in the Overseas Domestic

5 Convention Concerning Decent Work for Domestic Workers (No. 189), International Labour Organisation, adopted at the 100th Session of the International Labour Conference, Geneva, 2011 (ILO Domestic Work Convention).

6 Committee for the Elimination of All Forms of Discrimination Against Women, General Recommendation No. 26 on Women Migrant Workers, 5 December 2008, CEDAW/C/2009/WP.1/R (2008) (CEDAW General Recommendation).

7 Committee on the Protection of the Rights of All Migrant Workers and Members of Their Families, General Comment No. 1 on Migrant Domestic Workers, 23 February 2011, CMW/C/GC/1 (2011) (CMW General Comment).

8 This term is borrowed from Sikkink, *The Justice Cascade: How Human Rights Prosecutions Are Changing World Politics* (W.W. Norton & Co., 2011).

9 See Lutz, 'Gender in the Migratory Process', supra n.2, 1654; Anderson, *Doing the Dirty Work*, supra n.3.

10 The term 'border norms' is borrowed from Bosniak, *The Citizen and the Alien: Dilemmas of Contemporary Membership* (Princeton University Press, 2006).

11 Report of the Special Rapporteur on contemporary forms of slavery, including its causes and consequences, Gulnara Shahinia, UN Doc A/HRC/15/20 (18 January 2010), para. 47.

12 Anderson, 'Migration, Immigration Controls and the Fashioning of Precarious Workers' (2010) 24(2) *Work, Employment & Society* 300–317, 312.

Workers (ODW) visa regime in the UK and the politics and practice of human rights that has surrounded these changes. The move towards a more precarious migration status for migrant domestic workers marks a rejection of the reforms secured through sustained political activism by domestic workers advocates. It also highlights the contingency and instability of political moments that secure progressive change and legal recognition of migrant workers' human rights claims.

The reforms to the ODW visa follow on from the UK Government's failure to support the 2011 ILO Convention on Decent Work for Domestic Workers and its ambiguous commitment to the expansion of European Union (EU) anti-trafficking legislation.[13] These steps reflect a resistance to the 'cascade' of human rights standards that have sought to overcome the limits of migration status as a prerequisite to the exercise of rights.[14] A series of cases before the European Court of Human Rights[15] has highlighted the nexus between migration status and heightened risks of exploitation, as has the work of the CEDAW and Migrant Workers Committees. Limited access to secure migration status, however, remains the norm for many domestic workers. As the changes in the UK migrant domestic workers' visa regime reveal, states continue to invoke the 'deportability' of migrant workers.[16]

The move by the UK Government to introduce a highly precarious temporary status for migrant domestic workers and wider policy discourse on circular migration mark a resistance to the expansion of human rights norms to the realm of domestic work and to migrants.[17] This resistance is accompanied by appeals to protective norms that have shaped law's engagement with migrant women. The Modern Slavery Bill 2014, again, reiterates the Government's commitment to combating human trafficking and

13 See Statement to the House of Commons from Minister Damien Green, 22 March 2011, available at www.homeoffice.gov.uk/publications/about-us/parliamentary-business/written-ministerial-statement/eu-direct-human-trafficking-wms. The UK Government did not initially opt in to the proposed Directive.

14 See, for example, Inter-American Court of Human Rights Advisory Opinion on the 'Juridical Condition and Rights of the Undocumented Migrants' (Advisory Opinion OC-18/03, 17 September 2003, Inter-Am. Ct. H.R. (Ser. A) No. 18 (2003)). See also the work of the Global Forum on Migration and Development: Background Paper, 'Protecting Migrant Domestic Workers – Enhancing their Development Potential' (Prepared for Mauritius GFMD 2012, available at www.gfmd.org/docs/mauritius-2012), and 'Checklist to Support and Protect Domestic Workers', Mauritius Global Forum on Migration and Development (GFMD) 2012, available at www.gfmd.org/docs/mauritius-2012.

15 *Siliadin v France* (2006) 43 EHRR 16; *Rantsev v Cyprus and Russia*, Application No. 25965/04, Judgment of 7 January 2010; *C.N. and V v France*, Application No. 67724/09, Judgment of 11 October 2012; *CN* v. *The United Kingdom*, Application No. 4239/08, Judgment of 13 November 2012.

16 On the 'deportable alien', see Kesby, *The Right to Have Rights: Citizenship, Humanity, and International Law* (Oxford University Press, 2012), 111 *et seq*.

17 Dauvergne and Marsden, 'The Ideology of Temporary Labour Migration in the Post-Global Era', (2014) 18(2) *Citizenship Studies, Special Issue: Citizenship in a Globalized World: The Experience of Immigrant Democracies*, 224–242.

'modern slavery', yet leaves untouched the reforms made to the ODW visa that have further entrenched the precarious position of domestic workers.[18] The normative compulsion of preventing abuse is again appealed to as a justification for the failure to re-instate the full panoply of rights that had accompanied the ODW visa.

These appeals to protective norms do little to expand or support domestic workers in claiming and enacting rights, and ultimately pose only a limited challenge to the continuums of exploitation that define domestic work, particularly for those whose migration status is precarious or irregular.[19] Against this background, the *jurisgenerative* potential of human rights standards, heralded by many, continues to be limited.[20]

Decent Work standards, expanding human rights norms: a justice cascade?

As Carens has noted, migrant domestic workers are 'hard to locate on the map of democracy'.[21] The movement of migrant domestic workers across multiple jurisdictional boundaries, between states as well as from the 'public' domain into the 'private' domain of the home, is central to the constructed vulnerability of the domestic worker.[22] Law plays a dual role here, jealously guarding the public borders of the State through immigration laws while at the same time 'reifying the private borders of the home'.[23] The UN Special Rapporteur on the Human Rights of Migrants has pointed out that 'the lack of watchdog mechanisms and inadequate monitoring by

18 Home Office, Draft Modern Slavery Bill, Dec. 2013 Cm 8770. See also Joint Committee on the Draft Modern Slavery Bill, oral evidence 28 Jan. 2014, available at www.parliament.uk/business/committees/committees-a-z/joint-select/draft-modern-slavery-bill/written-evidence. (HC [1019] discussing the implications of the 2012 changes to the overseas domestic worker visa regime.)

19 The concern with international law's resort to protective norms, particularly in the realm of human trafficking, is evident in the work of Dianne Otto and others.

20 The term 'jurisgenerative' is borrowed from Robert M. Cover, The Supreme Court, 1981 Term – Foreword: Nomos and Narrative, 97 HARV. L. REV. 4 (1982). See also Benhabib, *Dignity in Adversity: Human Rights in Troubled Times* (Polity, 2011); Dauvergne and Marsden, 'The Ideology of Temporary Labour Migration in the Post-Global Era', in Shachar and Brahm Levey (eds.) *Citizenship in a Globalized World: Perspectives from the Immigrant Democracies* (2014) *Citizenship Studies* (special issue) 18(2): 224–242; Fudge 'Global Care Chains: Transnational Migrant Care Workers' (2012) 28(1) *International Journal of Comparative Labour Law and Industrial Relations* 63.

21 Carens, 'Live-In Domestics, Seasonal Workers, and Others Hard to Locate on the Map of Democracy' (2008) 16(4) *Journal of Political Philosophy* 419.

22 Fudge, 'Global Care Chains, Employment Agencies, and the Conundrum of Jurisdiction: Decent Work for Domestic Workers in Canada' (2011) 23 *Canadian Journal of Women & Law* 235.

23 Fudge, ibid., 243, referencing the work of Blackett, 'Promoting Domestic Workers: Human Dignity through Specific Regulation', in Fauve-Chamoux (ed.) *Domestic Service and the Formation of European Identity: Understanding the Globalization of Domestic Work, 16th–21st Centuries* (Peter Land, 2005).

the Government in the country of destination, the recruiting agencies and even consulates, mean that migrant domestic workers are cut off and abuses remain unseen'.[24]

For some, the movement to establish Decent Work standards for domestic work is doomed to failure, given the historical legacy of low status, low pay and exploitation associated with such work. Legal reforms, it is argued, cannot fully account for the wider 'realm of indignities' experienced by domestic workers, or the dynamics of power played out on 'concrete historicised bodies' that are gendered, raced and classed.[25] Migrant domestic workers are situated in the isolating and devalued 'privatised economy of household labour', where highly personalised and emotionally exacting work is undertaken in situations that are 'heavy with the histories of racialised subordination'.[26] Lack of enforcement and application restricts the potential for human rights norms to disturb the ongoing reproduction of such histories.[27] Against this background, the expansion of Decent Work standards to domestic work may provide a corrective, as Adelle Blackett has suggested, to the 'abstract articulations' of rights that traditionally overlook exploitation of domestic workers.[28] The refusal on the part of some governments and employers to support this expansion of rights, however, continues to postpone what is a significant political moment for domestic workers.

The ILO Convention on Decent Work for Domestic Workers: beyond noblesse oblige

This reification (and exclusion) of the household was one of the key issues that emerged in debates leading up to the adoption of the ILO Convention on Decent Work for Domestic Workers. The 2011 ILO Convention on Decent Work for Domestic Workers is the first dedicated international instrument to address the specificity of domestic work. As the Report that preceded the Convention notes, it is intended to mark a transition from paternalistic conceptions of 'good employers acting out of a sense of *noblesse oblige*', to

24 Report of the Special Rapporteur on the Human Rights of Migrants, Commission on Human Rights, 60th Session E/CN.4/2004/76 (January 2004).

25 Blackett, 'Introduction: Regulating Decent Work for Domestic Workers' (2011) 23 *Canadian Journal of Women & Law* 1, 43, citing Gutiérrez-Rodríguez, *Migration, Domestic Work and Affect: A Decolonial Approach on Value and the Feminization of Labor* (Routledge, 2010), 6.

26 Williams, 'Migration and Care: Themes, Concepts and Challenges' (2010) 9(3) *Social Policy & Society* 385, 386.

27 Ally, 'On Laws, Rights and Conventions: A Provocation', as part of Schwenken, Prügl, Rebeca Pabon, Claire Hobden and Shireen Ally 'Conversations' (2011) 13(3) *International Feminist Journal of Politics* 437, 457.

28 Blackett, 'Introduction: Regulating Decent Work for Domestic Workers' (2011) 23 *Canadian Journal of Women & Law*, 1, 44, citing Blackett, 'Situated Reflections on International Labour Law, Capabilities, and Decent Work: The Case of Centre Maraîcher Eugène Guinois' (2007) hors série, *Revue québécoise de droit international* 223, 242.

respect for domestic workers' rights.[29] The Convention seeks to extend core Decent Work standards concerning fair terms of employment and working conditions to the realm of domestic work. States are required to ensure that domestic workers enjoy equality with other workers regarding working time,[30] entitlements to minimum wage,[31] healthy and safe working conditions[32] and social security protection (including maternity).[33] It also requires states to introduce measures providing for the regulation of employment agencies[34] and for effective and accessible dispute resolution mechanisms for domestic workers.[35]

The only specific provision in the Domestic Work Convention relating directly to migration is found in Article 8, which provides that national laws or regulations specify that written job offers or contracts of employment are provided to domestic workers prior to their departure to the country where the work is to be performed.[36] The conditions under which migrant domestic workers are entitled to repatriation following the expiry or termination of their contract of employment are also to be specified pre-departure.[37] This requirement, while important, is relatively weak. It requires only that such terms and conditions be specified, but does nothing to address the inequalities of bargaining power between worker and employer. Article 7 of the Convention adopts a similarly minimal approach, requiring that domestic workers are informed of the terms and conditions of their work, but without specifying the terms and conditions.[38] Article 9 requires Members to ensure that domestic workers are 'free to negotiate with the employer whether to reside in the household'.[39] Such freedoms remain illusory, however, where immigration restrictions including access to public funds (such as affordable or social housing programmes) for migrants is restricted, and where minimum wage protections are not enforced or applicable. The proposed model contract of employment for domestic workers, noted in the accompanying Recommendation, seeks to overcome the minimal approach taken in the Convention itself.[40] Its inclusion in the non-binding text of the Recommendation, however, reflects the reluctance of states to take

29 International Labour Conference, 99th Session 2010, Report on Decent Work for Domestic Workers (Report IV(1)), 13.
30 Article 10.
31 Article 11.
32 Article 13.
33 Article 14.
34 Article 15(a).
35 Article 16.
36 ILO Domestic Work Convention, Article 8(1).
37 Ibid., Article 8(4).
38 Ibid., Article 7.
39 Ibid., Article 9(a).
40 ILO, Recommendation Concerning Decent Work for Domestic Workers (ILO Recommendation No. 201) Geneva, 16 June 2011, para. 6(3) (ILO Recommendation Concerning Decent Work for Domestic Workers).

concrete steps to realise the aspirations of a shift 'from status to contract' for domestic workers. Even these limited requirements attracted opposition from states, however. The UK Government argued that it was not, in its view, 'the duty of a government to ensure that terms and conditions of employment were understood by workers'.[41]

Despite the commitment to addressing disadvantage within the domestic work sector, the Convention's scope is deliberately limited. The specific difficulties facing agency workers, domestic workers in diplomatic households, irregular migrant domestic workers and workers categorised as 'au pairs' were highlighted repeatedly in the submissions made during the drafting process of the Convention.[42] These issues remain unresolved as the Convention continues to allow for 'de-juridifications' that could render its expansion of rights meaningless for such workers. Allowing for the possibilities of opting out, of excluding certain categories of domestic workers, was a concession to states and to employers' organisations, many of whom were opposed to the proposal to adopt a legally binding instrument.[43] The position of the EU during the negotiating process, for example, was to support the adoption of a Convention supplemented by a Recommendation, but to ensure flexibility in the text of the Convention itself.[44] This flexibility is found in Article 2 of the Convention, which allows for a sweeping measure of disentitlement with respect to 'limited categories of workers in respect of which special problems of a substantial nature arise'.[45] These special problems are not specified. A requirement of consultation with employers/employees (and where they exist, domestic workers' organisations) is intended to provide a check on the process of 'opting-out'. The office of the High Commissioner for Human Rights had specifically expressed concern at the wide discretion allowed by Article 2 during the drafting process.[46] Despite its concerns, the provision remained in the final text, and is a significant concession to the pursuit of greater flexibility (for employers and states) in defining the content of rights enjoyed by domestic workers.

The ILO has specifically acknowledged the need to address a wide spectrum of actors, both state and non-state, if the objectives of standard-setting initiatives such as the Domestic Work Convention and Recommendation are to be met. Recruitment agencies are key actors in this process. Article 15

41 International Labour Organisation, *Report of the Committee on Domestic Workers, Provisional Record No. 15*, (International Labour Conference, 100th Session), Geneva, June 2011 para. 895 (ILO, *Report of the Committee on Domestic Workers, Provisional Record No. 15*, 2011).

42 RESPECT Network, 'Introduction and Key Recommendations for an ILO Convention on Domestic Work' (May 2009) Amsterdam: Briefing Paper, Recommendations 3–4.

43 ILO Report IV(1) para. 15.

44 Ibid., para. 2.

45 ILO Domestic Work Convention, Article 2(2)(b).

46 ILO, *Decent Work for Domestic Workers*, Report IV(2A), International Labour Conference, 100th Session, Geneva, 2011, 21.

of the Convention specifically addresses the role of private recruitment agencies and notes measures required to safeguard against abusive practices by such agencies. This provision is particularly important for migrant domestic workers. The need for cooperation between states, to address exploitative practices in the context of transnational recruitment, is highlighted. However, the requirement of an 'employment relationship' in Article 1 of the Convention itself potentially restricts the application of the Convention to domestic workers categorised as self-employed, or those who are recruited through private agencies. The specific role of intermediaries such as recruitment agencies is widely recognised as a matter of concern, given the vagaries of domestic employment legislation and its application to agency workers. Although Article 15 of the Convention requires Members to adopt laws specifying the obligations of agencies towards domestic workers, considerable discretion is left in determining the scope of such obligations.

The regulation of employment agencies was one of the more contentious issues arising during the drafting process, with several non-government organisations (NGOs), workers' representatives and governments highlighting the importance of close monitoring. The government members of the Africa group (represented by South Africa) specifically identified the role of private recruitment agencies as a key concern. Human Rights Watch in its submission pointed to the need to ensure that employment agencies did not charge domestic workers for recruitment costs incurred by employers, a practice that frequently leads domestic workers to forced labour and servitude.[47] The issue of exorbitant fees charged by agencies was highlighted also by the Migrant Forum in Asia.[48] Despite recognition of these risks, the Convention itself does little to directly address abusive practices by agencies.

The adoption of the Domestic Work Convention, and the global momentum that led to its enactment as the first binding ILO instrument in more than a decade, is an important political moment. However, it is one that is marked by an enactment of limits. The exclusions and exemptions that remain within the ILO text reflect the continuing reluctance by some Members to acknowledge the domestic worker as a subject of rights and as more than a commodity or ingredient in an economic process. There is also a reluctance to acknowledge the imperative to re-draw gendered boundaries between public and private if international legal standards are to secure a movement beyond *noblesse oblige*. Taking this additional step also requires recognising the intersections of overlapping axes of discrimination – of 'race', gender and migration status.[49] Recognition of these intersections is evident in the work of UN human rights treaty bodies, which have some-

47 ILO, Report of the Committee on Domestic Workers, Provisional Record No. 15, 2011, para. 49.

48 Ibid., para. 50.

49 See written comments submitted by Interights to the European Court of Human Rights (pursuant to leave granted by the President of the Chamber in accordance with Rule 44 112 of the Rules of Court) in *Kawogo v UK*, para. 18.

what belatedly begun to address the sphere of domestic work. This gradual expansion of multilateral standards to encompass the realm of domestic work has the potential to move beyond the limits of bilateral attempts at reform, where the predictable trade-off between access to jobs and workers' rights too frequently kicks in.[50]

Human rights at the intersections: recognising the nexus with migration status

As Crenshaw has noted, 'the intersections of racism and sexism ... cannot be captured wholly by looking at the race or gender dimensions separately'.[51] Addressing the intersections of both expands the possibilities of human rights law's potential to address discrimination. Migration status, however, is often excluded from the scope of race discrimination prohibitions and is frequently ignored in analyses of discrimination that adopt a 'nationally insular approach'.[52] Notably, the reluctance to extend non-discrimination norms to the migration context is evident even in the Migrant Workers Convention, which does not include migration status in the list of non-discrimination prohibitions. The Migrant Workers Convention[53] has been described 'as a beacon of what has not been achieved in the realm of rights',[54] both because of its limited ratifications to date and the distinctions made between the rights of documented and undocumented workers. In the practice of UN human rights treaty bodies, including the Migrant Workers Committee, however, the significance of migration status as relevant to questions of racial and gender discrimination is increasingly probed, despite apparent textual exclusions from the treaty standards themselves.[55]

The obligations of effective deterrence that arise from forced labour, slavery and trafficking prohibitions are enshrined in several international and regional instruments, including CEDAW,[56] the International Covenant

50 Nisha Varia, 'Labour and Migration in International Law: Challenges of Protection, Specialization and Bilateralim, Remarks by Nisha Varia' (2011) 105 *Proceedings of the Annual Meeting (American Society of International Law)* 410, 411–412.

51 Crenshaw, 'Mapping the Margins: Intersectionality, Identity Politics, and Violence Against Women of Color' (1991) 43(6) *Stanford Law Review* 1241, 1241.

52 Bosniak, *The Citizen and the Alien: Dilemmas of Contemporary Membership* (Princeton University Press, 2006), 144, n.23.

53 International Convention on the Protection of the Rights of All Migrant Workers and Members of Their Families 1990, 2220 UNTS 3.

54 Dauvergne and Marsden, 'The Ideology of Temporary Labour Migration in the Post-Global Era', in Shachar and Brahm Levey (eds.) *Citizenship in a Globalized World: Perspectives from the Immigrant Democracies* (2014) *Citizenship Studies* (special issue) 18(2): 224–242.

55 Committee for the Elimination of All Forms of Racial Discrimination, General Recommendation No. 30 on Discrimination against Non-Citizens, 10 January 2004.

56 Convention on the Elimination of All Forms of Discrimination Against Women 1979, 1249 UNTS 13.

on Civil and Political Rights,[57] the Palermo Protocol,[58] and the Council of Europe Convention on Action Against Trafficking.[59] Developing obligations of due diligence at regional and international level has highlighted the nexus between states' positive obligations of prevention and non-discrimination norms, potentially of significance to migrant domestic workers. The European Court of Human Rights has repeatedly recognised that a state's positive obligations under the Convention go beyond the imposition of criminal sanctions and include policing and operative measures. In *Opuz v Turkey* the European Court of Human Rights, for the first time in Strasbourg case-law, linked states' obligations to combat domestic violence to Article 14 ECHR non-discrimination requirements.[60] More generally, the gradual expansion of indirect discrimination prohibitions suggests possible strategies for such challenges.[61] The *Jessica Lenahan* case before the Inter-American Court of Human Rights,[62] the *Campo Algondero* case[63] and others similarly point to the non-discrimination nexus. Given that the majority of domestic workers are women and many are migrants, a similar nexus between migration law, positive obligations and non-discrimination norms arises. The Advisory Opinion of the Inter-American Court on the application of Non-discrimination and Equality norms to Undocumented Migrants points to the transformative promise that underpins human rights standards. Fitting into the discrimination paradigm is not without its difficulties, however, and is a strategy that brings many pitfalls, particularly when required to identify an appropriate comparator,[64] or when faced with the possibility not of a legal remedy but of deportation.

In its General Comment on Migrant Domestic Workers, the Migrant Workers Committee outlines the specific role that immigration law plays in the production of vulnerability.[65] Overly restrictive immigration laws, they note, lead to higher numbers of migrant domestic workers who are undocumented or in an irregular situation, and thus particularly vulnerable to

57 International Covenant on Civil and Political Rights 1966, 999 UNTS 171.

58 Protocol to Prevent, Suppress and Punish Trafficking in Persons Especially Women and Children, supplementing the United Nations Convention Against Transnational Organized Crime (2000).

59 Council of Europe Convention on Action Against Trafficking in Human Beings 2005, 197 CETS.

60 Application No. 33401/02, Judgment of 9 June 2009.

61 *D.H. and Others v. the Czech Republic,* Application No. 57325/00, 7 February 2006.

62 *Jessica Lenahan (Gonzales) v. United States*, Inter-American Court on Human Rights, Judgment of 21 July 2011.

63 *Gonzalez ('Cotton Fields') v Mexico*, Inter-American Court on Human Rights, Judgment of 16 November 2009.

64 Edwards, *Violence Against Women Under International Human Rights Law* (Cambridge University Press, 2010), in particular Chapter 4, 'Equality and Non-Discrimination on the Basis of Sex', 140.

65 CMW General Comment, paras. 21, 22 and 27.

human rights violations.[66] Similar vulnerabilities arise where migration laws tie a worker's migration status to the continued sponsorship of a particular employer, with the result that domestic workers may risk deportation if they leave an abusive employment relationship.[67] Any such arrangement can 'unduly restrict' liberty of movement and increase exploitation and abuse, 'including in conditions of forced labour or servitude'.[68] Migration status may also limit access to rights such as family reunification. Where visa or work permit permissions impose limits on access to public funds, rights to education, healthcare and housing remain illusory.[69] The nexus between discrimination, vulnerability and migration status is also recognised in CEDAW's General Recommendation No. 26 on Women Migrant Workers. CEDAW notes that while States Parties are entitled to control their borders and regulate migration, they must do so 'in full compliance' with their international obligations. Those obligations include 'the promotion of safe migration procedures and the obligation to respect, protect and fulfil the human rights of women throughout the migration cycle'.[70]

CEDAW has also called on states to ensure that visa schemes do not indirectly discriminate against women by excluding or limiting options for certain female-dominated occupations, such as domestic work.[71] The changes introduced in the UK Overseas Domestic Worker visa regime, however, ignore this call, revealing the continuing willingness of states to circumvent human rights standards and resort to what Paul Berman has described elsewhere as 'sovereigntist territorial prerogatives'.[72]

Migrant domestic workers in the UK: exclusions from rights

Limited recognition of domestic work: a concession

Until 1979, resident domestic workers in the UK came within the scope of the general work permit regime operating under the 1971 Immigration Act.[73] In 1980, when the issuing of work permits for 'unskilled workers'

66 CMW General Comment, para. 21.

67 CMW General Comment, para. 21.

68 Ibid.

69 See, generally, Spencer and Pobjoy, *The Relationship between Immigration Status and Rights in the UK: Exploring the Rationale*, Centre on Migration, Society and Policy Working Paper No. 86 (University of Oxford, 2011).

70 CEDAW General Recommendation, para. 3.

71 CEDAW General Recommendation, paras. 19 and 26(b).

72 P Berman, *Global Legal Pluralism: A Jurisprudence of Law Beyond Borders* (Cambridge University Press, 2012).

73 Statement of Immigration Rules for Control on Entry. EEC and Other Commonwealth Nationals. Laid before the Houses of Parliament on 25 January 1973 (HC 81). For a brief history of entry to the UK to work and the development of the work permit scheme, see Clayton, *Immigration and Asylum Law* (5th ed., Oxford University Press, 2012).

ended,[74] a limited exception was made for domestic workers who had worked for their employers for at least 12 months prior to coming to the UK.[75] Given the important reproductive function carried out by domestic workers, allowing for such a concession was justified in the 'national interest' so as to ensure that productive, highly skilled migrants would continue to choose the UK as a preferred destination.[76] (Many years later, a similar rationale was to surface in the case-law of the Court of Justice of the European Union on the free movement rights of EU citizens and their third-country national spouses.)[77] Under the concession scheme, employers were permitted to bring domestic workers into the UK either as a 'visitor' or as a 'person named to work with a specified employer'.[78] A degree of confusion surrounding the appropriate immigration status to be granted was evident in the varying statuses granted to domestic workers on entry.[79] In general, however, it was presumed that the employment rights of domestic workers and their migration status were linked to their employer, increasing the potential for exploitation and abuse, despite the recognised 'national interest' served through their work.[80]

Enacting rights: the ODW visa

In 1998, the newly elected Labour Government announced a scheme to regularise the position of domestic workers who had entered under the concession scheme.[81] In 2002, the ODW visa scheme was introduced,[82] following an extensive advocacy campaign by migrant domestic workers' NGOs, including the Waling-Waling, Kalayaan and the Commission for Filipino Migrant Workers organisations.[83] Under the ODW visa scheme, migrant domestic workers were permitted to change employers, a key element of the campaign for reform. Employment protections were also recognised as

74 Clayton, ibid., 385.

75 Earl Ferrers (Minister of State, Home Office) *HL Deb Written Answers*, 24 July 1990.

76 Lord Reay, HL Deb col 1052 (28 November 1990).

77 C-60/00 *Carpenter* [2002] ECR I-6279.

78 See Anderson, *Doing the Dirty Work*, supra n.3, 89.

79 See Anderson, ibid. Section 3(1)(c) of the Immigration Act 1971.

80 Anderson, *Britain's Secret Slaves* (London: Anti-Slavery International 1993). See also Anderson, *Doing the Dirty Work*, supra n.3, 89.

81 See Announcement by Mr Mike O'Brien MP (Immigration Minister) on 23 July 1998. HC Deb col 611W (23 July 1998).

82 According to the Immigration Directorate's Instructions (Chapter 5, Section 12: Domestic Workers in Private Households, December 2006), the amended criteria were implemented administratively from 17 October 2001 before they were formally incorporated into the Immigration Rules on 18 September 2002 (HC 395 of 1994 as amended by Cm 5597 of 22 August 2002).

83 Waling-Waling was established in 1984 and became a self-organised group with a membership of domestic workers. The supporters of the migrant domestic workers formed Kalayaan in 1987. The Commission for Filipino Migrant Workers (CFMW) was founded in 1979.

applying to domestic work and, as with other categories of migrant workers, domestic workers could apply to have their dependants join them in the UK.[84] The possibility of qualifying for indefinite leave to remain was also recognised, subject to meeting generally applicable criteria such as the requirement of continuous employment.[85] While these hurdles were not insignificant and could pose barriers to secure migration status, a route out of temporary residence was at least, in principle, available.[86]

Labour market mobility for domestic workers on the ODW visa was, however, limited, as visa extensions were dependent on securing continuous employment in the domestic work sector,[87] thus limiting possibilities for moving out of a traditionally lower-paid and under-valued employment sector. The eligibility criteria also limited the potential impact of the visa scheme; only domestic workers employed for one year or more in the house of their employer or a connected household were eligible to apply. The requirement of no recourse to public funds meant that, in practice, many domestic workers had no option but to accept 'live-in' arrangements, thus exacerbating the isolated nature of the work and heightening risks of abuse. Thus, while the ODW visa provided important employment rights protections, it did not fully resolve the precarious status of migrant domestic workers.

In 2006, the Labour Government proposed a new 'Points Based System' of immigration,[88] as part of which it was proposed that domestic workers would receive six-month, non-renewable business visitor visas only and lose the right to change employers.[89] Following an extensive campaign led by Kalayaan and other NGOs,[90] the Government agreed to postpone the introduction of changes to the ODW visa pending a review of the national anti-trafficking strategy.[91] The Government also affirmed their commitment to minimising risks of abuse or exploitation in any process of reform. In 2009, the House of Commons Home Affairs Select Committee, in its Report on Human Trafficking in the UK, concluded that the retention of the existing ODW visa and the protections it offered was the single most important issue in preventing forced labour and trafficking of domestic workers.[92] Given the particular vulnerability of migrant domestic workers

84 This was not set out in the Immigration Rules but was accepted practice.

85 Paragraph 159G of the Immigration Rules.

86 Kalayaan, Annual Report 2009–2010, 15. See also Kalayaan, Annual Report 2010–2011, 16.

87 Paragraph 159EA of the Immigration Rules.

88 See, generally, 'A Points-Based System: Making Migration Work for Britain' (2006).

89 The proposals were raised in a Westminster Hall debate on Migrant Domestic Workers. HC Deb cols 101–107WH (10 May 2006).

90 Kalayaan and Oxfam, 'The New Bonded Labour? The Impact of the Proposed Changes to the UK Immigration System on Migrant Domestic Workers' (Oxfam and Kalayaan, 2008). See also Campaign Statement of Kalayaan (January 2007).

91 UK Border Agency, 'Government Response to the Consultation on Visitors' (June 2008).

92 House of Commons Home Affairs Select Committee, Sixth Report of Session 2008–2009, *The Trade in Human Beings: Human Trafficking in the UK*, HC 23-I, 14 May 2009, para. 59.

to abuse, the Committee argued that the preservation of the ODW regime would be necessary for much longer than the two-year period proposed by Government.[93] In 2010, the UN Special Rapporteur on the Human Rights of Migrants specifically commended the effectiveness of visa protections for migrant domestic workers in the UK and recommended that its protections be extended to cover domestic workers in diplomatic households.[94]

Reform: enacting exclusion

The issue of reform, delayed by the previous Labour Government, came to the fore again in 2011. In June 2011, a consultation paper on overseas domestic workers published by the Liberal Democratic–Conservative Coalition Government proposed abolishing the special entry route for domestic workers, abolishing the special ODW visa or significantly restricting its operation to a six-month, non-renewable entry visa and removing the right to change employers (in effect, returning to the earlier Labour Government proposals),[95] noting that the UK was 'more generous in its provision for ODWs than other EU countries'.[96] This 'generosity', it seemed, was not to be commended. Documented abuses as well as levels of unemployment in the UK domestic labour market were appealed to as support for the case to abolish the ODW visa.[97] The announcement of the proposed reforms coincided with the UK Government's decision to abstain from voting on the ILO Domestic Worker's Convention, a move that attracted significant criticism from domestic workers' advocates.[98]

The stated rationale for the proposed reforms reveals the continuing characterisation of domestic work as low-skilled and of little economic value.[99] Migrant domestic workers, the Government argued, were 'generally doing low skilled work'. Continuing to allow 'unrestricted low skilled entry for an extended period' ran counter to the Government's policy of seeking to attract highly skilled migrants and limiting access to settlement routes.[100] This policy can also be seen to fit with broader trends at EU level to encourage and facilitate preferential immigration routes for 'highly qualified

93 Ibid.

94 UN Human Rights Council, *Report of the Special Rapporteur on the Human Rights of Migrants, Addendum: Mission to the United Kingdom of Great Britain and Northern Ireland*, 16 March 2010, A/HRC/14/30/Add.3, 15 and 16, and recommendation para. 76.

95 Ibid., 13.

96 UK Border Agency, 'Employment-Related Settlement, Tier-5 and Overseas Domestic Workers: A Consultation' (June 2011) (Consultation Paper), 30.

97 Ibid.

98 See Williams, 'Behind Closed Doors: The Plight of the UK's Domestic Workers', *Guardian* online, 15 June 2011, available at www.guardian.co.uk/lifeandstyle/the-womens-blog-with-jane-martinson/2011/jun/15/domestic-workers-uk-obstructive.

99 Consultation Paper, supra n.96, 29.

100 Ibid.

workers' and their family members.[101] The categorisation of skills levels in this context is potentially a highly gendered exercise. The stated concerns to protect demand-led labour migration ignore the continuing demand for domestic workers. The Consultation Paper pointed to the existence of the National Referral Mechanism as sufficient to identify victims of trafficking and responding to abuses experienced by domestic workers. A route to settlement, such as that offered by the ODW visa, was not considered an appropriate response. The level of documented abuses of migrant domestic workers was presented, in itself, as a reason to cease the operation of the ODW visa. This argument, in particular, seems difficult to sustain given the acknowledged protections that it offered to migrant domestic workers, including, in particular, the right to change employers.[102]

Again, we see the reluctance to acknowledge the nexus between access to safe migration routes and states' positive obligations to deter and prevent human rights abuses. The proposed reforms were strongly resisted by NGOs, who argued that the changes would remove crucial protections from migrant domestic workers.[103] Central to the debates on the impact of reform proposals is the disputed role that immigration laws and policies are presumed to play.[104] The constructed vulnerability of the migrant domestic worker is instrumentalised by the State to justify the imposition of further immigration restrictions. While advocates for the retention of the ODW visa highlighted immigration restrictions as likely to contribute to further abuse and exploitation of domestic workers, the Government invoked controls on immigration as essential to curbing abuse by unscrupulous employers.[105] This argument was also made by the Government in its response to the OSCE Special Representative's Report on her 2011 country visit.[106]

In the House of Commons debates on the proposed reforms, MPs arguing in favour of the retention of the ODW visa emphasised the critical role played by the right to change employer in limiting the potential for exploitation. The proposed reforms, it was noted, would lead to an increase in abuse and illegality, and would 'dramatically increase the power that the

101 The Stockholm Programme – An Open and Secure Europe Serving and Protecting Citizens (2010/C 115/01), para. 6.1.

102 Consultation Paper, supra n.96, 30.

103 Kalayaan Statement, 'Government Proposes Return to Slavery for Migrant Domestic Workers in the UK' (2011). See also Kalayaan 'Response to Consultation – Questions on MDWs' (5 August 2011).

104 See 'Consultation on Employment-Related Settlement, Tier 5 and Overseas Domestic Workers: (9 June, 2–9 September 2011) Summary of the Findings from the Consultation' (Home Office, 2012).

105 Anderson, 'Mobilizing Migrants, Making Citizens: Migrant Domestic Workers as Political Agents' (2010) 33(1) *Ethnic and Racial Studies* 60, 70–73.

106 Report by OSCE Special Representative and Co-ordinator for Combating Trafficking in Human Beings, following her visit to the UK, 7–10 March 2011, SEC.GAL/200/11, 18 January 2012, Appendix 1, p. 12.

employer has over the worker'.[107] Despite these arguments, the Government continued to refuse to recognise the links between migration routes, migration status and vulnerability to abuse. The issuing of immigrant visas, they argued, was 'not the way to deal with that'.[108]

A series of changes to the Immigration Rules applicable to domestic workers came into effect on 6 April 2012.[109] Against the trend of expanding human rights norms for migrant domestic workers, the reforms introduced significantly increase the precariousness of the migrant domestic worker's position. Domestic workers will now be permitted to enter and stay in the UK for a maximum period of six months only.[110] Critically, the right to change employer is removed,[111] as is the possibility of sponsoring dependants or seeking longer-term settlement in the UK.[112] In introducing these changes, the Government signalled its intention to align the domestic worker migration route with wider migration policies and to return it to its original purpose, 'to allow visitors and diplomats to be accompanied by their domestic staff – not to provide permanent access to the UK for unskilled workers'.[113] Central to the Government's position is the view that the domestic worker's reproductive labour requires limited skills and is easily replaced. The intimate connections, relationships and caring skills involved in much of domestic work are denied, as are the wider protections afforded to other workers. The confinement to a temporary status, combined with increasing policy discourse on circular migration, facilitates further curbs on family reunification as the domestic worker is denied the possibility of claiming family unity rights.

Migrant domestic workers employed in diplomatic households have not enjoyed the right to change employer, even prior to the reforms introduced in 2012. Their migration status was and continues to be tied directly to their employment with a named diplomatic or international civil servant.[114] In 2010, the UN Special Rapporteur on the Human Rights on Migrants specifically recommended that the UK Government consider extending the right to change employers to domestic workers in diplomatic households

107 HC Deb col 101WH (10 May 2006).

108 Ibid.

109 'Statement of Changes in Immigration Rules, Presented to Parliament Pursuant to Section 3(2) of the Immigration Act 1971', HC 1888 (15 March 2012).

110 Paragraphs 159A(iv) and 159B of the Immigration Rules.

111 Paragraph 159E of the Immigration Rules provides: 'An extension of stay as a domestic worker in a private household may be granted for a period of six months less the period already spent in the UK in this capacity'.

112 Paragraph 159G(i) of the Immigration Rules.

113 Home Office Announcement, 'Immigration (Employment-Related Settlement, Overseas Domestic Workers, Tier 5 of the Points Based System and Visitors)', 29 February 2012, 2.

114 Paragraph 155 of the Immigration Rules, which was deleted in 2008 (HC 1113, para. 39), provided that in order to extend their stay in the UK, such workers had to show that they were still engaged in the employment for which the entry clearance was granted.

as a safeguard against 'abusive practices'.[115] In 2011, the OSCE Special Representative and Co-ordinator for Combating Trafficking in Human Beings included a similar recommendation in the report on her UK country visit.[116] These recommendations were ignored, however. Instead, further limits on the rights of domestic workers in diplomatic households were enacted; the route to settlement that had previously been available after a five-years residence period has now been removed.[117]

The changes to the ODW regime and the return to a highly temporary and tied status for domestic workers has been noted with concern in the UK evaluation report of the Group of Experts on Action Trafficking in Human Beings (GRETA).[118] In its response, the Government argued that the removal of the right to change employer will not affect its ability to take other positive measures to combat trafficking.[119]

This argument, however, refuses to acknowledge the 'chilling effect' that immigration controls can and do play on accessing legal remedies. Elsewhere the GRETA report notes the limited engagement with the UK's National Referral Mechanism on human trafficking and concerns expressed by NGOs that this is, at least in part, due to the absence of an immigration firewall and the ever-present threat of deportation.[120] Given the very temporary nature of the immigration routes, it is likely that an increasing number of migrant domestic workers will find themselves in an irregular situation. As Noll has noted, in such cases human rights law provides little assistance.[121] The absence of a 'firewall' between employment, social security or other legal remedies and migration laws ensures that the disciplinary and punitive reach of immigration controls function as limits to the claiming of rights.

115 UN Human Rights Council, *Report of the Special Rapporteur on the Human Rights of Migrants, Addendum: Mission to the United Kingdom of Great Britain and Northern Ireland*, supra n.94, para. 76(a).

116 Report by OSCE Special Representative and Co-ordinator for Combating Trafficking in Human Beings, following her visit to the UK, 7–10 March 2011, SEC.GAL/200/11, 18 January 2012, Recommendation 5, p. 8.

117 Home Office Announcement, supra n.113, 2. Paragraph 245ZR(d) of the Immigration Rules.

118 See *Report concerning the Implementation of the Council of Europe Convention on Action against Trafficking in Human Beings by the United Kingdom*, GRETA (2012) 6 (Strasbourg, 12 September 2012), Appendix I: List of GRETA's proposals, para. 8, 83.

119 Ibid. United Kingdom authorities' Comments on the Report concerning the implementation of the Council of Europe Convention on Action against Trafficking in Human Beings by the United Kingdom, 97–98, para. 19.

120 Ibid., para. 231/p. 54.

121 Noll, 'The Laws of Undocumented Migration' (2010) 12(2) *European Journal of Migration and Law* 143.

Domestic work, the public and the private: work like 'no other'

Prior to the final adoption of the ILO Convention, the UK Government had signalled its commitment to a 'workable convention' that could be ratified by as many states as possible and would protect 'vulnerable domestic workers worldwide'.[122] Despite this commitment, the UK Government was one of eight states to abstain from the final vote on the Convention.[123] Ultimately, the Government concluded that the Convention failed to acknowledge the specificity of domestic work or the particular difficulties concerning the application of labour rights in the domestic household.[124] Speaking in the House of Commons, the Minister for Employment Relations commented that the 'main sticking point' for the Government was the potential application of health and safety legislation to private homes.[125] Such a legislative disincentive to employment of domestic workers could, he argued, force elderly or disabled individuals into residential homes thereby undermining Government policy to support independent living through direct payments to recipients of care supports.[126]

In refusing to support the 2011 ILO Domestic Work Convention, the Government was concerned to protect its own care and welfare policies, as well as to shield employers in the domestic sphere from what, it argued, were unnecessary and burdensome regulatory obligations. The shift towards direct cash payments has been a key feature of social care policy in the UK over the last decade, facilitating a trend towards outsourcing of care work to private actors including migrant women. Direct payments in the social care system are cash payments given to service users in lieu of community care services[127] and are presented as facilitating greater choice and independence in sourcing care supports.[128] A system of direct payments has been in place since 1996,[129] premised on an increasing trend towards 'personalisation' of care, including through allocation of personal budgets and direct

122 HC Deb col WA 469W (23 May 2011).

123 The other states that abstained from the vote were El Salvador, Malaysia, Panama, Singapore, Thailand, the Czech Republic and Sudan. See Fiona MacTaggart MP: HC Deb col 269WH (29 June 2011).

124 As quoted by Fiona MacTaggart MP: HC Deb cols 269–293WH (29 June 2011).

125 HC Deb cols 288–289 (Ed Davey MP) (29 June 2011).

126 Ibid.

127 See Regulations 7 and 8 of the Community Care, Services for Carers and Children's Services (Direct Payments) (England) Regulations 2009 (No. 1887 of 2009).

128 *Guidance on Direct Payments for Community Care, Services for Carers and Children's Services* (Department of Health, 2009), 8.

129 Direct payments were introduced in relation to social care services for adults through the Community Care (Direct Payments) Act 1996. This Act was repealed (in relation to England) by the Health and Social Care Act 2001. Direct payments are now governed by the 2001 Act and the Children Act 1989.

payments.[130] Williams has argued that direct cash payments of this kind have encouraged the development of a particular form of care or domestic help: home-based, often low-paid, commodified and generally accessed privately through the market.[131] At the same time, the trend towards the outsourcing of care, she notes, has expanded employment opportunities for newly arrived migrant women workers, creating yet another link in a wider transnational political economy of care.[132] The employer-driven nature of the market for care workers, however, contributes to the potential for exploitation of migrant domestic workers particularly in a context where the usual Decent Work standards are deemed not to apply.[133]

The claimed specificity of domestic work, as work that takes place in the domestic household, was also central to the Government's decision not to support the ILO Convention. Echoing sentiments expressed in earlier eras in the context of debates on domestic violence, the Minister for Employment Relations questioned why the Government would wish to pass 'quite an intrusive law',[134] one that would give to health and safety inspectors a 'new right to visit millions of homes'. The evidence of the need for such a change, he argued, was weak – households being 'low risk in health and safety terms'.[135] The previous Government had baulked at taking such a measure and had continued to uphold the exemptions applicable to domestic households from the operation of the 1974 Health and Safety Act.[136] The increased vulnerability of domestic workers, the Minister argued, arose not from health and safety concerns but rather from the actions of individual employers that were already covered in other legislation.

This argument, however, ignores the legislative exemptions relating to domestic work that continue to operate in the UK and that provide a protective shield to unscrupulous employers. Domestic workers are excluded from certain aspects of the regulation of working time under the Working Time Regulations 1998, for example.[137] Deductions may be made from the minimum wage payment if accommodation is provided,[138] effectively allowing

130 *A Vision for Adult Social Care: Capable Communities and Active Citizens* (Department of Health, November 2010), 8.
131 Williams, 'Markets and Migrants in the Care Economy' (2011) 47 *Soundings* 22, 25.
132 Ibid.
133 Gordolan and Lalani, 'Care and Immigration: Migrant Care Workers in Private Households' (Kalayaan, September 2009), 39.
134 HC Deb cols 269–293WH (29 June 2011).
135 Ibid.
136 See Section 51 of the Health and Safety Act 1974.
137 Regulation 19, Working Time Regulations 1998 (No. 1833 of 1998), which provides that Regulations 4(1) and (2), 6(1), (2) and (7), 7(1), (2) and (6) and 8 do not apply in relation to a worker employed as a domestic worker in a private household. These Regulations cover the maximum weekly working time, length of night work, health assessment and transfer of night workers to day work, and weekly rest period.
138 Regulations 36 and 37 of the Minimum Wage Regulations 1999 (No. 584 of 1999).

for payments 'in kind' for the live-in domestic worker.[139] Perhaps one of the most striking of these exemptions has been that provided by Regulation 2(2) of the National Minimum Wage Regulations, which allows for payments less than the national minimum wage where a domestic worker is treated as 'a member of the family'.[140]

A new provision introduced into the revised Immigration Rules is the requirement to provide written terms and conditions of employment as part of the pre-entry application process, and to commit to complying with the terms of the National Minimum Wage Act 1998 and supporting Regulations.[141] The strengthening of pre-entry protections is a feature of the 2011 ILO Domestic Work Convention, which the Government refused to support.[142] Given this refusal, it is unclear how effective pre-entry clearance measures will be in practice or whether there is any political will to monitor their impact on the prevention of abuse. A previous report of the House of Commons Home Affairs Select Committee on Human Trafficking expressed scepticism as to the effectiveness of pre-departure interviews with domestic workers in preventing abuse, noting that enforcement was patchy at best.[143] The 'family member' exemption from the operation of the minimum wage requirements continues to apply, however.[144] And, as was noted by domestic workers' advocates, access to UK employment protections or remedies for failure to comply with minimum wage requirements are greatly limited by the temporary and tied nature of the new visa arrangements.

The family member exemption, perhaps more than any other, reinforces the public–private divide that limits the enforcement of Decent Work

139 Report on Decent Work for Domestic Workers (Report IV(1)), supra n.28, 7.

140 Regulation 2(2) provides that work for the purposes of the Regulations does not include work relating to the employer's household done by a worker where:

(i) the worker resides in the family home of the employer for whom he works;

(ii) that the worker is not a member of that family, but is treated as such, in particular regards to the provision of accommodation and meals and the sharing of tasks and leisure activities;

(iii) that the worker is neither liable to any deduction, nor to make any payment to the employer, or any other person, in respect of the provision of the living accommodation or meals; and

(iv) that, had the work been done by a member of the employer's family, it would not be treated as being performed under a worker's contract or as being work because the conditions in sub-paragraph (b) would be satisfied.

141 Paragraph 159A(v) of the Immigration Rules.

142 ILO Provisional Record, 100th Session, 15 June 2011, Report of the Committee on Domestic Workers, para. 895.

143 House of Commons, Home Affairs Select Committee, Sixth Report of Session 2008–2009, *The Trade in Human Beings: Human Trafficking in the UK*, HC 23-I, 14 May 2009, paras. 116–118.

144 UK Border Agency, *Entry Clearance Guidance*, WRK2.1.9, available at www.ukba.homeoffice.gov.uk/policyandlaw/guidance/ecg/wrk2/wrk2-1/#header9.

standards for domestic workers.[145] It is a line that is, of course, deeply gendered and reflects continuing categorisation of domestic work as work 'like no other'.

Just like one of the family: enacting exclusions

A series of cases before the UK Employment Appeals Tribunal highlights the difficulties that arise when the family member exemption is applied.[146] Where the work done could be characterised as similar to the everyday work that characterises intimate domestic life, it was removed from the scope of employment law protections reserved for the public domain. In *Ms Julio v Ms Jose,* the Tribunal accepted Ms Julio's evidence that she was not at any time paid the agreed monthly salary,[147] but found that she was treated as 'a member of the family as regards to the provision of accommodation, meals and the sharing of tasks and leisure activities'.[148] The 'family member' exemption from the minimum wage regulations was therefore applicable. In the case of *Ms Nambalat v Mr Taher and Mrs Tayeb*, the Tribunal found that there were distinct 'phases' in the employment relationship, during which Ms Nambalat's work duties varied widely. Despite these variations, the Tribunal concluded that the 'family member' exemption nonetheless applied.[149] In the case of *Ms Udin v Mr and Mrs Chamsi-Pasha*, variations in the working and living conditions of the claimant were found by the Tribunal to have changed the nature of the employment relationship. Financial difficulties encountered by the employers had led to a 'downsizing' of accommodation space and more difficult living conditions for Ms Udin for limited periods. For these periods only, the Tribunal concluded that the family member exemption did not apply, and Ms Udin was therefore entitled to a remedy for the unauthorised deductions from her wages during this time.[150]

On appeal, each of the claimants argued that the Employment Tribunal had erred in law in its interpretation of the family member exemption.[151] The narrowest possible interpretation, it was argued, should be given to this exemption so as to ensure consistency with the statutory language and compliance with the public policy good of eliminating gender and racial discrimination, given that the majority of domestic workers were women from minority ethnic communities.[152] It was also argued that a narrow

145 Kalayaan/Lalani, 'Ending the Abuse: Policies that Work to Protect Migrant Workers' (May 2011), 22.
146 Appeal No. UKEAT/0553/10/DM, Judgment of 8 December 2011 (EAT judgment).
147 EAT judgment, para. 19, quoting from the Tribunal's decision.
148 EAT judgment, para. 21, quoting from the Tribunal's decision.
149 EAT judgment, para. 32, quoting from the Tribunal's decision.
150 Ibid.
151 EAT judgment, para. 39.
152 EAT judgment, paras. 39 and 40.

interpretation was necessary to meet the State's positive obligations under Article 4 ECHR, in line with the judgment of European Court of Human Rights in *Siliadin v France*.[153] The Employment Appeals Tribunal (EAT) did not specifically comment on the Article 4 ECHR arguments, but did accept however that a narrow interpretation must be given to the family member exemption.[154] The dignity with which the domestic worker is treated, the degree of privacy and autonomy afforded and the extent to which, if at all, exploitation occurs were also relevant.[155] The core question was whether the worker is 'integrated into the family'.[156] If the answer is yes, then the limits of human rights protections appear to be reached. In each of the three cases before it, the Employment Appeals Tribunal concluded that the family member exemption applied and the domestic workers (all of whom were migrants) were not entitled to payment of the national minimum wage.[157]

That 'integration into the family' could trigger an exemption from a core labour standard reveals a continuing reluctance, as the European Court of Human Rights has noted elsewhere, to apply human rights norms 'within personal relationships or closed circuits'.[158] Until recently, the UK Border Agency's Instructions to entry clearance officers noted that non-payment of the national minimum wage was not a valid reason for a refusal to issue an ODW visa. The House of Commons Home Affairs Select Committee, in its Report on Human Trafficking in the UK, criticised this practice, commenting that it 'makes a mockery of the concept of a legal minimum wage'.[159] Changes to the Immigration Rules introduced in April 2012 only partly address this criticism. Applicants for an ODW visa now have to demonstrate that the employer has agreed to pay the minimum wage in accordance with the National Minimum Wage Regulations.[160] However, the family member exemption continues to apply, giving legal standing to the paradox inherent in many domestic work employment relationships; employers delegate intimate reproductive labour to domestic workers, expecting unconditional availability and care, while remaining unwilling to comply with Decent Work standards.

The draft Modern Slavery Bill 2014 does not reinstate the right to change employer, or provide a route to long-term residence, despite a

153 (2006) 43 EHRR 16. EAT judgment, para. 41.
154 EAT judgment, para. 46.
155 Ibid.
156 EAT judgment, para. 45.
157 EAT judgment, para. 58. In relation to Ms Udin, the EAT over-turned the majority finding of the Employment Tribunal, concluding that in the overall context of the family's circumstances, the changing conditions did not result in Ms Udin ceasing to be treated as a member of the family. EAT judgment, para. 57.
158 *Opuz v Turkey*, Application No. 33401/02, Judgment of 9 June 2009, para. 132.
159 House of Commons, Home Affairs Select Committee, Sixth Report of Session 2008–2009, *The Trade in Human Beings: Human Trafficking in the UK*, HC 23-I, 14 May 2009, para. 53.
160 Paragraph 159A(v) of the Immigration Rules.

recommendation from the Joint Select Committee on the Bill to reverse the changes to the ODW visa. This, they argued, would 'at the very least allow organisations and agencies to remove a worker from an abusive employment situation immediately'. It would also facilitate prosecutions of modern slavery, by removing the 'chilling effect' of a fear of deportation.[161] Concerning diplomatic domestic workers, the Committee recommended that the Government consider the merits of granting visas to diplomatic domestic workers only where they have contractual arrangements directly with the Embassy or other diplomatic mission, so as to facilitate workers being able to secure remedies against diplomatic employers.[162] Both of these recommendations were rejected by the Government. Reiterating their determination to 'stamp out' all forms of modern slavery, including slavery, servitude and forced labour faced by domestic workers, they conclude that the previous ODW visa arrangements potentially encouraged abuse by allowing for longer-term residence.[163] Pointing to the 'substantial safeguards' that exist in the ODW route, as reformed, they note the requirement to comply with national minimum wage regulations, but do not acknowledge the exemptions from such safeguards that apply to 'live-in' domestic workers who fall within the family member exemption.[164] They also note that it is not Government policy to facilitate 'low-skilled' immigration to the UK.[165]

There is in the Government response no acknowledgement of the disputed categories of skilled/unskilled, or of the appeals to rights standards in both oral and written submissions from domestic workers' advocates. The responses to abuse of workers, instead, continue to focus on prosecutorial strategy and enforcement of criminal law prohibitions. To date the positive obligations jurisprudence of the European Court of Human Rights has also largely remained confined within this more familiar comfort zone of civil and political rights enactment, failing to address the everyday exploitation of migrant domestic workers.

Litigating Article 4 of the European Convention on Human Rights

The Coroners and Justice Act 2009 introduced into the domestic law of the UK the offence of holding another person in slavery or servitude or requiring them to perform forced or compulsory labour.[166] The introduction of this offence sought to remedy the legislative gap that arose in cases where

161 *Report of the Joint Select Committee on the Modern Slavery Bill*, 8 April 2014, para. 227, citing written evidence from Human Rights Watch, available at www.publications.parliament.uk/pa/jt201314/jtselect/jtslavery/166/16610.htm.

162 Ibid. para. 228.

163 The Government Response to the Report from the Joint Committee on the Draft Modern Slavery Bill: Session 2013–14 HL Paper 166/HC 1019, Cm 8889, June 2014, p. 28.

164 Ibid. p. 27.

165 Ibid. p. 28.

166 Section 71 Coroners and Justice Act 2009.

trafficking had not occurred or the trafficking element could not be proven to a criminal standard.[167] A series of cases before the European Court of Human Rights highlight the inadequacies of the legal framework in place prior to the adoption of the 2009 Act and the challenges of enforcement of forced labour, servitude and slavery prohibitions, particular in a migration context. These cases build on the Court's evolving jurisprudence under Article 4, following the landmark *Siliadin* judgment.

In *Siliadin*, the Court recognised for the first time that Article 4 could give rise to positive obligations for states, including obligations to ensure that effective criminal sanctions were in place and enforced at the domestic level.[168] A key question that had arisen in the domestic legal proceedings was how to demarcate the boundaries of everyday intimate labour in the domestic sphere from working conditions contrary to Article 4. The French Civil Court of Appeal, in concluding that exploitation had taken place, was anxious to clarify that *Siliadin* was not a member of the family and was not treated as such.[169] The public tests of rights compliance could, therefore, kick in. In contrast, the Court found that *Siliadin* had not been subject to working conditions that were 'incompatible with human dignity'. These conditions they noted were 'the lot of many mothers'.[170] The Court's presumption that the usual standards of human dignity could not apply, therefore, served to distinguish domestic work as 'work like no other'.

These distinctions came into play again in the subsequent case of *Osman v Denmark*,[171] where the European Court of Human Rights was required to distinguish between domestic care work provided by a minor in a family context and the boundaries of human trafficking. Osman, a Somali national, had lived in Denmark from the age of 7. At the age of 15, she was brought by her father to Kenya and left at the Hagdera refugee camp in Northern Kenya, to care for her paternal grandmother. After two years, she left the camp and applied to be reunited with her family in Denmark. The Court found that the Danish authorities' refusal to reinstate her residence status constituted an unjustifiable interference with her rights to private and to family life.[172]

The AIRE centre, representing the applicant, had sought to argue that Osman had been subject to intra-familial human trafficking and that the State had failed in its obligation to investigate and prosecute the offence

167 Crown Prosecution Service, Legal Guidance (2009) 'Slavery, Servitude and Forced or Compulsory Labour', available at www.cps.gov.uk/legal/s_to_u/slavery_servitude_and_forced_or_compulsory_labour.

168 (2006) 43 EHRR 16. EAT judgment, para. 41.

169 See, generally, Van Walsum, 'Labour, Legality and Shifts in the Public/Private Divide' (Paper presented at Seminar on Gender, Migration and Human Rights, EUI Florence, 18–20 June 2012) 9 (copy on file with the authors).

170 *Siliadin*, para. 44.

171 *Osman v Denmark*, Application No. 38058/09, Judgment of 14 June 2011.

172 Ibid., in particular paras. 51–77.

of trafficking.[173] The Court rejected this argument, however, noting that neither the applicant nor her mother had complained of trafficking to the Danish authorities. This conclusion ignores the positive obligation on states to identify victims of trafficking, recognised as a core obligation under the Council of Europe Convention on Action Against Trafficking and an element of the positive obligations of prevention and deterrence implied by Article 4 ECHR at least since *Rantsev*.[174] In its judgment, the Court sought to distinguish the work done as part of everyday family life from the exploitation that constitutes an element of human trafficking offences.[175] Its conclusions, however, fail to acknowledge the role played by gender in determining the kind of work or harm that might be defined as exploitative, or as merely a family role. Neither does it address the wider issue of cultural expectations concerning appropriate family roles and responsibilities or the intersections of gender, 'race' and age as overlapping axes of potential discrimination and disadvantage.[176]

The issue of intra-familial trafficking has also come before the Court in the cases of *C.N. and V. v France*[177] and in *C.N. v UK*. The case of *C.N. and V.* concerned the treatment of two sisters aged 16 and 10 years, originally from Burundi, who were living with their aunt and uncle in Paris, following the death of their parents in Burundi's bloody civil war. Both sisters were required to undertake extensive domestic work and the older sister C.N. was also required to undertake care work for the disabled son of her relatives. Reflecting again the continuum of exploitation that is frequently found in domestic work, the Court noted that it was necessary to distinguish 'forced or compulsory labour' from work that could 'reasonably be required in respect of mutual family assistance or cohabitation, taking into account, among other things, the nature and amount of work in issue'.[178] The Court noted that the older sister C.N. had to perform, under threat of being returned to Burundi, activities that would have been described as work if performed by a remunerated professional. In respect of her treatment, the Court concluded that France had failed to meet its positive obligations to put in place an effective legislative and administrative framework to combat servitude and forced or compulsory labour. The younger sister V. had attended school, developing social networks that were ultimately central to the Court's finding that no violation had occurred with respect to her situation.[179] This finding was arrived at despite the aunt having been

173 Ibid., paras. 46 and 62.

174 *Rantsev v Cyprus and Russia*, Application No. 25965/04, Judgment of 7 January 2010.

175 Supra n.165, para. 64.

176 See, generally, Columbia Law School Sexuality and Gender Law Clinic, 'Sent Away: The Trafficking of Young Girls and Women within the Family Unit' (May 2010).

177 *C.N. and V. v France*, supra n.15, paras. 90–93.

178 Ibid. para. 74.

179 Ibid., para. 92.

convicted by a domestic court for aggravated assault of V.[180] The Court's finding suggests a failure to acknowledge the relative youth of V. as a key issue in assessing the reasonableness of the demands made of her, and the likely impact of coercive threats.

The absence of an effective legislative and administrative framework to meet the State's positive obligations under Article 4 ECHR has arisen under a series of cases in the UK. These cases also highlight the difficulties of establishing credibility and of demonstrating the significance of the harms endured by migrant domestic workers. The case of *C.N. v United Kingdom*[181] involved a Ugandan applicant who had come to the UK with the assistance of a relative to escape alleged physical and sexual violence. On arrival in the UK, her passport was taken from her by her relative and not returned.[182] She later began work as a live-in carer for an elderly couple, having been introduced to a private recruitment agency. C.N. claimed not to have received any of the remuneration paid to the agent.[183] She left her live-in carer position after several years having fallen ill, and sought asylum. She was denied asylum, in part because of a finding of a lack of credibility.[184] A complaint was submitted to the police concerning her treatment by her employers, but it was found that there was insufficient evidence to substantiate the allegation of trafficking, though it was accepted that there was dispute over payment of wages and that her relative had 'kept more than he should have done'.[185] Further requests from C.N.'s solicitor to consider prosecutions for *jus cogens* offences of slavery or forced labour were rejected.[186]

Of note are comments made by the police authorities that the situation was one where 'one criminal (her uncle) has taken all the proceeds of their crime'.[187] The reference to 'their crime' reveals a preoccupation with the irregularity of C.N.'s employment. Elsewhere, the police noted that C.N.'s identity and travel documents were false, suggesting again that the illegality of the applicant's entry to and presence in the UK somehow weakened her claims.[188] As C.N. argued before the European Court of Human Rights, the suggestion that the lack of payment was no more than 'an absence of "honour among thieves"', betrayed a fundamental disregard of the ILO's key indicators of forced labour and 'a troubling ignorance of the vulnerabilities of illegal immigrants'.[189] In correspondence with C.N.'s

180 The diplomatic immunity enjoyed by Mr M., a former Burundi Government minister and a UNESCO employee, was waived by UNESCO, as was that of his wife. See ibid., paras. 22 and 23.
181 Supra n.15.
182 Ibid., paras. 5–7.
183 Ibid., paras. 10 and 48.
184 Ibid., para. 14.
185 Ibid., paras. 15–18.
186 Ibid., paras. 21–24.
187 Ibid., para. 25.
188 Ibid., para. 26.
189 Ibid., para. 49.

solicitor, the police commented that they were 'not aware' of any specific offence of forced labour or servitude in UK law, though they noted that 'regulation of working conditions are controlled by such areas as health and safety legislation'.[190] There is no acknowledgement and perhaps not even an awareness on their part that the usual protections of health and safety law so confidently invoked here do not apply to domestic workers.

The Court found the UK to have violated Article 4 ECHR.[191] The Court's judgment on the meaning of servitude is an important one. It recognises 'domestic servitude' as a specific offence, distinct from trafficking and exploitation, 'which involves a complex set of dynamics, involving both overt and more subtle forms of coercion, to force compliance'.[192] Due to the absence of a specific offence in domestic law, the Court found that the authorities were unable to give sufficient weight to these factors and to meet their obligation to carry out an effective investigation into C.N.'s complaints.[193] Drawing on Rantsev, they noted that a duty to investigate was triggered wherever a 'credible suspicion' arose that rights had been violated. In this case, the Court was particularly critical of the police authorities' failure to interview key actors, notably C.N.'s relative and the private recruitment agent. What was required under Article 4, they said, was a 'thorough investigation', one premised on an understanding of 'the many subtle ways an individual can fall under the control of another'.[194] The Court was also critical of the failure to give any weight to C.N.'s complaints that her passport was taken from her, her wages withheld and that she was frequently threatened with reporting to the immigration authorities. All of these were factors, as the Court noted, that came within the scope of the ILO's indicators of forced labour.[195]

The duty of effective investigation also arose in the case of O.O.O. *and others v Commissioner of Police for the Metropolis*.[196] In this case four Nigerian women complained that they had been brought to the UK as children and forced to undertake extensive domestic work, including child care. Each of the women complained that they had been regularly subject to physical and emotional abuse. Although they had sought protection and assistance from the police, their complaints were not pursued. The High Court accepted that the four claimants, who had alleged treatment contrary to Articles 3 and 4 ECHR on the part of their employers, were concerned

190 *C.N. v The United Kingdom*, para. 30.

191 The applicant had also alleged violations of Article 8 and Article 13 (read in conjunction with Articles 4 and 8). The Court found that no separate issues arose under Articles 8 and 13, given its findings on Article 4.

192 *C.N.* v. *The United Kingdom*, para. 80.

193 Ibid., paras. 80–81.

194 Ibid., para. 80.

195 Ibid.

196 O.O.O *and others v Commissioner of Police for the Metropolis* [2011] EWHC 1246 (QB).

about their migration status in the UK and that this concern had impacted on their willingness to cooperate in a police investigation. The Court found, however, that 'reasonable sensitivity' on the part of the police authorities could have overcome this obstacle.[197] A duty of effective investigation arose on the part of the police, they said, whenever a credible allegation was received, 'however that information comes to their attention'.[198] The duty of effective investigation arising under Articles 3 and 4 ECHR, the Court concluded, had not been met in this case.

Concluding remarks

For irregular or temporary migrants, the recognition of such a positive duty to investigate is critical. The difficulty, however, is that investigation, and/or the claiming of rights, may lead not to the possibility of remaining but to deportation. For those who are identified as victims of trafficking, rights to remain may be triggered.[199] Outside of the trafficking framework, however, 'deportability' remains a constant limit to rights. That migrant domestic workers continue to enact rights through a process of claim making before the European Court of Human Rights reveals the continuing resonance and force of rights claims. States, employers and others continue to resist such claims, however, and, in particular, refuse to acknowledge the nexus between denials of rights and migration status. Claiming rights through human rights litigation in domestic and international courts can lead to the creation of 'contact zones' in which an 'alternative legality' is presented, drawing on the transformative promise of human rights norms.[200] The claims presented reveal the potential to position domestic work firmly within the world of work, and highlight the injustice of failing to apply generally applicable workplace and human rights norms. The obstacles to presenting such cases and claims are many, however, particularly for migrant domestic workers whose status may be tied to that of their employer, their presence within the territory of the state dependent on the goodwill of an unscrupulous employer or perhaps irregular. The isolated and privatised nature of domestic work also limits the emergence of 'contact zones' within which alternative legalities may be presented.

Given the high levels of irregularity and undeclared work in the domestic work sector, a key issue at the intersections of migration, gender and 'race' is the application and enforcement of employment protections to migrant domestic workers in irregular situations. In the UK, the generally applicable

197 Ibid., paras. 170–177.

198 Ibid. para. 163.

199 See, generally, GRETA evaluation report, supra n.118, para. 220, discussing difficulties relating to the standard of proof applied to the identification of victims of trafficking and consequences for eligibility for residence permits.

200 De Sousa Santos, *Toward a New Legal Common Sense: Law, Globalization, and Emancipation* (Cambridge University Press, 2002), 472.

employment protections do not apply, especially where the worker is deemed to have participated voluntarily and taken an 'active part in' the illegal conduct.[201] In *Hounga v Allen*,[202] the Court of Appeal held that the applicant, a Nigerian citizen employed in the UK as an au pair, could not bring a racial discrimination claim against her employers as she was knowingly working unlawfully in the UK. Although the Court accepted that she had suffered ill-treatment, including physical abuse in the course of her employment,[203] they found that she was precluded from bringing forward a claim that was 'clearly connected or inextricably bound up or linked with her own illegal conduct'.[204] The case was criticised as the prohibition of racial discrimination is not dependent in UK law on the existence of a valid employment contract. More generally, of course, the protections afforded by human rights treaties including the European Convention of Human Rights do not admit of such sweeping exclusions. In July 2014, the UK Supreme Court reversed the decision of the Court of Appeal, finding that to uphold the defence of illegality ran counter to the greater public policy interest in countering human trafficking, and protecting its victims, including against discrimination.[205] The judgment is a significant one in seeking to advance the human rights of migrants, including irregular migrants. It is limited, however, to the specific context of human trafficking, and not all irregular migrants will fit the category of trafficked person, albeit they may be subject to exploitation. It remains to be seen whether the reach of Article 4 ECHR and positive obligations jurisprudence to counter human trafficking may further reinforce migrants' rights.

In *Siliadin*, the European Court of Human Rights recognised states' positive obligations in the context of Article 4. It failed, however, to recognise that such obligations could extend to the regularisation of a victim's migration status and to positive obligations of rehabilitation.[206] The nexus between migration routes and states' positive obligations of prevention and protection were given more consideration in *Rantsev v Cyprus and Russia*,[207] a case involving trafficking for the purposes of sexual exploitation. Specifically the Court found that Article 4 requires states to put in place adequate measures to regulate businesses used as a cover for human trafficking and to ensure that domestic legislation provides 'practical and effective protection of the rights of victims and potential victims of trafficking'.[208] The Court found that the Cypriot Government had violated Article 4 by not

201 *Zarkasi v Anindita*, Employment Appeal Tribunal, 18 January 2012.
202 [2012] EWCA Civ 609.
203 Ibid., para. 35.
204 Ibid., para. 61.
205 *Hounga (Appellant) v Allen and another (Respondents)* [2014] UKSC 47, para. 52.
206 See Cullen, '*Siliadin v. France*: Positive Obligations under Article 4 of the European Convention on Human Rights' (2006) 6 *Human Rights Law Review* 585.
207 Application No. 25965/04, Judgment of 7 January 2010.
208 Ibid. para. 284.

regulating the 'cabaret artiste' industry and by maintaining a visa regime for cabaret artistes that did not provide effective protection against trafficking.[209] On this reading, destination states may be found in breach of their Convention obligations continuing to operate immigration schemes that put migrant domestic workers at risk of treatment contrary to Article 4.[210]

The links between limited opportunities for legal migration for domestic workers and the high level of irregularity in the sector have been emphasised by the EU Fundamental Rights Agency, amongst others.[211] Irregularity, as they note, leads to high levels of insecurity, producing susceptibility to exploitation and difficulties in accessing rights protections.[212] In response to concerns of abuse and exploitation of migrant domestic workers, however, it is open to states to respond by expanding immigration controls rather than seeking to remedy the disadvantages that continue to attach to precarious migration status. As Dauvergne notes, 'Once an argument is shifted to the terrain of rights, the right of the nation to shut its borders tends to overshadow the rights claims of individuals.'[213] The 'deportability' of the alien persists as a constant threat to the claiming and enjoyment of rights.

The recent changes introduced in the ODW visa in the UK reveal the continuing willingness of states to limit migration options for domestic workers. Against the background of such resistance from states, the potential of human rights law to provide an effective bulwark against exclusion in the migration context must be questioned. Borders proliferate the texts of human rights law and, as De Sousa Santos argues, exclusion rather than exploitation has become the central mechanism of disentitlement from law's protections. His comment appears particularly relevant to migrant domestic workers. Exclusions and exemptions that operate in employment laws, in laws and policies on access to social security, in immigration and citizenship laws and in the scope of diplomatic immunity protections reinforce the invisibility and vulnerability of domestic workers. These exclusions take

209 Concerning Cyprus, the Court found, had violated its procedural obligations under Article 2 ECHR, 'because of the failure to conduct an effective investigation into Ms Rantseva's death' (paras. 241–242). The Court also found that the procedural obligations under Article 2 included a duty of transnational cooperation and investigation.

210 Ibid., para. 495.

211 EU Fundamental Rights Agency, 'Migrants in an Irregular Situation Employed in Domestic Work: Fundamental Rights Challenges for the European Union and Its Member States' (EU FRA, 2011); also Council of Europe Parliamentary Assembly Committee on Migration, Refugees and Population, Report on 'Protecting Migrant Women in the Labour Market' (Doc. 12549, 24 March 2011), para. 23.

212 EU Fundamental Rights Agency, *idem*. See also Cyrus, 'Being Illegal in Europe: Strategies and Policies for Fairer Treatment of Migrant Domestic Workers', in Lutz (ed.) *Migration and Domestic Work: A European Perspective on a Global Theme* (Ashgate, 2008).

213 Dauvergne and Marsden, supra n.28, 27.

the form and shape of de-juridifications that limit the application of human rights norms to domestic work and to migration status.[214]

Assessing the process of law reform in the UK law, it might be argued that the position from 1998 to 2012 was an anomaly of sorts, the product of a short-lived 'political moment' and a powerful advocacy campaign that successfully enacted domestic workers' rights.[215] The ODW visa, though imperfect, provided a better 'place in the world'[216] for migrant domestic workers – a route to settlement, the possibility of changing employers and of sponsoring family dependants. The reforms introduced by the UK Government have removed these possibilities, returning migrant domestic workers again to a deeply unequal employment relationship and a precarious migration status. Is the status of the migrant domestic worker diminished then to that of 'bare life'? As yet, it is unclear whether human rights law can effectively resist such processes of exclusion or whether the deployment of law continuously reproduces 'categories of illegal at its boundaries',[217] limiting the transformative promise of human rights norms.

Human rights law, if recognising the nexus between migration status, access to safe migration routes and the enjoyment of rights, has the potential to be transformative. States continue to resist this potential, however. The process of enacting rights, in courts and through political activism, is a difficult and uncertain one, but one that can be 'empowering'.[218] Reforms secured are contingent and reversible, as the story of the ODW visa reveals. In the context of migrant domestic workers in the UK, the limiting of a migration pathway reflects the potential for coercive exercises of state power that reverse reforms secured through sustained political activism. Such reversals, however, may yet be challenged, at which point the inescapable nexus between the state's migration laws, migration status and human rights violations cannot be denied.

214 See generally, Blackett, 'Introduction: Regulating Decent Work for Domestic Workers', supra n.28.

215 Rancière, *Disagreement: Politics and Philosophy* (University of Minnesota Press, 2004).

216 Arendt, *The Origins of Totalitarianism* (Andre Deutsch, 1986), 296–297.

217 Dauvergne, *Making People Illegal: What Globalization Means for Migration and Law* (Cambridge University Press, 2007), 37.

218 On the transformative potential of rights and their limits, see Benhabib, *Dignity in Adversity: Human Rights in Troubled Times* (Polity, 2011).

5 Obstacles to Claiming Rights: Migrant Domestic Workers in Asia's World City, Hong Kong

Nicole Constable

Introduction

In December 2005, while Hong Kong was hosting the fifth Ministerial Conference of the World Trade Organization, I attended a talk at the Hong Kong Foreign Correspondents' Club (FCC) by Global Commission on International Migration (GCIM) co-chairs Jan Karlsson and Mamphela Ramphele. A local Filipina journalist had invited me, and several domestic worker advocates and migrant activists I knew were also in the audience. Karlsson and Ramphele presented the findings of the recently released first major Global Commission on International Migration (GCIM) report, "Migration in an Interconnected World: New Directions for Action" (GCIM 2005), and, as they explained, they hoped to "hear Asian views" on the subject. They ended their presentation with comments about Hong Kong as a model for "successful migration." They spoke of Hong Kong as an attractive destination and as Asia's preferred destination for foreign domestic workers (FDWs). Indeed, the speakers echoed what I had long heard, since I began conducting research among foreign domestic workers in Hong Kong in the early 1990s: that Hong Kong is exemplary as a place to work compared with other Asian and Middle Eastern or Gulf regions.

The most commonly cited reason for Hong Kong's model status is Hong Kong's officially mandated "foreign domestic helper" standard employment contract, which must be signed by the worker and the employer and which stipulates key obligations on both sides.[1] The contract stipulates that the employer must pay Hong Kong's minimum monthly wage for foreign domestic helpers (FDHs), must provide adequate shelter in the employer's home, and must provide a mandated weekly day off.[2] Recognizing the rule

1 "Foreign domestic helper" (FDH) is the official local term. Many domestic worker activists prefer "worker" as "helper" minimizes their role as employees and workers. Unless referring to government forms and usage, I use the term "worker." A sample of the standard employment contract is posted on the Hong Kong Immigration Department website at: www.immd.gov.hk/en/forms/forms/id407_detail.html (accessed June 21, 2014).

2 The Minimum Allowable Wage for FDHs with new contracts beginning in October 2013, was raised to HK$4,010 per month (approximately US$520) in September 2013. This is a

of law, Hong Kong also allows migrant workers the right to organize and protest, and they can avail themselves of legal processes to claim their labor rights. Moreover, Hong Kong law prohibits local employment agencies from charging foreign domestic workers more than 10 percent of a month's wages as fees. Although these positive features are commonly cited and recognized by employers, local lawmakers, foreign domestic workers, scholars, and others I have spoken to over the years, as well as by the GCIM speakers that day, the story clearly does not end there.

What I remember best about the FCC event, and what I documented in my field notes at the time, are the responses of many domestic worker activists during and after the talk. They said that the speakers completely overlooked the problems and the failures of the Hong Kong system. Yes, there is an employment contract, but workers are often underpaid, overworked, and cannot prosecute their employers unless they are willing and able to invest huge amounts of time while they are prohibited from working and earning much-needed money to support themselves and their dependent family members. Hong Kong may have maximum agency fees, but many workers are seriously overcharged by employment agencies. As the audience pointed out, the GCIM speakers overlooked the difficulties of family separation and the fact that temporary migrants necessarily remain temporary in the "host" community as they do not qualify for permanent residence, no matter how many years they work there. Although the GCIM speakers advocated for skilled and unskilled workers to receive the same treatment, they seemed to ignore the real differences between the legal and social status of skilled and unskilled migrant workers in Hong Kong.[3]

As my companions noted at the time, yes, Hong Kong has a standard employment contract and some good laws and policies in theory. On paper Hong Kong looks like a very good place to work, and for many domestic workers it is. Activists readily admit that it is generally better than many other places. Stories abound comparing the freedoms of Hong Kong with the constraints of working in some Middle Eastern or Gulf states.[4] At that time, Hong Kong also came out ahead in popular views of the violence suffered by workers in the Middle East versus the safety of those in Hong Kong, but, as discussed below, by 2013 that view was being qualified or called into

2.3 percent increase from the previous year, but only HK$150 above the 1998 rate (*SCMP* Sept. 30, 2013).

3 A key difference is that other workers who remain in Hong Kong legally for seven years can apply for "right of abode" or permanent residency. Also, they are not usually required to leave the territory before changing employment.

4 Hong Kong often comes out on top compared with the desirability of "Saudi" (common shorthand for Middle Eastern countries among workers). Yet some women preferred to work in the Middle East because employers were sometimes more protective of them there. They understood constraints on their mobility as forms of protection and care by employers, not as lack of freedom. By contrast, the liberties of Hong Kong were frightening or overwhelming to some workers.

question. A common comparison was often made with Singapore as well, and Hong Kong usually came out on top. Wages are higher in Hong Kong. Workers can organize and protest in Hong Kong, but not in Singapore. Singapore (at that time) had no mandated weekly day off, but Hong Kong did. Singapore requires regular pregnancy tests and if the worker is pregnant she is required to leave.[5] In Hong Kong, by contrast, domestic workers are subject to the maternity protections of the Employment Ordinance (Cap. 57).[6] Many receiving countries permit workers only a limited number of contracts, but the number of times a FDH contract can be renewed in Hong Kong is technically unlimited, and some have worked as domestic workers there for decades, with ten or more contracts.

As this chapter argues, as activists and critics in Hong Kong have long claimed, and as is often the case for law in general, legal protections may look good on paper, but they are really only as good as they are in practice and if they are enforced. Positive though some aspects of migrant worker policies may appear and valuable as they are in promoting Hong Kong as an ideal Asian destination, Hong Kong's rights, I argue, are often hard to claim and difficult to enforce. There is a troubling underside to what seemed good to the GCIM representatives. Looking directly *at* the policies and comparing them with regions that do not have them at all – rather than looking *beneath* the surface at whether and how those policies are applied, enforced, or experienced by domestic workers – results in an unreasonably positive picture. Below, I point to some of the policies and some of the obstacles workers face in claiming their rights. This chapter also describes how, in the decade since the 2005 GCIM report when Hong Kong was widely considered by some as an "ideal" destination and a model of good practice, this image has become tarnished. In recent years the failures of Hong Kong's system for the employment of migrant domestic workers have been aired and questioned in an increasingly critical global arena.

In the following section, I turn to a recent incident of domestic worker abuse that placed Hong Kong in the international media spotlight in 2013 and 2014. This involved Erwiana Sulistyaningsih, an Indonesian domestic worker, who was named in April 2014 as one of *Time*'s 100 most influential people for speaking up for the rights of migrant workers (*Time* 2014). The case against Erwiana Sulistyaningsih's employers (DCCC 421/2014, set for pre-trial review in District Court on July 10, 2014), points to some of the most serious problems of physical abuse, overwork, underpayment, and debt faced by Hong Kong domestic workers today. Although her case is exceptionally disturbing and violent, it has brought to light and illustrated,

5 See "Work Permit Application Form for a Foreign Domestic Worker" (Ministry of Manpower 2013 p. 17, no. 7) at www.mom.gov.sg/Documents/services-forms/passes/WP_Appln_Form_for_FDW.pdf (accessed June 21, 2014).

6 See "Maternity Protection" at www.labour.gov.hk/eng/public/wcp/MaternityProtection.pdf (Feb. 2014) and www.labour.gov.hk/eng/legislat/contentB2.htm for the full text of the Employment Ordinance (accessed Aug. 29, 2014).

in a way that is difficult to ignore, the severity of potential problems and the underlying problems that can deter domestic workers from leaving abusive employers and instead tolerating horrendous working and living conditions.

Next, I outline some of the main criticisms of the Hong Kong system and how, by 2014, these specific criticisms have become widespread, voiced not only by local Hong Kong domestic workers and advocates, as was the case in earlier decades, but also by a wide range of international and local groups who are speaking loudly, in unison, and in conversation with each other. The criticisms are not new, but what is new is the global participation in the choir of voices that are reaching a broader audience. In addition to local research reports from activist groups and migrant worker unions (AMC 2007; ATKI 2005; Mission for Migrant Workers 2012), recent Amnesty International (2013), United Nations (UN) (2013, 2014), and Trafficking in Persons (TIP) (2013) reports have criticized many aspects of the situation of foreign domestic workers in Hong Kong.

In the concluding section I argue that the solution does not lie solely in improved knowledge, enforcement, and reform of Hong Kong's laws and policies. Instead, I argue that there is a more fundamental problem. Hong Kong has developed a system of governmentality in which local citizens benefit from the market at the expense of migrant workers, outside others, who constitute "neoliberal exceptions" (Ong 2006). As Aihwa Ong describes,

> [...] exceptions to neoliberalism can be modes for protecting social safety nets or for stripping away forms of political protection ... In Southeast Asia, exceptions to neoliberalism exclude migrant workers from the living standards created by market-driven policies. In other words, exceptions to neoliberalism can both preserve welfare benefits for citizens and exclude noncitizens from the benefits of capitalist development.
>
> (2006: 4)

Hong Kong's policy makers, I argue, thus face an ethical choice in whether and how to shift policies so as to better protect the labor rights and human rights of global citizens from whom so many of their own local citizens benefit. The current system denies migrant workers their basic rights as workers and as human beings.

Erwiana Sulistyaningsih

The story of Erwiana Sulistyaningsih's alleged horrific abuse took place over a period of almost eight months, from her arrival in Hong Kong in May 2013 until her eventual departure on January 10, 2014. In January 2014, upon her return to Indonesia, disturbing graphic images of her burned, bruised, blackened, scarred, and emaciated body spread like wildfire through the internet and the press in Hong Kong, Indonesia, and many other parts of the world, threatening to tarnish the notion of Hong Kong as a prime labor migration destination, and as a proud, self-ascribed Asian World City. As activists were quick to assert, Erwiana Sulistyaningsih's story graphically illustrates the limits of Hong Kong's migrant worker system and the risks faced by foreign workers in the self-ascribed Asian "World City."

In January 2014, before and after photographs of Erwiana Sulistyaningsih, 23, spread rapidly through the blogosphere. The pretty young Indonesian everywoman, with a clear complexion and a gentle smile, contrasted with the emaciated woman that was shown as she lay prone on a stretcher or in a hospital bed in Sragen, Central Java, with swollen and discolored skin, a gaunt and scarred face, and oozing scabs and wounds on her hands, feet, arms, and legs. Facebook commentators wondered why – with her face, arms, ankles, and feet, all of her revealed skin, severely discolored with burns, bruises, and scars, and with her obviously weakened and skeletal form – no officials had stopped her on her way out of Hong Kong, in striking contrast to the level of policing of those who try to enter the city. On the evening she left Hong Kong, Erwiana Sulistyaningsih could barely walk and required

> assistance from a friend to walk through Hong Kong airport because much of her body, including legs and feet, were covered in cuts and burns, according to Sringatin, spokeswoman for the Association of Indonesian Migrant Workers. Her employer had given her HK$100 and a t-shirt and asked her not to speak with any Indonesians before boarding the plane, said Sringatin.
>
> (*SCMP* Jan. 13, 2014)

No longer able to work, her employer had sent her off. Upon return to her home region of Central Java, she was admitted to a hospital in the city of Sragen in a critical condition.

While Erwiana Sulistyaningsi was in the hospital in Sragen, Indonesian President Dr. Susilo Bambang Yudhoyono made a phone call to her and her father and "pledged to cover her medical costs." He told Erwiana and her father, Rohmad, that he would help them both overcome the ordeal. Rohmad is quoted as saying to the press:

> I asked the president for help. The president said that he supports Erwiana and told us not to worry because the government would take care of all the costs. He also spoke with Erwiana briefly and he asked her if she felt any discomfort or any pain. She said he sounded concerned and he said that he would support her. [Rohmad added,] I was happy that the president called me, but it was because of something very unhappy that it happened. It was because this has happened to my daughter. Erwiana is not the only domestic helper who has been hurt. The Hong Kong government has many problems. ...
>
> (*SCMP* Jan. 21, 2014)

The phone call from the President prompted further comments from Erwiana Sulistyaningsih, echoing her father's comments and expressing disappointment that it takes a tragedy to draw the government's attention to the plight of migrant workers.

While in the hospital, a support network grew around Erwiana Sulistyaningsih. This included the growing rapport that she developed with Indonesian domestic worker activist networks in Java and in Hong Kong who offered her support and assistance in pursuing her case. As more photographs of Erwiana Sulistyaningsih in the hospital circulated, visited by activists such as Iwenk, an Indonesian domestic worker who had returned from Hong Kong to Indonesia and continues to be a member of ATKI (the Association of Indonesian Migrant Workers), and later by Hong Kong members of ATKI, the International Migrant Alliance, and the Asian Migrant Coordinating Body (AMCB), she was seen smiling, with her wounds slowly healing. Meanwhile, domestic workers and activists in Hong Kong formed the Justice for Erwiana campaign.[7] They marched through the city on numerous occasions to protest domestic worker abuses, and to demand that charges be pressed against Erwiana Sulistyaningsih's employer.

Following huge protests in Hong Kong, charges were finally levied against Erwiana Sulistyaningsih's employer. Hong Kong police investigators traveled to the Sragen hospital to interview Erwiana. Her employer, Lan Wan-tung, 44, a mother of two, was then arrested on January 20, 2014, as she was attempting to leave Hong Kong for Thailand. She was charged with one count of grievous bodily harm with intent, two counts of assault, and four counts of criminal intimidation of three domestic workers including Erwiana (Channel News Asia 2014). The first court hearing was delayed and rescheduled for April 29, 2014. On that date, Lan was charged with additional counts against Erwiana, including "failing to pay wages for seven months and not allowing public holiday leave or rest days" (*Newsweek* 2014).[8]

Meanwhile, encouraged by activists to speak out, Erwiana Sulistyaningsih and other domestic workers spoke publicly about the abuse they had experienced, including several women who had also worked for Lan Wan-tung. In January 2014, 28-year-old Bunga spoke at a Justice for Erwiana protest and said she worked for the same employer and had suffered similar beatings and threats in 2010. At the protest in Causeway Bay, as described in the *South China Morning Post*,

> Bunga said she experienced 10 months of beatings working for Erwiana's alleged abuser. "One time the employer got so angry she dragged me to the balcony and threatened to throw me off it. She made me beg for my life," Bunga said. "I told her that she could beat me as

7 The full name of the campaign is "Justice for Erwiana and Other Migrant Workers."
8 As of this date, the case is not available in Hong Kong's public judicial records.

> much as she wanted but I went on my knees and begged her not to kill me because I had a son." Bunga said she was never allowed outside the Tseung Kwan O flat and would be locked in when the family went out. "The woman threatened to pay the Indonesian police money to kill my entire family if I talked to others about the beatings," she said. She was eventually helped to leave by an employment agency, but the agency pressed her not to press charges. "I'm speaking out now because I feel so sad I didn't do anything to help Erwiana," she said. Erwiana was also not permitted to leave the home and the employer also threatened to "kill her family" if she told of her treatment.
>
> (*SCMP* Jan. 16, 2014)

Almost a month after leaving Hong Kong, on February 5, 2014, Erwiana left the hospital in a wheelchair, her many scars and discolored skin still visible. In early April, she returned to Hong Kong, with her father and a friend, to provide prosecutors with evidence against her former employer. Upon her return to Hong Kong, the media reported that she was taken to the Indonesian Consulate, against her wishes and contrary to her plans to stay in a shelter provided by the Mission for Migrant Workers, a Hong Kong domestic worker activist organization whose director, Cynthia Abdon-Tellez, had visited Erwiana in Indonesia. This move, as well as attempts to convince Erwiana Sulistyaningsih to use a lawyer assigned by the Indonesian Consulate as opposed to the one she had chosen, resulted in public criticism from the Justice for Erwiana campaign, and fears that the consulate was trying to treat the case as an isolated event rather than address the wider underlying issues (HK Helpers Campaign 2014). On her second night in Hong Kong, she was permitted to stay in the Mission-sponsored shelter and she retained attorney Melville Boase, who has supported migrant domestic workers in Hong Kong for several decades.

Unlike the image of Hong Kong as the ideal destination for migrant workers in general, and domestic workers in particular, Erwiana Sulistyaningsih's story has given activists and non-governmental organizations (NGOs) an opportunity to highlight many of the interconnected problems that domestic worker grassroots organizations and advocates have pointed to since at least the 1990s. For several months (and still as I write in May 2014) Erwiana Sulistyaningsih has been the subject of masses of media reports, blogs, protests, and online discussions. Many issues have been aired, including those concerned with Hong Kong's reputation, and many, as discussed below, saw Erwiana's experiences and those of other abused workers as linked to or exacerbated by Hong Kong's long-criticized domestic worker policies. Indeed, for advocates and critics, Erwiana Sulistyaningsih has become a symbol of the failures and dangers of Hong Kong's "model" system for its temporary migrant workers, and, I would argue, also a vivid representation of the underlying problems of temporary labor migration schemes more generally.

Rules and recommendations

As noted above, during the past 25 years, the number of domestic worker grassroots groups, workers' unions, activists and advocates, NGOs and charity organizations calling for reforms to some of Hong Kong's domestic worker policies has grown, and the chorus of voices has become louder and its constituents have diversified well beyond the local migrant workers activists. Data gathered from local studies and surveys of domestic workers and of clients of service providing groups, such as the Mission for Migrant Workers, ATKI, IMWU (Indonesian Migrant Workers Union), fueled also by the International Migrants Alliance (IMA) and AMCB, groups that have grown in size, scope, and international visibility, have provided ample quantitative and qualitative data to illustrate the existence of problems that laws and policies do not appear to adequately resolve, and that have been argued to make the situation worse.

The years 2013 and 2014 are a watershed of sorts, as Hong Kong has gained the public spotlight first in the case of Kartika Puspitasari that came to court in Fall 2013 (*SCMP* Sept. 19, 2013). She was found to have been tied to a chair and made to wear adult diapers while her employers went on vacation; her employers – described by the judge as "cruel" and "vicious" – were found guilty of systematic abuse over a period of two years (*SCMP* Jan. 13, 2014).[9] The other case is that of Erwiana Sulistyaningsih described above which created an ideal focal point through which to illustrate how Hong Kong's policies and regulation regarding temporary migrant workers fail to produce safe working and living condition for workers, and in fact may promote the sorts of unsafe conditions that result in the abuse and vulnerability of workers. These stories, whose

> stomach churning images [of] scarred and abused workers circulate through the on and offline media[,] are visible reminders of Hong Kong's failures as the abuses to invisible workers in private homes are revealed and made highly and widely visible. Hong Kong's exalted status as a migrant receiving region is clearly put into question.
>
> (McBride 2014)

Many criticisms have been voiced since the 1990s (see Constable 1997), but what is new is the extent to which international agencies have joined locals in recent years, adding legitimacy, gravitas, and credibility to their claims, and helping local advocates and activists to frame the critique in the internationally legible language of human rights and, more recently, "trafficking."

9 Her employers, Tai Chi-wai and Catherine Au Yuk-shan were jailed for 3 years and 3 months and 5½ years, respectively (*SCMP* 19 Sept. 2013). See DCCC 251/2013 (in Chinese) at: http://legalref.judiciary.gov.hk/lrs/common/ju/judgment.jsp (accessed June 21, 2014).

The two back-to-back cases of abuse, in a sense, literally raised the visibility of the issues and helped to illustrate how various policy issues on the employment of migrant domestic workers are linked.

For example, during the past several years, U.S. government "Trafficking in Persons Reports" (TIP 2013, 2012, 2011, 2010) have reported on the abuses faced by foreign domestic workers in Hong Kong.[10] Despite the Hong Kong government's continued assertion that existing laws are sufficient to deal with the problem, the last several years of TIP reports claim that the Hong Kong government does too little to address the problem. At the hundredth meeting of the International Labor Organization (ILO) Conference in 2011, the ILO passed new instruments to protect the rights of domestic workers, namely Convention on Domestic Workers (No. 189) and Recommendation (No. 201) (discussed in Chapter 2 of this volume). Drawing input from domestic worker organizations including those in Hong Kong, the Convention on Domestic Workers drew added international attention to the cause. Other influential external reports included an Amnesty International report (Amnesty International 2013), which lent further international legitimacy to local Hong Kong activists' claims and recent UN reports (2013, 2014).

Most recently, the HK Helpers Campaign (HKHC) (HKHC 2014), a Hong Kong group of activists who established their online presence in 2014, as Erwiana's story was coming to light, clearly and coherently voiced many common concerns and criticisms and posted a number of studies, reports, and materials to support their claims. The HKHC website serves as a repository of information about domestic workers and their rights, bringing together many of the key shared concerns of activist organizations, NGOs, domestic worker activists, and labor union demands (HKHC 2014). HKHC describes itself as an "independent Hong Kong campaign formed by a group of local activists to promote the rights of local Foreign Domestic Workers." Their objective "is to *amplify* the voices of helpers by linking them, and relevant NGOs, with those in the media, law, politics and academia" (emphasis in original). Their "ultimate aim is to apply pressure to successfully achieve our three basic campaign points. To (1) scrap the

10 According to the 2013 Trafficking in Persons (TIP) Report on Hong Kong, echoing several of the previous years' reports: "Some foreign domestic workers in the territory, particularly those from Indonesia and the Philippines, face notable indebtedness assumed in their home countries as part of the terms of job placement, which have the potential to lead to situations of debt bondage. Foreign domestic workers from the Philippines and Indonesia are generally charged the equivalent of approximately $1,950 and $2,725, respectively, by recruiters in their home countries, debts which may comprise more than 80 percent of workers' salaries for the first seven to eight months of employment. During that period, some workers may be unwilling to report abusive employers for fear of losing their jobs. Several of Hong Kong's domestic worker employment agencies have charged fees in excess of Hong Kong law and illegally withheld passports, employment contracts, and bank debit cards of domestic workers until their debt has been paid – factors that could facilitate labor trafficking in the territory" (TIP 2013).

'two-week' law, (2) to enforce maximum working hours and (3) to end illegal agency fees." These objectives and three campaign points echo some of the most common issues among activists and advocates. The first and third points are critically relevant to the recent cases of abuse.

The first policy objective of the HKHC is to abolish the two-week rule and the live-in requirement. The two-week rule is part of the New Conditions of Stay which were introduced in 1987.[11] The rule dictates that foreign domestic workers who resign or whose contracts are terminated by their employer must leave Hong Kong within two weeks of the termination date of their contracts. Originally introduced allegedly to prevent domestic workers from "job hopping" (i.e., resigning from one job and taking on another one), the rule in fact discourages domestic workers from leaving difficult or abusive work situations (Hong Kong Human Rights Monitor 1996/97; Constable 2007, 2014; Kennelly 2008).[12]

The "live-in" requirement, part of the standard employment contract, stipulates that domestic workers must live with their employers.[13] In the 1990s I commonly encountered exceptions to the rule, and its enforcement appeared very lax or non-existent. In the 1990s, and especially in recent years, the rule was more strictly enforced and far fewer exceptions were officially granted. Supporters of the rule, including Joseph Law of the Hong Kong Employers of FDHs Association and Michael Lee of the Liberal Party, say it helps to prevent domestic workers from working illegally part-time, ensures that they are available when their employers need them, helps curb workers' potential misbehavior, and prevents them from getting into trouble and getting pregnant.[14] The live-in requirement has also been defended as a means to protect local domestic workers from foreign competition, since foreign domestic workers are understood to fill the live-in niche and the local workers to fill the live-out and part-time niche.

Critics have responded in a number of ways, pointing to the intersection of gender, age, and race in the infantilizing of domestic workers. One criticism is simply that workers are adults entitled to the protection of

11 See *Immigration Department Guidebook for the Employment of Domestic Helpers from Abroad* at: http://www.immd.gov.hk/en/services/hk-visas/employ-domestic-helpers-from-abroad/guidebook.html (accessed June 21, 2014.

12 The UN Human Rights Committee (2013) and the UN Economic and Social Council (2014) recommend repealing the two-week rule and the live-in requirement to reduce discrimination against and abuse of foreign domestic workers in Hong Kong. See UN Economic and Social Council, UN Doc. E/C.12/CHN/CO/2, May 23, 2014, para. 43; UN Human Rights Committee, Concluding Observations on the Third Periodic Report of Hong Kong, China, UN Doc. CCPR/C/CHN-HKG/CO/3, April 29, 2013, para. 21.

13 See Employment Contract for a Domestic Helper Recruited from outside Hong Kong: www.immd.gov.hk/en/forms/forms/id407_detail.html.

14 Excerpt from RTHK Radio 3 "Michael Lee on the '2-week' & 'Live-in' Rules" at: https://soundcloud.com/t-grundy/michael-lee-on-the-2-week-live. See also http://hongwrong.com/helper-employers "Employer Groups Protest Against Improved Rights for Domestic Workers" (both accessed June 21, 2014).

rights and freedoms that are denied when they are required to remain with their employers and are treated like irresponsible children. Another major criticism is that the live-in requirement helps to isolate domestic workers, making them more vulnerable to abuse. As in most cases of domestic abuse, household members are the most likely perpetrators. Allowing people to leave the home, and to do so legally, is necessary and helps to avoid conflicts in many small and intensely crowded flats.

In the HKHC's words:

> Both the "two-week" and "live-in" rules are unfair, discriminatory and prevent foreign domestic workers from escaping abusive situations. The majority of helpers are abused in some manner, yet they are made to live with their bosses and must leave or return home within a fortnight if not in employment. Helpers are not allowed to attain permanent residency and are excluded from the universal minimum wage.
>
> (HKHC 2014)[15]

This perspective is echoed in the 2013 Amnesty International Report:

> There is little doubt that regulations like the Two-Week Rule and the live-in requirement increase migrant domestic workers' vulnerability to human and labour rights violations and limit their ability to access redress mechanisms in Hong Kong. This has been recognized by several UN human rights expert panels, including the Committee on Economic, Social and Cultural Rights (2005), Committee on the Elimination of Discrimination against Women (2006), Committee on the Elimination of Racial Discrimination (2009) and Human Rights Committee (2013). All of these UN bodies have specifically called on the Hong Kong government to review or repeal the Two-Week Rule. The latter two also called for the repeal of the live-in requirement.
>
> (Amnesty International 2013: 13)

ILO Convention 189 concerning Decent Work for Domestic Workers (article 9(a)) also criticizes mandatory live-in requirements, considering it a key risk factor leading to abuse. The Hong Kong Confederation of Trade Unions (HKCTU), and the Federation of Asian Domestic Workers (FADWU), in their 2012 ILO submissions raised similar concerns:

> The live-in requirement has made migrant domestic workers more prone to working and sexual abuses. There is no law defining decent accommodation. There is no way for workers to complain specifically

15 See Section 7 (point 3) of the Minimum Wage Ordinance Cap. 608 where FDWs are specifically excluded from the local minimum wage at: www.hklii.hk/eng/hk/legis/ord/608/s7.html (accessed June 22, 2014).

> on indecent accommodation to the Labour Department which governs working conditions. [...] There are reportedly cases when workers sleep in the living room, in kitchens, in toilets and inside the wardrobe.
>
> (Amnesty International 2013: 89)

The Hong Kong SAR government responded to the UN Human Rights Committee's assertions that foreign domestic workers are not provided enough protections, asserting that:

> The live-in requirement is the cornerstone of our policy on importing FDHs. ... HKSAR Government's established policy is to accord priority to the local workforce in employment; importation of workers should only be allowed where there is genuine manpower shortage in a particular trade or occupation that could not be filled locally. Under this general principle, FDHs were allowed to work in Hong Kong to meet the shortfall of local live-in domestic workers. Such live-in requirement is made clearly known to the FDHs before their admission into the HKSAR, and specified in the Standard Employment Contract signed by the FDHs before they assume duty.
>
> (Amnesty International 2013: 89–90)[16]

Living and working conditions in private homes are difficult to monitor and highly isolating, which further render domestic workers vulnerable to abuses. A common complaint of live-in domestic workers, besides isolation, and poor and crowded living conditions, is the number of hours they work and often the irregularity of those hours. Workers have long described being always on call with no time they can count on as their own. For many, even their sleep hours are regularly interrupted (Constable 1997, 2007). According to the HK Helpers Campaign,

> Hong Kong's foreign domestic workers are often expected to be "on call" 24/7. On average, helpers work 102 hours per week and some do not get a weekly rest day. They earn just HK$4,010 (US$517) per month and are powerless to negotiate working conditions. Furthermore, helpers may be excluded from upcoming "maximum working hours" legislation.
>
> (HKHC 2014)[17]

Further criticisms relate to the fact that FDWs' minimum allowable wage is far lower than they would earn if they were accorded Hong Kong's

16 See also "HKSAR Government Welcomes Constructive Dialogue with UN Human Rights Committee", Press Release, March 28, 2013, available at: www.info.gov.hk/gia/general/201303/28/P201303280704.htm (accessed April 29, 2014).

17 See Hong Kong Labour Department "Statutory Minimum Wage" at: www.labour.gov.hk/eng/news/mwo.htm (accessed June 21, 2014).

hourly minimum allowable wage for local workers. Local workers must be paid at least HK$30 per hour. The recent Amnesty International survey of Indonesian domestic workers in Hong Kong found that they worked on average 17 hours a day (Amnesty International 2013: 55).[18]

Since my earliest research with foreign domestic workers in the early and mid-1990s, illegal agency fees, especially for Indonesian domestic workers, have become a growing problem. Although Hong Kong law deems it illegal for employment and recruitment agencies to charge a domestic worker more than 10 percent of one month's salary,[19] agencies in Hong Kong, associated with overseas-based agencies and local loan agencies, have devised ways to charge Indonesian workers up to almost seven months of their salary. As described by HK Helpers Campaign:

> It is illegal to charge foreign domestic workers excessive fees yet recruitment agents, placement agencies in Hong Kong and loan companies collude to evade regulators, burden helpers and maximise profit. As many helpers work 7 to 8 months to repay loans, it is considered, by definition, "bonded labour" – a form of slavery.
>
> (HKHC 2014)

Many organizations such as the Mission for Migrant Workers and Helpers for Domestic Helpers have painstakingly helped domestic workers to document their experiences with illegal overcharging and their cases have been brought to the attention of Hong Kong authorities, especially during the past three years. As reported in *Bloomberg BusinessWeek*:

> Since 2010, domestic workers have filed about 2,000 complaints a year with the Philippine consulate in Hong Kong, seeking help to recoup placement fees after losing their jobs, says the consulate's labor attaché, Manuel Roldan.[20] Hong Kong Labor Department spokeswoman Lily Chan says her department received 54 complaints last year and 27 in the first nine months of 2012 about overcharging by employment agencies. Two firms were convicted, resulting in fines of HK$50,000 and a loss of licenses, she says, adding in an e-mail: "We are concerned about

18 Based on working 17 hours a day for six days a week at HK$30 per hour, a local worker would earn HK$3,060 per week. At the current FDH rate, a foreign domestic worker would be making HK$9.8 per hour (given the FDH wage of HK$4,010 per month). Even if one were to deduct the value of her room and board (which is difficult to assess), she is still earning far less per hour than local workers.

19 Legco Paper No. CB(2)870/13-14(01) p. 3, para. 9 (Feb. 27, 2014) at: www.legco.gov.hk/yr13-14/english/panels/mp/papers/mp0227cb2-870-1-e.pdf (accessed June 21, 2014).

20 At that time Filipinos were the second largest group of foreign domestic workers in Hong Kong, following Indonesians. The Mission for Migrant Workers (2013) reports far more complaints from Indonesian domestic workers than from Filipinos.

> this situation and have raised this issue to the relevant governments' attention."
>
> (*Bloomberg BusinessWeek* Nov. 15, 2012)

Of critical importance to cases such as those of Kartika Puspitasari and Erwiana Sulistyaningsih are the combined problems of living in highly isolated and isolating conditions, having little distinction between work time and non-work time, fearing the two-week rule's required departure from Hong Kong if their contracts are terminated or they are fired (without enough time to change employers), and owing huge sums of money to loan agencies, or fearing greater debts from agency fees should they lose their current jobs. As I have argued elsewhere, the two-week rule, contrary to its intent of ensuring that domestic workers remain temporary workers and return home when their contracts end, instead encourages domestic workers to remain in Hong Kong longer as illegal overstayers (Constable 2014). Moreover, critics have argued that the rule does not serve the stated purpose of preventing "job-hopping" by domestic workers, since the more urgent problem in most cases seems to be the termination of the contract of domestic workers by their employers, in conjunction with agencies that offer employers the opportunity to change workers at no charge. If workers are replaced more frequently, it is the agencies that stand to gain from it, not the workers. Moreover, if the two-week rule prevents workers from job-hopping, it also makes it extremely difficult for domestic workers like Erwiana Sulistyaningsih and Kartika Puspitasari to leave abusive employers and find better ones.

Protections that are theoretically offered to domestic workers in Hong Kong are among the main factors that deter them from pursuing their rights. If workers do try to pursue their rights, they face the additional problems of not being allowed to work legally while they seek unpaid salaries or other benefits through the labor tribunal, a process that can take several months and sometimes a year or more. Workers must then rely on charity or on friends for food and shelter unless they want to risk being caught working illegally. Many domestic workers tolerate very poor work conditions and a range of emotional and physical abuses for fear that if they report them they will lose their jobs, they cannot stay and find new ones, and they have no source of income with which to pay back debts or support family members abroad if they decide to pursue their claims.

Indifference and exclusion

Since the early 1990s, demands to abolish the two-week rule, to allow workers to change employers in Hong Kong, to curb the role of agencies, and to raise wages and regulate work hours have been repeatedly voiced by domestic workers and their supporters, with limited results (see Constable 1997, 2007). Critics have repeatedly argued that foreign domestic workers cannot afford the time and cost of pursuing justice. The lack of response reflects in part what Estelle Kennelly describes as part of Hong Kong's wider "culture of indifference" (2008). I would argue that this "indifference" arises from a deeper problem: governmental adherence to neoliberal exclusions that support the entitlements of privileged locals at the expense of excluded migrant workers who help to provide the "good life" for locals (Agamben 1998; Ong 2006).

The too readily accepted division between those who benefit from the profits of neoliberal policies and those who are restricted by them is the main obstacle to Hong Kong's foreign domestic workers, in particular, and migrant workers, in general, claiming their rights. Many local employers, local citizens, most local law makers, and government bureaucrats who enforce laws and policies passively accept that there are differences between the human and labor rights of temporary migrant workers and those of local citizens. The presumed difference is intimately linked to temporary workers' lack of entitlement and to what Aihwa Ong describes as neoliberal policies of "exception" in which states impose "market criteria on citizenship" (2006: 1). Neoliberal policies in Hong Kong construct temporary migrant workers as exceptions to the rule, in terms of their rights as workers. Although they are accorded certain rights as temporary workers, their rights are not the same as those of local workers, and they cannot access them or claim them as easily as locals.

As discussed above, unlike local citizens and unlike many other noncitizen workers, foreign domestic workers do not receive the local minimum wage (they have their own lower one); they are required to "live-in" with their employers; they cannot bring their family members with them to Hong Kong; they are not free to change employers if they have a bad one or find a better one; and their temporary residence can never become a route to permanent residency or legal citizenship.[21] Unlike locals who "belong" or other categories of workers who are permitted to bring their family members with them to Hong Kong, and who can eventually apply for permanent residency, foreign domestic workers constitute a special category of "temporary migrant workers" who might in fact stay and work in Hong Kong for several decades but who are not permitted to apply for right of abode.[22] Migrant domestic workers are not treated as adult subjects. They are disciplined, controlled, their movements and their freedoms curbed. Given the "live-in requirement," they often lack privacy and freedom of other

21 See Constable 2014: 173–180 for discussion of the legal debates regarding foreign domestic worker right of abode.

22 See Court of Final Appeal final judgment on March 25, 2013 regarding Evangeline B. Vallejos (FACV/19/2012) at: http://legalref.judiciary.gov.hk/lrs/common/search/search_result_detail_frame.jsp?DIS=86304&QS=%24%28Vallejos%29&TP=JU and regarding Daniel Domingo (FACV20/2012) at: http://legalref.judiciary.gov.hk/lrs/common/search/search_result_detail_frame.jsp?DIS=86312&QS=%24%28Vallejos%29&TP=JU (both accessed June 21, 2014).

adults and workers. Moreover, while local workers can claim legal protections without losing their homes and their right to work, foreign domestic workers have no legal right to work while they pursue remedies for rights violations. Secretary for Labour and Welfare Matthew Cheung Kin-chung reportedly said that "foreign domestic helpers have the same access to legal protection as local workers, and urged helpers to report cases of abuse to the government" (*SCMP* Jan. 17, 2014). Encouraging migrant domestic workers to report abuse and pursue their rights without providing a means for them to do so is simply disingenuous.

Such rules and policies – forms of governmentality – may sound good on the surface but they serve to ensure that migrant workers remain in Hong Kong only temporarily. Such rules and policies are part of a wider apparatus used to regulate and reinforce the precarious migratory status of foreign domestic workers in Hong Kong. Such apparatus creates and underscores their exceptionalism – the idea that they really do not share or deserve the same rights, privileges, and social status as locals. The notion of "difference" in relation to foreign domestic workers in Hong Kong is also built on, I argue, a sort of humanitarian reasoning that posits them as less human than their employers (Constable 2014; Fassin 2012). Their work is understood by locals as a privilege, a sort of charity offered to the poor, for which they are expected to be grateful. Employment, as a form of "gift" to the less privileged poor from Southeast Asia, presumes a response of gratitude paired with an assumption that those who are ungrateful for the privilege of work should leave. The underlying attitude is that "equality" and workers' rights do not apply – or do not apply in the same way – to foreign domestic workers; notions of social difference are key and foundational.

The laws and policies regulating the employment of foreign domestic workers might accord them in theory certain rights, but they are tied, as noted earlier, to the "market driven logic of exception" and exclusion (Ong 2006: 5). This raises ethical questions about rights, equity, and human protections. Asian neoliberal governments, Ong has argued, have created particular spaces of exception, where the benefits apply to only certain categories of people – in this case Hong Kong locals and employers – and the costs are borne by another category of people – temporary migrant workers from Indonesia, the Philippines, and elsewhere – who are legally underpaid and overworked relative to locals. The dependence of Hong Kong on underpaid guest workers comes at a cost not only for the workers, but also indirectly for Hong Kong as a city that prides itself on its modernity and its free-market economy. Were Hong Kong to add a legal live-out option, many workers and their employers, some of whom are doing it anyway, would be relieved. Raising foreign workers' wages to the hourly minimum level of local ones would also allow Hong Kong to test whether indeed local workers might be willing to live-in for a fair wage. Granted the number of foreign workers might drop, but those who would remain might have better working and living situations. Of course, those locals who face the greatest challenge are the working Hong Kong families who cannot afford to pay domestic workers higher wages. But perhaps that is the key problem that local policy makers should carefully consider.[23] Most countries have far shorter working hours than Hong Kong. With fewer working hours, Hong Kong men and women would have time to spend at home, with children or to attend to household work, as is the case in many other countries where household help is rare and working hours are shorter.

In sum, this chapter began with the rosy image of Hong Kong as a destination for migrant workers, and moved on to the obstacles faced by migrant domestic workers in securing decent work and in vindicating their rights. Domestic workers may be reluctant to report abuse because of their debts and financial needs. The employment process usually includes high fees, often requires workers to sign loan agreements, and constitutes what has been called debt bondage. The live-in requirement makes it difficult for workers to escape and report abuse. The two-week rule requires that domestic workers return home within two weeks of the termination of their contracts. Since two weeks is rarely long enough to find a new employer, workers are loathe to resign from even a bad situation. Moreover, if a worker does file a case against her employer, she is no longer permitted to work while her case is in progress. It will mean months without an income and with mounting living costs and visa renewal costs. These factors help to explain why some workers chose to overstay their visas and work illegally for more money. They also help explain why workers like Kartika Puspitasari and Erwiana Sulistyaningsih found it impossible to leave abusive employers.

Erwiana's youth, innocence, the graphic detail of her injuries, and her painful departure from Hong Kong may help to make her the focal point for reform. She is perhaps a "perfect victim" in the sense of her youth and innocence.[24] She is an apt symbol of Hong Kong's failed protections and regulations that I have argued, in the bigger picture, serve ultimately to protect the rights of Hong Kong citizens to avail themselves of cheap and precarious labor more than to protect precarious workers from local abuses.

Over the years, many of the criticisms directed at Hong Kong's law and policy framework regulating the employment of foreign domestic workers have fallen on deaf ears. The underlying problem is that an ethics of privilege, often bolstered by racism, is not an ethics of equality. Activists in 2014

23 Some outspoken labor activists and politicians have expressed support. Leo Tang Kin-wa, organizing secretary at the Hong Kong Confederation of Trade Unions, criticized the live-in policy. He asked: "Why did this case just come to public attention after the helper returned to Indonesia? It is because Hong Kong has failed to provide a safe environment for workers. She was forced to live with her employers ..." Similarly, Fernando Cheung Chiu-hung of the Labour Party said the two-week rule should be revisited.

24 As Carol Chan argues in an analysis of Indonesian migrant worker injuries and abuses (Chan 2014), within the Indonesian context some workers are blamed or their morals questioned in relation to "failed migrations," but others are seen as "perfect victims" because of their perceived youth, their innocence, and the extent of their injuries.

are hopeful that local citizens and law makers will be moved to advocate for change, partly from the shame of the cases of Kartika Puspitasari and Erwiana Sulistyaningsih, partly through a coalescence of concerns shared by a range of different activist and advocate groups. True reform will not be easy, but Hong Kong's reputation as a world city – especially one that struggles to define its independence and distinction from China – would benefit in multiple ways from such reforms.

References cited

Agamben, Georgio. 1998. *Homo Sacer: Sovereign Power and Bare Life*, trans. Daniel Heller-Roazen. Stanford, CA: Stanford University Press.

AMC, ILO Indonesia, Oxfam HK. 2007. The Continuing Systematic Extortion of Indonesian Migrant Workers in Hong Kong, an In-Depth Study. www.ilo.org/wcmsp5/groups/public/@asia/@ro-bangkok/@ilo-jakarta/documents/publication/wcms_116888.pdf Accessed May 1, 2014.

Amnesty International. 2013. Exploited for Profit, Failed by Governments: Indonesian Migrant Domestic Workers Trafficked to Hong Kong. www.amnesty.org/en/library/asset/ASA17/029/2013/en/d35a06be-7cd9-48a1-8ae1-49346c62ebd8/asa170292013en.pdf Accessed May 1, 2014.

ATKI (Association of Indonesian Migrant Workers in Hong Kong). 2005. *Second Survey of the Conditions of Indonesian Migrant Workers in Hong Kong*. Hong Kong: ATKI.

Bloomberg BusinessWeek. "Indentured Servitude Hong Kong Style" (Nov 15, 2012): www.businessweek.com/articles/2012-11-15/indentured-servitude-hong-kong-style Accessed June 21, 2014.

Chan, Carol, 2014. "Tolerable Violence": Gendered Morality, Neoliberal Development, and Female Labor Migration from Indonesia. Unpublished paper. University of Pittsburgh.

Channel News Asia March 25, 2014. Hong Kong Maid "Torture" Case Adjourned until April 29. www.channelnewsasia.com/news/asiapacific/hong-kong-maid-torture/1048158.html Accessed March 25, 2014.

Constable, Nicole. 1997. *Maid to Order in Hong Kong: Stories of Filipino Workers*. Ithaca, NY: Cornell University Press.

Constable, Nicole. 2007. *Maid to Order in Hong Kong: Stories of Migrant Workers* (second edition). Ithaca, NY: Cornell University Press.

Constable, Nicole. 2014. *Born Out of Place: Migrant Mothers and the Politics of International Labor*. Berkeley: University of California Press; Hong Kong: Hong Kong University Press.

Fassin, Didier. 2012. *Humanitarian Reason: A Moral History of the Present*. Berkeley: University of California Press.

GCIM (Global Commission on International Migration). 2005. Migration in an Interconnected World: New Directions for Action. www.queensu.ca/samp/migrationresources/reports/gcim-complete-report-2005.pdf Accessed May 1, 2014.

Helpers for Domestic Helpers. 2013. Agency Fees LEGCO Submission.

HKHC (HK Helpers Campaign). 2014. About Us. http://hkhelperscampaign.com/about-us Accessed May 1, 2014.

Hong Kong Human Rights Monitor 1996/97 Newsletter. The Two-Week Rule. www.hkhrm.org.hk/english/reports/enw/enw0796d.htm Accessed June 21, 2014.

Kennelly, Estelle. 2008. Culture of Indifference: Dilemmas of the Filipina Domestic Helpers in Hong Kong. PhD dissertation. University of St. Andrews. http://research-repository.st-andrews.ac.uk/bitstream/10023/509/6/Estelle%20Kennelly%20PhD%20thesis.pdf Accessed June 21, 2014.

McBride, Meredith. 2014. Hong Kong's Misguided Laws Failing to Halt Abuse of Foreign Domestic Helpers. *SCMP* Jan. 15, 2014. www.scmp.com/comment/insight-opinion/article/1406060/hong-kongs-misguided-laws-failing-halt-abuse-foreign Accessed June 21, 2014.

Mission for Migrant Workers. 2012. Mission for Migrant Workers Data and Statistics 2011. FMW Ltd, St. John's Cathedral, 4–8 Garden Road, Central, HK.

Mission for Migrant Workers. 2013. Live-In Policy Increases Female FDW's Vulnerability to Various Forms of Abuse. http://issuu.com/mfmw/docs/primer_live-in_english/1?e=8079376/225401 Accessed June 21, 2014.

Newsweek. April 29, 2014. More Charges in Erwiana Sulistyaningsih Abuse Case that Shocked Hong Kong. www.newsweek.com/more-charges-erwiana-sulistyaningsih-abuse-case-shocked-hong-kong-249009 Accessed May 1, 2014.

Ong, Aihwa 2006. *Neoliberalism as Exception: Mutations in Citizenship and Sovereignty*. Durham, NC: Duke University Press.

RTHK Radio. Jan. 22, 2014. Backchat. http://programme.rthk.hk/channel/radio/programme.php?name=radio3%2Fbackchat&d=2014-01-22&p=514&e&m=episode&contentindex=1Accessed May 1, 2014.

SCMP (*South China Morning Post*). Aug. 4, 2013. Survey Reveals Extent of Abuse of Foreign Maids in Hong Kong. www.scmp.com/news/hong-kong/article/1294210/survey-reveals-extent-abuse-foreign-maids-hong-kong?page=all Accessed May 1, 2014.

SCMP (*South China Morning Post*). Sept. 19, 2013. Domestic Helper Kartika Puspitasari Tells Court of Horrific Abuse over Two Years. www.scmp.com/news/hong-kong/article/1312504/domestic-helper-kartika-puspitasari-tells-court-horrific-abuse-over Accessed May 1, 2014.

SCMP (*South China Morning Post*). Sept. 30, 2013. Anger over HK$90 Rise in Monthly Minimum Wage for Domestic Workers. www.scmp.com/news/hong-kong/article/1321571/anger-over-hk90-rise-monthly-minimum-wage-domestic-helpers?page=all Accessed May 1, 2014.

SCMP (*South China Morning Post*). Jan. 13, 2014. Indonesian Helper, 23, in Critical Condition after Alleged Beatings by Hong Hong Employers. www.scmp.com/news/hong-kong/article/1404697/indonesian-helper-23-critical-condition-after-alleged-beatings-hong Accessed May 1, 2014.

SCMP (*South China Morning Post*). Jan. 16, 2014. She Threatened to Throw Me Off the Balcony': Second Domestic Helper Alleges Employee Beatings. www.scmp.com/news/hong-kong/article/1406833/second-maid-claims-abuse-hands-english Accessed May 1, 2014.

SCMP (*South China Morning Post*). Jan. 17, 2014. Labour Minister Pledges to Punish Unscrupulous Maid Agencies after Beating Allegations. www.scmp.com/news/hong-kong/article/1407638/labour-minister-pledges-punish-unscrupulous-maid-agencies-after Accessed Aug. 29, 2014.

SCMP (South China Morning Post). Jan. 21, 2014. "Torture" Employer Linked to Alleged Abuse of Five Different Hong Kong Maids 1410402). www.scmp.com/

news/hong-kong/article/1410402/torture-employer-linked-alleged-abuse-five-different-hong-kong-maids Accessed Aug. 29, 2014.

Time. April 23, 2014. Erwiana Sulistyaningsih. http://time.com/70820/erwiana-sulistyaningsih-2014-time-100 Accessed May 1, 2014.

TIP (Trafficking in Persons Report). 2010. Office to Monitor and Combat Trafficking in Persons. www.state.gov/j/tip/rls/tiprpt/2010 Accessed Aug. 29, 2014.

TIP (Trafficking in Persons Report). 2011. Office to Monitor and Combat Trafficking in Persons. www.state.gov/j/tip/rls/tiprpt/2011 Accessed Aug. 29, 2014.

TIP (Trafficking in Persons Report). 2012. Office to Monitor and Combat Trafficking in Persons. www.state.gov/j/tip/rls/tiprpt/2012 Accessed Aug. 29, 2014.

TIP (Trafficking in Persons Report). 2013. Office to Monitor and Combat Trafficking in Persons 2013. www.state.gov/j/tip/rls/tiprpt/2013 Accessed Aug. 29, 2014.

UN Committee on Economic, Social and Cultural Rights. Concluding Observations on the Second Periodic Report of China, Including Hong Kong, China and Macao, China. E/C.12/CHN/CO/2, May 23, 2014.

UN Human Rights Committee, Concluding Observations on the Third Periodic Report of Hong Kong, China, UN Doc. CCPR/C/CHN-HKG/CO/3, April 29, 2013.

Acknowledgments

I have benefitted immensely from the help and insights of more domestic workers, activists, advocates, and scholars than I can name, but they include members of the Asia Pacific Mission for Migrants, Association of Indonesian Migrant Workers, Barnes and Daly (law firm), Christian Action, Helpers for Domestic Helpers, HK Helpers Campaign, Hong Kong Pathfinders, Mission for Migrant Workers, Open Door, The SUN, United Filipinos in Hong Kong, and many others.

6 Access to Justice for Undocumented Migrant Domestic Workers in Europe: The Consequences of Constructed Illegality

Clíodhna Murphy

Introduction: the social construction of labour and the undocumented migrant domestic worker

Recent years have seen the rise of a transnational "economy of care",[1] whereby migrant women are employed to perform the domestic and care work which is frequently outsourced to privately paid workers in industrialised states. The commodification of domestic labour (propelled, in the European context in particular, by female participation in the labour force, and state welfare policies which delegate care to the market)[2] does not involve any fundamental restructuring of labour market or state supports for family responsibilities. The institution of privately paid domestic work allows governments to continue to situate this work solely within the private sphere and away from the responsibilities of the State. In this way, it fails to address what Fineman has termed the "social debt" which arises from the essential social good of caretaking labour.[3]

Aside from discussions of the ethics of domestic work, this form of labour is, in Anderson's words, "a site where the social construction of labour is revealed and contested".[4] Despite the vital nature of the functions which they perform in contemporary European societies, domestic workers are susceptible to a "decent work deficit", including working long hours without sufficient rest, low pay and lack of access to maternity and sickness

1 See Fiona Williams, "Towards a Transnational Analysis of the Political Economy of Care" in Rianne Mahon and Fiona Robinson (eds) *Feminist Ethics and Social Policy: Towards a New Global Political Economy of Care* (UBC Press, 2011); Fiona Williams, "Migration and Care: Themes, Concepts and Challenges" (2010) 9(3) *Social Policy & Society* 385.

2 See, for example, Helma Lutz and Eva Pallenga Mollenbeck, "Care, Gender and Migration: Towards a Theory of Transnational Domestic Work Migration (2011) 19(3) *Journal of Contemporary European Studies* 349.

3 Martha Fineman,"Contract and Care" (2000–2001) 76 *Chicago-Kent Law Review* 1403, 1411.

4 Bridget Anderson, "Immigration and Domestic Work: Between a Rock and a Hard Place" in *Us and Them: The Dangerous Politics of Immigration Controls* (Oxford University Press, 2013) 159, 159.

protections.[5] The reasons for this are complex and include the traditionally low prestige of domestic work, its association with unpaid, "unskilled" work performed by women, and problems with enforcing labour laws developed in response to the industrial context in respect of employment within the home.

In parallel with the on-going development of protective international standards for domestic workers, in particular the International Labour Organisation's (ILO's) landmark Convention on Domestic Work,[6] recent research has highlighted the persistent gap between such standards and the actual living and working conditions of migrant domestic workers in Europe.[7] Migrant domestic workers are particularly vulnerable to forms of labour exploitation, due to the intersection of gendered, racial and classed inequalities, reinforced by employment law and the restrictions of immigration status.[8] Domestic labour is "treated as exceptional"[9] in the labour migration policies of most European states. The lack of explicit recognition of the demand for migrants to carry out domestic work[10] in the migration policies of most EU Member States means that domestic workers enter Europe with a wide range of migration statuses outside the regular work permit system.[11] Most of these statuses are precarious in the sense of being of a limited duration and/or being dependent in some way on the legal status of another person. In addition to the proliferation of precarious statuses, inadequate legal channels of migration for domestic workers produce high levels of irregularity, which in turn leads to insecurity, producing susceptibility to exploitation and difficulties in accessing key rights.[12]

5 As discussed in International Labour Conference, 99th Session, 2010, *Decent Work for Domestic Workers* (Report IV(1)).
6 Convention Concerning Decent Work for Domestic Workers, International Labour Organisation, adopted at the 100th session of the International Labour Conference, Geneva, 2011.
7 See, generally, Anna Triandafyllidou (ed.) *Irregular Migrant Domestic Workers in Europe: Who Cares?* (Ashgate, 2013).
8 See, generally, Clíodhna Murphy, "The Enduring Vulnerability of Migrant Domestic Workers in Europe" (2013) 62(3) *International and Comparative Law Quarterly* 599.
9 Anderson (n4) 160.
10 "Rights of Migrant Domestic Workers in Europe" (UN Human Rights, Office of the High Commissioner Europe Regional Office, 2010), 10.
11 Maria Galotti, "The Gender Dimension of Domestic Work in Western Europe", No. 96 *International Migration Papers* (International Labour Office, Geneva, 2009). These include admission by way of temporary work permits, au pair programmes, spousal or dependent residence permits, and as "private servants" in diplomatic households.
12 EU Fundamental Rights Agency (EUFRA) "Migrants in an Irregular Situation Employed in Domestic Work: Fundamental Rights Challenges for the European Union and Its Member States" (EUFRA, July 2011), 19. See also Norbert Cyrus, "Being Illegal in Europe: Strategies and Policies for Fairer Treatment of Migrant Domestic Workers" in Helma Lutz (ed.) *Migration and Domestic Work: A European Perspective on a Global Theme* (Ashgate, 2008).

Against this background, this chapter focuses on a specific issue at the intersection of migration and employment law: the application and enforcement of employment standards to undocumented migrant domestic workers. This is a vexed issue in Ireland and the UK, in particular, where the courts have found that as such workers are employed under an "illegal" contract of employment, they are not entitled to the protection of the applicable employment legislation, especially where the worker was aware of and "took an active part in" the illegality.

Given the complex matrix of societal, political and legal factors involved, entrenched care inequalities cannot be dealt with through regulation alone. However, the legal position of irregular migrant domestic workers highlights how the law continues to reinforce the vulnerability of these employees, illustrating the "ambivalence of domestic work in employment".[13] In terms of the interplay between migration and employment law, the construction of domestic workers as unskilled undesirable migrants has a series of consequences resulting, in the UK and Ireland, in access to justice being blocked through operation of law. This provides an important illustration of the interconnectedness of the social construction of labour with immigration and employment law, and the impact of this relationship on individual rights protection.

This chapter first briefly sets out the legal and conceptual background by giving some examples of the way in which migration law systems in Europe currently construct "illegality" in the sphere of domestic work. It then outlines the approach taken in the UK and Ireland to illegal contracts of employment and assesses the implications for undocumented domestic workers of recent jurisprudence on this issue, focusing on cases involving domestic workers. The analysis shows that the underlying rationale for the approach taken in the common law countries is the high priority accorded to maintaining the integrity of the immigration system, compounded in the Irish case by the legislative criminalisation (until 2014) of both the migrant and the employer for working without an employment permit.

The next section of the chapter demonstrates that while this approach appears to be viewed in most of the recent UK and Irish legal decisions as inevitable from a public policy perspective, there is in fact a diversity of approaches to the issue of employment protections for undocumented workers within the EU. In this regard, it points to the legal position in France, where, in common with most European jurisdictions, all undocumented workers are in principle entitled to a minimum level of labour protection. The integrity of the employment protection system is preserved to a greater degree under this model.

In its final sections, the chapter considers whether the divergent approaches offered by these jurisdictions can be reconciled, in light of European human rights law. It concludes that EU action in this sphere, as embodied in the

13 Anderson (n4) 176.

Employers' Sanctions Directive,[14] does not effectively address the problems created by the legal/illegal dichotomy at the heart of national immigration systems. However, it is suggested that there may be some potential to challenge the obstacles to access to justice for irregular migrant domestic workers exposed to slavery, servitude or forced labour, by reference to Article 4 of the European Convention on Human Rights. It is argued that a complete absence of employment protections for certain undocumented domestic workers constitutes a violation of states' positive obligations, under Article 4, to protect individuals from slavery, servitude and forced labour.

Restricting secure migration routes: precarious statuses and the construction of illegality in the domestic work sector

As Duvell, among others, insists, irregular migration "is not an independent social phenomenon but exists in relation to state policies and is a social, political and legal construction".[15] In addition to controlling who is permitted to cross national borders, states also construct the consequences of breaching border rules, with state responses based on the creation of a legal/illegal dichotomy which governs access to rights, welfare and other public goods.[16] As will be seen in the next section, one of the most serious consequences of this state construction of illegality is the potential exclusion of individual migrants from protective state regulation, particularly in the sphere of employment. This section explores how immigration law systems produce illegal migrant domestic workers in Europe.

The labour migration policies of most European states are characterised by their failure to explicitly acknowledge the demand for migrants to perform domestic work. In Ireland, for example, the only route currently open to individuals to migrate as domestic workers is as a domestic servant to a diplomat – although no regulated system exists for the entry of diplomatic migrant domestic workers and there is no work permit or employment contract required prior to admission.[17] Diplomatic domestic workers are particularly vulnerable to exploitation due to their dependence on their employer for their migration status, together with the immunity from litigation of the diplomat.[18]

14 Directive 2009/52/EC of the European Parliament and of the Council of 18 June 2009 providing for minimum standards on sanctions and measures against employers of illegally staying third-country nationals (Employers' Sanctions Directive).

15 Franck Duvell, "Paths into Irregularity: The Legal and Political Construction of Irregular Migration" (2011) 13 *European Journal of Migration and Law* 275, 276. See also Franck Duvell, *Illegal Immigration in Europe: Beyond Control?* (Palgrave Macmillan, 2006).

16 Duvell, "Paths into Irregularity: The Legal and Political Construction of Irregular Migration," ibid 290.

17 See Migrant Rights Centre of Ireland, "Protections for Migrant Domestic Workers Employed by Foreign Diplomats in Ireland: Time for Reform" (MRCI, December 2010).

18 For a case study of trafficking of domestic workers by diplomats in the US context, see Janie Chuang, "Achieving Accountability for Migrant Domestic Worker Abuse" (2010)

The tendency to restrict secure channels of migration for domestic workers is also evident in the temporary migration statuses available to migrant domestic workers in the UK and France. In the UK, live-in domestic workers can enter the UK with their employers and stay for a maximum of six months,[19] and domestic staff can enter France as "seconded workers" for periods of three months at a time.[20] These statuses are time-limited and not open to renewal, and do not provide for family reunification or a path to settlement.[21] Outside of these restricted overseas domestic workers visas, which are intended to ensure that wealthy individuals travelling to the UK and France can bring their domestic staff with them for short periods, there are no legal migration routes specifically available to domestic workers.

The position in Ireland, the UK and France reflects the general picture in EU Member States: as domestic work is not ascribed any economic value, no incentive is provided to attract migrant domestic workers and the resulting available immigration statuses fall far short of meeting the demand for such workers. In Southern European countries such as Italy and Spain, this has occasioned the acceptance, in practice, of high levels of irregularity in the domestic work sector and large-scale regularisation programmes, as well as the introduction of quotas for migrant domestic workers.[22]

Employers continue to seek out migrant domestic workers, with the European Parliament's resolution of 2014 on undocumented women migrants acknowledging that "the increased demand for workers in the domestic and care sectors is attracting a large number of women migrants, many of whom are undocumented".[23] It has been reported (by the EU

88 *North Carolina Law Review* 1628, 1641. See also Angelica Kartusch/German Human Rights Institute, "Domestic Workers in Diplomats' Households: Rights Violations and Access to Justice in the Context of Diplomatic Immunity" (German Human Rights Institute, 2011). In Ireland, see *Kifordu v Udoka*, Labour Court Determination MWD1310, 23 July 2013.

19 See, in particular, paras 159A–159E of the UK Immigration Rules. See also Home Office Announcement, "Immigration (Employment-related Settlement, Overseas Domestic Workers, Tier 5 of the Points Based System and Visitors)", 29 February 2012.

20 Article L1262-1 of the Labour Code, together with Circular NOR IMIM0900078C of August 3, 2009.

21 For a detailed exploration of the UK case study, see Siobhán Mullally and Clíodhna Murphy, "Migrant Domestic Workers in the UK: Enacting Exemptions, Exclusions, and Rights" (2014) 36(2) *Human Rights Quarterly* 397.

22 See Margarita León, "Migration and Care Work in Spain: The Domestic Sector Revisited", *Social Policy and Society* (2010) 9(3) (July): 409–418, 413 and 414; Francesca Scrinzi, "Migrations and the Restructuring of the Welfare State in Italy: Change and Continuity in the Domestic Work Sector" in Lutz (ed.) *Migration and Domestic Work: A European Perspective on a Global Theme* (Ashgate, 2008) 29; Franca Van Hooren, "When Families Need Immigrants: The Exceptional Position of Migrant Domestic Workers and Care Assistants in Italian Immigration Policy" (2010) 2(2) *Bulletin of Italian Politics* 21.

23 European Parliament Resolution of 4 February 2014 on undocumented women migrants in the European Union (2013/2115(INI), Recital Q. The Recital also states: "the undocu-

Fundamental Rights Agency, among others)[24] that the au pair migration route is often used as a way to recruit domestic workers, and that the employment of au pairs has been steadily growing in some countries in Europe during the last decade for this reason.[25] The au pair phenomenon reinforces Lutz's observation that the general lack of explicit recognition in migration policies of the need for migrants to carry out domestic work[26] does not mean that this does not take place: these workers are present in Europe, and "endure the difficult conditions of life in a twilight zone", often with an irregular migration status.[27]

Reflecting Castles' general point that "the more that states and supranational bodies do to restrict and manage migration, the less successful they seem to be",[28] the links between insufficient legal channels of migration for domestic workers and the high level of irregularity in the sector have been emphasised by the EU Fundamental Rights Agency, among others.[29] Empirical research carried out in the specific field of domestic work reveals high levels of irregularity across Europe.[30] The Parliamentary Assembly of the Council of Europe has recognised the gaps in human rights protection caused by such irregularity and has urged Member States to develop independent visa schemes for migrant domestic workers and care workers which would allow legal entry, provide a standardised working contract and allow for a change of employer.[31] However, governments are reluctant

mented women working in this sector are most vulnerable to low pay, mental abuse, withholding of wages and passports and sometimes even physical abuse at the hands of their employers".

24 Danish Centre Against Human Trafficking, "Au Pair and Trafficked? – Recruitment, Residence in Denmark and Dreams for the Future, A Qualitative Study of the Prevalence and Risk of Human Trafficking in the Situations and Experiences of a Group of Au Pairs in Denmark" (Danish Centre Against Human Trafficking, 2010); Office of the Special Representative and Co-ordinator for Combating Trafficking in Human Beings, Organization for Security and Co-operation in Europe, "Unprotected Work, Invisible Exploitation: Trafficking for the Purpose of Domestic Servitude" (Organisation for Security and Co-operation in Europe, 2010). In the Irish context, see Migrant Rights Centre of Ireland, "Part of the Family? The Experiences of Au Pairs in Ireland" (MRCI, October 2012).

25 EUFRA report (n12). See also, OSCE, ibid.

26 Silvia Gonzalez del Pino, "Rights of Migrant Domestic Workers in Europe" (UN Human Rights, Office of the High Commissioner Europe Regional Office, 2010), 10.

27 Helma Lutz, "Introduction: Migrant Domestic Workers in Europe" in Helma Lutz (ed.) *Migration and Domestic Work: A European Perspective on a Global Theme* (Ashgate, 2008) 1, 6.

28 Stephen Castles, "Why Migration Policies Fail" (2004) 27(2) *Ethnic and Racial Studies* 205, 205.

29 EUFRA report (n12). See also Migrant Rights Centre of Ireland, "Profile Report on Undocumented Migrants in Ireland" (MRCI, 2011). Domestic work was the second largest job sector for undocumented migrants surveyed.

30 See Anna Triandafyllidou (ed.), (n7), which is based on an EU-wide study funded by the EU Fundamental Rights Agency.

31 Pernille Frahm, *Protecting Migrant Women in the Labour Market* (Report of the Committee on Migration, Refugees and Population, Council of Europe Doc. 12549, 24 March 2011).

to acknowledge the role of immigration law in reinforcing the vulnerability of migrant domestic workers and creating illegality. In recent debates on the overseas domestic workers visa in the UK, for example, those arguing against the retention of a relatively secure migration status for domestic workers stated that the job of protecting these workers is more appropriately achieved through employment law or anti-trafficking mechanisms, stating that "immigration is not the way to deal with that".[32]

Blocking access to employment protections for migrant domestic workers in an irregular situation: illegality and public policy

Recent years have witnessed a move, particularly at the international level, to better regulate domestic work and precipitate a paradigm shift away from considering domestic work as a "form of labor market engagement unsuited to the standard array of labor law protections".[33] One outcome of this increased international interest in domestic work has been the adoption of the ILO Convention on Domestic Work, which came into force in August 2013.[34] At the national level, however, there are two factors, as identified by Mantouvalou, which continue to exclude undocumented migrant domestic workers from developments in the regulation of domestic work: the migrant's anxiety about deportation and their wish to remain invisible to the authorities; and the rules of employment law, which can create "further precariousness".[35]

As already mentioned, a key issue in common law countries has been that much employment law centres on the concept of the contract of employment, which, it has been found, is tainted with illegality in the case of undocumented migrants (particularly those who knowingly participate in the illegal work, at the inception of the contract). The basic principle of the doctrine of illegality in the contract was stated as far back as 1775, when Lord Mansfield CJ declared in *Holman v Johnson*:

> No court will lend its aid to a man who founds his cause of action upon an immoral or an illegal act. If, ... the cause of action appears to arise *ex turpi causa*, or the transgression of a positive law of this country, there the court says he has no right to be assisted. It is upon that ground that

32 Joan Ryan MP, House of Commons, 10 May 2006, col 106WH.

33 Deirdre McCann, "New Frontiers of Regulation: Domestic Work, Working Conditions and the Holistic Assessment of Non-Standard Work Norms" (2012–2013) 34 *Comparative Labour Law & Policy Journal* 167, 168.

34 For analysis, see, generally, Einat Albin and Virginia Mantouvalou, "The ILO Convention on Domestic Workers: From the Shadows to the Light" (2012) 41(1) *Industrial Law Journal* 67.

35 Virginia Mantouvalou, "Human Rights for Precarious Workers: The Legislative Precariousness of Domestic Labour" (2012–2013) 34 *Comparative Labour Law & Policy Journal* 133, 142.

> the court goes; not for the sake of the defendant, but because they will not lend their aid to such a plaintiff.[36]

Employment law scholars have questioned whether such longstanding, general principles of contract law are sufficiently flexible to be applied to the modern employment relationship without producing "artificial reasoning and unsatisfactory results".[37] A number of recent cases involving irregular migrant workers, explored below, clearly illustrate the difficulties which arise from a formalistic application of the doctrine of illegality.

The UK approach

One of the outcomes of the *Holman v Johnson* approach, in the modern UK context, is that where an employee has knowingly participated in an employment contract which is illegal in its inception, they are unable to avail of the employment protections which would be triggered by the contract. The application of the doctrine of illegality in the context of immigration law has been the subject of recent decisions on claims taken by domestic workers, the facts of which vividly illustrate the difficulties experienced by this group. In the Employment Appeals Tribunal (EAT) decision in *Zarkasi v Anindita*,[38] the claimant was an Indonesian domestic worker recruited from Indonesia to work for a family in the UK.[39] When she left her employer in the UK and brought a number of employment claims, it was found by an employment tribunal that she had voluntarily participated in an arrangement to enter the UK by pretending to be someone else in order to work for her employer, meaning that the employment of contract was unlawful and thus unenforceable, as were any statutory rights dependent on it.[40] This was in spite of its factual finding that "in general terms the Claimant was exploited. She was young, relatively poorly educated and vulnerable in a foreign country in which she had no right to be, let alone to work."[41] The EAT endorsed the Employment Tribunal's decision, thereby accepting that the rather minimal participation of this "vulnerable" migrant domestic worker in immigration fraud (which, it was found, had been orchestrated by her employer) rendered any access to redress for the exploitation she had suffered impossible. The EAT also resisted the applicant's argument that employment and contract law must be read in light of international human rights law obligations.[42]

36 [1775] COWP 341, as cited by Goff LJ in *Tinsley v Milligan* [1994] 1 AC 340.

37 Simon Deakin and Gillian S Morris, *Labour Law* (6th ed., Hart Publishing, 2012), 113.

38 Appeal No. UKEAT/0400/11/JOJ, Decision of the EAT of 18 January 2012.

39 Ibid [5], quoting Employment Tribunal decision.

40 *Zarkasi* (n38) [9].

41 *Zarkasi* (n38) [7], quoting Employment Tribunal decision.

42 *Zarkasi* (n38) [27–35]. The argument was essentially that the Employment Tribunal should have taken into account her human trafficking claim before determining that the

One of the striking features of the *Zarkasi* decision was that the EAT emphasised the availability of other routes by which the claimant could seek redress, outside the employment protection system – even though her complaints were employment-centred.[43] The EAT concentrated on the possibility of actions for false imprisonment, trespass, assault or harassment for which she might be entitled to damages which could include the value of her labour as she had been promised but as she had not received, together with the potentiality of aggravated and exemplary damages.[44] In reality, these actions are both potentially costly and untested in this context, and do not reflect the nature of the applicant's complaints as based in an employment context.

The decision reveals a high level of deference to the legislature and its role in making public policy, with the EAT accepting the illegality of the contract as a *fait accompli* without examining the broader public policy issues around labour exploitation, economic duress and the public interest in preserving the integrity of the system of employment protections. These points do not appear to have been raised in argument, and it seems that the applicant accepted as a given that the employment contract would be deemed illegal. This was an opportunity missed: while the applicant had entered the UK using false papers and in breach of a tourist visa, the provisions of the Immigration Act 1971 which criminalise this conduct do not expressly specify what the effect of a breach should be on any contractual claim taken by the person.[45] Moreover, section 21 of the Immigration, Asylum and Nationality Act 2006, which creates the offence of employing a migrant who is not entitled to accept the employment, does not criminalise the migrant but, rather, the employer, and also fails to specify the consequences of the illegal employment for the enforcement of employment law. In principle, therefore, it would be left to the court or tribunal to interpret the legislation to determine whether it impliedly provides for the consequences of the illegality for the contract of employment, which would open the door to a fuller analysis of public policy issues than that which was undertaken in *Zarkasi*.

Hounga v Allen

The concept of illegality has also been considered in the context of attempts use equality legislation to obtain a remedy for discrimination resulting from irregular immigration status, even though the statutory tort of race discrimination does not necessarily depend on a valid contract of employment. In

contract of employment could not be enforced because to rely on it would be to rely on a contract rendered illegal by law.

43 *Zarkasi* (n38) [29–30].

44 Ibid.

45 See sections 24A(1) and 26(1) of the Immigration Act 1971.

Hounga v Allen,[46] the applicant had accepted the findings of the tribunal and of the EAT that the defence of illegality precluded any claim which might arise under the contract of employment. However, the Court of Appeal went one step further and decided that the applicant (a Nigerian au pair, described as "a young, illiterate person of uncertain age although with a good command of English"[47]) could not bring a race dismissal discrimination claim as she was working illegally.

Ms Hounga's dismissal discrimination case relied on the argument that her employers had taken advantage of her illegal status and the fact that she had no right to be employed in the UK to treat her less well than a hypothetical white British comparator, thus, in the view of the Court of Appeal, "making a direct link between the discriminatory treatment of which she complained and the circumstances in which she came to be, and was, employed by the Allens".[48] The Court of Appeal held that the applicant was an equal participant (with the employers) in an illegal contract of employment, with the approach of the Court encapsulated in its finding that:

> whilst one inevitably has sympathy for Ms Hounga as a young person of whom unfair advantage was probably taken, there is no escaping the tribunal's findings that she knew what she was doing and knew it to be wrong and illegal.[49]

This judgment was strongly criticised as being "inconsistent with authority" and involving "a faulty application of illegality principles",[50] and in 2014 the Supreme Court upheld the domestic worker's appeal.[51] The primary basis for the Supreme Court decision, as outlined in the judgments of Lord Wilson (with whom Lady Hale and Lord Kerr agreed) and Lord Hughes (with whom Lord Carnwath agreed), was that, in the particular facts of this case, there was an insufficiently close connection between the appellant's immigration offences and her claims for the statutory tort of discrimination, meaning that the "inextricable link" between the facts giving rise to the claim and the illegality, required by tort law, had not been established. Her immigration offences merely provided the "context" within which the tort was committed.[52]

There was significant disagreement among the members of the Supreme Court as to the precise basis for their unanimous overall finding that the appeal should be upheld. Lord Hughes was careful to specifically confine his

46 [2012] EWCA Civ 609.
47 Ibid [34].
48 *Hounga* (n46) [61].
49 *Zarkasi* (n46) [62].
50 Alan Bogg and Tonia Novitz, "Race discrimination and the doctrine of illegality" (2013) 129 *Law Quarterly Review* 12, 12.
51 [2014] UKSC 47.
52 Ibid [67].

judgment to tort cases, distinguishing the tort claims under consideration from the contractual claims initially made in the employment tribunal and the EAT, dependent on a lawful contract of employment, which claims had "rightly not been pursued either in the Court of Appeal or in this court".[53] Lord Wilson, on the other hand, engaged in a more wide-ranging analysis of the public policy dimensions of the doctrine of illegality, finding not only that "the considerations of public policy which militate in favour of applying the defence so as to defeat Miss Hounga's complaint scarcely exist",[54] but also that the decision of the Court of Appeal to uphold the defence of illegality in this case "runs strikingly counter to the prominent strain of current public policy against trafficking and in favour of the protection of its victims".[55] Lord Wilson placed great importance on his conclusion that Miss Hounga's case was, effectively, one of trafficking for the purposes of forced labour, bringing it within the scope of the UK's international obligations in this regard, including Article 4 of the ECHR. He even went so far as to state that the public policy considerations involved in trafficking cases could have possibly yielded a different result, had the contractual claims for unfair dismissal and unpaid wages been pursued in the appellate courts.[56]

The approach of Lords Wilson and Kerr and Lady Hale could provide a basis for a more nuanced application of the doctrine of public policy in purely contract-based claims, at least in cases involving trafficking. In particular, Lord Wilson dismissed as "fanciful" the argument that the award of compensation in this case would "compromise the integrity of the legal system by appearing to encourage those in the situation of Miss Hounga to enter into illegal contracts of employment".[57] However, it is difficult to assess if and how this strand of reasoning will develop in future cases, given that Lords Hughes and Carnwath explicitly disagreed with the idea that the law of trafficking provided a specific basis for allowing the appeal.[58] It was also their trenchant view (echoing the comments of earlier courts) that even if one assumed that Miss Hounga was subjected to forced labour, she had not been compelled to commit the relevant immigration offences, meaning that any contract of employment was substantively illegal.[59]

Ultimately, despite the strong statements on trafficking and public policy in Lord Wilson's judgment, the Supreme Court judgment in *Hounga* is (purposefully) narrow and does not, in the short term, have a real impact on access to justice for undocumented workers in the context of general employment law claims. Post-*Hounga*, the defence of illegality will not automatically operate to exclude tort claims related to their employment

53 Ibid [54].
54 Ibid [45].
55 Ibid [52].
56 Ibid [24].
57 Ibid [44].
58 Ibid [67].
59 Ibid [59].

taken by undocumented migrants; however, the wider legal landscape has been left intact.

Diffusion of the UK approach to illegality to Ireland

The issue has been less litigated in Ireland, with the first Irish High Court decision on the employment rights of irregular migrant workers handed down in August 2012. In his judgment in *Hussein v The Labour Court*,[60] Hogan J recognised that the treatment of migrant workers "poses considerable difficulties with regard to the regulation of the labour market and the enforcement of public policy".[61] Nonetheless, he applied the principle that the contract of employment is void for illegality, basing the decision on the construction of the relevant employment permits legislation.

The case involved a challenge to a series of determinations of the Labour Court by Mr Hussein, who had employed an undocumented migrant worker, Mr Younis, in his restaurant for a number of years. The Labour Court had awarded Mr Younis compensation of €91,134 for breaches of employment legislation relating to information on terms of employment, working time regulations and payment of the minimum wage. The Rights Commissioner and the Labour Court had accepted Mr Younis' claim (which echoes claims often made in the domestic work context) that he had been required to work for seven days a week for a number of years and was paid "what amounted to pocket money".[62] Hogan J upheld the employer's appeal, finding that the effect of section 2 of the Employment Permits Act 2003, which criminalises both the employer and the employee for employment without a work permit, was to make any contract between an employer and a non-EU migrant worker who does not have permission to work in Ireland "substantively illegal".[63] In particular, the judge went on to note how the legislation did not have any "saving clause", which would have excused any illegality and the decision was "inescapable".

In contrast to the situation of the applicants in *Zarkasi* and *Hounga*, it was accepted by the Labour Court that Mr Younis was not aware of his irregular status: he was not a willing participant in the illegality, the entire fault for which lay with the employer. However, the wording of section 2 meant that the extent of the employee's knowledge of the irregularity was irrelevant: as Hogan J observed, it provides that an employee "automatically commits an offence if he or she does not have a work permit irrespective of the reasons for that failure".[64] This is a strict liability offence for the

60 [2012] IEHC 364.
61 Ibid [1].
62 *Hussein* (n66) [2].
63 *Hussein* (n66) [13–18].
64 *Hussein* (n66) [16].

employee, hence why an even stricter approach has been applied in Ireland than in the UK.

As is the case with the relevant UK legislation, the Employment Permits Act 2003 criminalises individuals for engaging in employment without a work permit, without dealing with the status of the contract of employment for labour law or civil law purposes. Hogan J, however, clearly felt constrained by the statute, which he saw as setting out the policy of the Oireachtas in respect of such contracts. He did not engage in assessing the public policy issues around the doctrine of illegality, as he considered these to have been dealt with by the legislature. Hogan J believed that he was compelled to effectively read these implications for civil law into the statute. The approach taken, whereby the judge purported to apply strict rules, does not reflect the public policy nuances of the doctrine of illegality, as it does not even consider the question of the impact on employment protections or take into account individual rights. Rather, it reflects a deferential approach to the role of the legislature in regulating immigration. As in *Zarkasi* and the Court of Appeal judgment in *Hounga*, the value of protecting the immigration system, which is the presumed priority of the legislature, was raised over the aims of the employment regulation system, without any explicit discussion of this approach. As already discussed, despite the limitations of the Supreme Court decision in *Hounga*, Lord Wilson's judgment provides an important counterpoint to this logic, particularly in cases involving victims of trafficking. However, in the context of the current legislative framework in Ireland, it seems doubtful that Lord Wilson's approach will have a significant impact on the application of the illegality doctrine by Irish judges in future cases.

Hogan J was clearly uncomfortable with the decision, which resulted in Mr Younis being "the victim of the most appalling exploitation in respect of which he has no effective recourse"[65] and took the unprecedented step of sending the judgment to the Minister for Jobs, Enterprise and Innovation (among others)[66] for review. The Employment Permits (Amendment) Act 2014, enacted in July 2014, addresses some of the issues at the heart of the *Hussein* decision. Section 3 provides for a defence for the employee to the charge of having been employed without an employment permit, where they can show that they took all reasonable steps to ensure compliance with the section. In addition, section 4 permits the foreign national to take a civil claim for compensation against the employer, "notwithstanding the illegality of the contract",[67] again where it can be proved that they took all reasonable steps to comply with the requirement to have an employment permit, and provides that the Minister may take such an action on behalf of the employee. These changes have been welcomed by migrant rights organi-

65 *Hussein* (n66) [23].
66 *Hussein* (n66) [24].
67 Explanatory memorandum to Employment Permits (Amendment) Act 2014, 2.

sations.[68] However, the Act's approach of providing a "carve-out" for civil, remuneration-related claims taken by undocumented workers, who played no part in the breach of the 2003 Act, leaves the basic conceptual framework intact. The contract of employment remains illegal and, most significantly, those employees who do not take "all reasonable steps" to ensure that an employment permit is obtained remain unprotected. The 2014 Act effectively brings the law in Ireland into line with that of the UK, still leaving those who are implicated in the illegality unprotected by Irish employment legislation.

In the UK and Ireland, the culmination of the policy choices which have led to domestic workers being effectively excluded from the work permit system is thus a pathway into illegality, with consequent exclusion from employment protections and resulting in state-constructed vulnerability to labour exploitation. The State is, in this way, complicit in the creation and perpetuation of the decent work deficit for migrant domestic workers in an irregular situation. The intersection of exclusionary approaches to domestic work and migrant labour places migrant domestic workers in a highly vulnerable position, as illustrated by the facts in *Zarkasi* and *Hounga* in particular. The question that arises from all of this is whether other legal approaches provide an alternative which results in greater protection for the vulnerable, irregular migrant worker.

Alternative normative approaches? Preserving the integrity of the employment protection system by penalising the employer

In contrast to the position in the UK and Ireland, in France, all undocumented workers (even those who have knowingly participated in the breach of immigration law) are in principle entitled to a minimal level of labour protection despite the fact that they are illegally employed. This reflects the position in most jurisdictions across Europe that migrant domestic workers should enjoy certain labour rights "regardless of whether they hold a stay permit".[69] In France, the worker's rights are the same as other employees' as regards the employer's obligations in respect of maternity leave, working time, breaks and holiday leave, health and safety and in calculating length of service.[70] The undocumented worker has the right to a decent salary (that cannot be lower than the guaranteed minimum wage), payment for overtime, annual paid holidays and fixed compensation if the employment ends (this compensation cannot be less than one month's salary).[71] The Labour Code

68 MRCI, "New Bill Tackles Exploitation of Migrant Workers in Ireland", MRCI Press Release, 28 April 2014.

69 See, generally, Triandafyllidou (n7) 210; EUFRA report (n12).

70 Article L8252-1 of the Labour Code.

71 *Groupe d'Information et de Soutien des Immigrés* ("Gisti"), *Sans papiers mais pas sans droits* (Gisti Notes Pratiques, 5th ed.), at 53; Platform for International Cooperation on Undocumented Migrants ("PICUM"), "Basic Social Rights of Undocumented Migrants

stipulates[72] that, no matter what the circumstances, the employer is the only party responsible for hiring an undocumented worker, with the undocumented worker seen as a victim, meaning that, contrary to the position in the UK and Ireland, any undocumented worker can bring an action against an employer for withheld wages as well as other employment violations.

In addition, the Labour Code goes some way to dealing with the difficulties that arise for individuals seeking employment redress who then become subject to immigration sanctions, providing that when someone is deported a designated body can pursue the unpaid wages on their behalf.[73] This was introduced in 2011 (among other things) by the so-called "Besson Law"[74] as part of the package of measures implemented to transpose the Employers' Sanctions Directive (which does not apply to the UK, Ireland or Denmark), which is considered in detail below. The changes introduced to implement the Directive, although intended to deter irregular migration by making it more difficult for irregular migrants to obtain jobs, improved the position of irregular workers in France in terms of accessing basic employment protections.[75]

Notwithstanding these advances, it seems that financial compensation for withheld wages and other labour-related matters is often difficult to obtain in practice for undocumented workers in France.[76] Proving the existence and the duration of the work is a significant obstacle, as is an increasing tendency of employment tribunals to consider migrant workers in an irregular situation as independent contractors, who can be pursued for engaging in undeclared work.[77] The French system also does not effectively deal with the most important practical barrier, identified by Mantouvalou and others, to the realisation of undocumented migrant domestic workers' employment rights: fear of discovery and subsequent deportation.

Despite these difficulties, the system in France (with its comprehensive labour code) shows the advantages of expressly dealing with the question of the position of undocumented migrant workers in employment legislation, rather than failing to address the issue and leaving it to the courts to extrapolate the civil law consequences of immigration and criminal law provisions. The focus on the employer as the wrongdoer shifts the focus from the individual responsibility of the migrant in breaching immigration law,

in France", available at http://picum.org/picum.org/uploads/file_/Basic%20Social%20Rights%20study%20-%20France.pdf (accessed 2 September 2014).

72 Article L8251-1 of the Labour Code.

73 Article L8252-4 of the Labour Code.

74 *Loi n° 2011-672 du 16 juin 2011 relative à l'immigration, à l'intégration et à la nationalité* (NOR:IOC/K/10/03689/L).

75 See para. 5-2-12 of "Practical Measures for Reducing Irregular Migration in France: A Study of the French Contact Point of the European Migration Network" (European Migration Network, October 2011).

76 Gisti (n77) 53.

77 Ibid. PICUM (n77). See also Gisti (n77) 53. Articles L-8221–L-8224 of the Labour Code.

and the policy reasons for maintaining the integrity of national borders, to the employer as a threat to employment law. Most importantly, it shows that the approach of the courts in the UK and Ireland in prioritising the enforcement of immigration regulation by way of penalising the employee for their complicity in the illegality cannot be assumed to be the only way to deal with the issues surrounding irregular migrant work.

"Semi-legalisation" of irregular migrant workers in EU law: the Employers' Sanctions Directive

EU law also requires avenues of redress to be put in place for irregular migrant workers in certain limited circumstances, although the normative context for this is quite different to that in French law. The protection of the basic right to pay for irregular migrants is, in the EU setting, a by-product of immigration law. Directive 2009/52/EC providing for minimum standards and measures against employers of illegally staying third-country nationals (the Employers' Sanctions Directive) aims to counter the "pull factor" for illegal migration into the EU of the "possibility of obtaining work in the EU without the required legal status",[78] through a "general prohibition on the employment of third-country nationals who do not have the right to be resident in the EU,[79] accompanied by sanctions against employers who infringe that prohibition".[80] The Directive has a number of planks, including a requirement for states to criminalise the employment of irregular migrant workers where the infringement is accompanied by particularly exploitative working conditions or involves the employment of a minor (Article 9).

The key part of the Directive, from the perspective of this chapter, is the provision that employers who have breached the prohibition on employing irregular migrants[81] are liable to pay any outstanding remuneration for the employee(s), any taxes or social security contributions which would have been paid in the event of legal employment and any cost arising from sending the back payments to the country which the employee has returned to.[82] Illustrating the perception that differentiated considerations apply in the domestic work context, Article 4(3) provides that Member States may provide for reduced financial sanctions where the employer is a natural person who employs an illegally staying third-country national for his or her private purposes (and where no "particularly exploitative working conditions are involved").

78 Recital 2 of the Employers' Sanctions Directive.

79 Recital 3 of the Employers' Sanctions Directive.

80 Recitals 2 and 3 of the Employers' Sanctions Directive. See, generally, Steve Peers, "Legislative Update: EC Immigration and Asylum Law – Attracting and Deterring Labour Migration: The Blue Card and Employer Sanctions Directives" (2009) 11 *European Journal of Migration and Law* 387–426.

81 Contained in Article 3 of the Employers' Sanctions Directive.

82 Articles 5 and 6 of the Employers' Sanctions Directive.

The Directive does not address the application of labour law rules other than pay to irregular migrant workers, highlighting that this is primarily an immigration measure rather than an instrument driven by concerns around issues relating to undeclared work from the perspective of employment or social affairs.[83] In respect of employment law rules other than those covered in the Directive, Peers argues that "to the extent that labour law has been harmonised by EC law then it follows from the EC law principle of effectiveness as regards EC social policy that irregular migrants should be covered by the relevant legislation".[84] This argument is supported by the findings of the Court of Justice of the EU in *Tümer*.[84a] However, even if this were found to be the case, this would result in only a limited range of protection in practice as the coverage of EU labour law is fragmented and incomplete.[85]

Overall, EU law cannot reconcile the diverging approaches taken in the UK and Ireland and elsewhere to the enforceability of the employment rights of irregular migrant workers.[86] As a result of the opt-outs secured by the UK and Ireland in the sphere of immigration law, the Employers' Sanctions Directive does not apply to these jurisdictions (or to Denmark). Even if it did, the Directive does not completely solve the basic problem of the illegality of the contract, which could still be considered to be unlawful or illegal by virtue of Article 3's general prohibition on employment of irregular migrant workers. While it would carve out a useful, but limited, exception requiring the enforcement of employment rights in the case of remuneration-related claims, ultimately, the Directive as a whole reinforces the legal/illegal dichotomy at the heart of national immigration regulation which is the root cause of the difficulties around claiming employment protection. It is not, therefore, particularly useful in terms of providing redress for forms of employment-related breaches not expressly mentioned in the

83 Sergio Carrera and Elspeth Guild, "An EU Framework on Sanctions Against Employers of Irregular Migrants: Some Reflections on the Scope, Features and Added Value", Centre for European Policy Studies Policy Brief No. 140 (CEPS, August 2007).

84 As he points out, they are not expressly excluded from any EU social legislation, and their inclusion within the scope of the legislation would further its objectives of avoiding unfair competition as between Member States and ensuring a high level of protection for employees. Steve Peers, "Legislative Update: EC Immigration and Asylum Law – Attracting and Deterring Labour Migration: The Blue Card and Employer Sanctions Directives" *European Journal of Migration and Law* (2009) 11 387–426.

84a Case C-311/13 *Tümer* (Judgment of the Court of Justice of the European Union of 5 November 2014). For analysis, see Steve Peers, "Irregular migrants and EU employment law", at http://eulawanalysis.blogspot.co.uk/2014/11/irregular-migrants-and-eu-employment-law.html (last accessed 9 November 2014).

85 See, generally, Catherine Barnard, *EU Employment Law* (4th ed., Oxford University Press, 2012).

86 For a general discussion of some of the criticisms of the Employers' Sanctions Directive, see Irina de Sancho Alonso, "Access to Labour Rights for Undocumented Workers" in Carrera and Merlino (eds), *Assessing EU Policy on Irregular Immigration under the Stockholm Programme* (CEPS, 2009), 10.

Directive itself, or providing an alternative normative framework for dealing with illegal work.

The protection afforded to workers by the Directive is limited, and the European Commission report on the transposition of the Directive has found that most Member States have not yet implemented the protective elements of the Directive in a satisfactory manner.[86a] Nonetheless, it has been argued that the Employers' Sanctions Directive requires a "semi-legalisation", or acceptance of the undocumented migrant worker's employment status.[87] The employment relationship is not completely invalidated, as it is under the UK and Irish approach, and there is a window for certain claims under the contract of employment, at least those relating to pay, to be recognised. Thus, even though this "semi-legalisation" of the employment contract does not allow for the continuation of the employment contract, the EU regime is more favourable to undocumented workers than the UK or the Irish approach. In spite of their shortcomings, it has been shown that both the French and the EU regimes have some positive characteristics, most importantly in illustrating that it is not inevitable, from a public policy perspective, to completely exclude undocumented migrant workers from the protection of employment law.

The actual and potential impact of Article 4 of the European Convention on Human Rights

There are various arguments that can be made against the strict stance of the courts in Ireland and the UK, some of which have been touched on in the preceding sections. Responding to the Court of Appeal judgment in *Hounga*, Bogg and Novitz argued that the reasoning of the courts is based on a misinterpretation of the doctrine of illegality, particularly in the context of tort claims.[88] It remains to be seen whether the Supreme Court judgment in that case will have some impact, beyond tort cases, on the application of the doctrine of illegality, particularly where serious human rights violations and international law obligations are at issue. More generally, allowing the employment law system to be flouted without consequence is corrosive to the rule of law and the labour law regulation system.

From a human rights law perspective, the failure to provide any employment law protection for a significant cohort of irregular migrant workers could constitute a breach of states' positive obligations under Article 4 of the

86a Communication from the Commission to the European Parliament and Commission on the application Directive 2009/52/EC of 18 June 2009 providing for minimum standards on sanctions and measures against employers of illegally staying third-country nationals (Brussels, 22.5.2014, COM(2014) 286 final), 10.

87 Andreas Inghammer, "The Employment Contract Revisited. Undocumented Migrant Workers and the Intersection between International Standards, Immigration Policy and Employment Law" (2010) 12 *European Journal of Migration and Law* 193.

88 Bogg and Novitz (n52) 1.

European Convention on Human Rights (ECHR) to protect those within its territory from slavery, servitude and forced or compulsory labour. A series of ECHR cases have highlighted states' positive human rights obligations to protect against severe labour exploitation in the context of the Article 4 prohibition of slavery and forced labour. All of the decided cases to date have involved migrant domestic workers. In *Siliadin v France*,[89] in which the applicant was a domestic worker from Togo, the Court held that France had breached Article 4 in not having criminal law provisions that would allow for the penalisation and effective prosecution of such acts, noting that criminal sanctions are the only effective deterrent in these situations.[90] In *CN and V v France*[91] and *CN v United Kingdom*,[92] the Court built on the positive obligations findings in *Siliadin* and developed its conceptions of "forced labour" and "servitude". In *CN and V v France*, the Court acknowledged the particular vulnerabilities created by immigration status, and stated that threats to report undocumented migrants to the authorities or send them back to their country of origin can constitute the "penalty", the menace of which can lead to labour being "forced".[93] In *CN v UK*, the Court emphasised the positive obligation to adequately investigate claims of slavery, servitude and forced labour.[94]

Although this line of jurisprudence is, as yet, relatively undeveloped, the Court has been consistent in its approach of focusing on the State's obligation to provide "practical and effective protection"[95] against Article 4 violations, by putting in place "a legislative and administrative framework to effectively combat servitude and forced labour".[96] Each of the specific jurisdictions examined in this chapter (the UK, Ireland and France) have introduced or amended criminal prohibitions on forms of forced labour in response to the *Siliadin* judgment.[97] The experience to date within the criminal law anti-trafficking framework shows how difficult criminal prosecution in these types of cases can be, however.[98] In Ireland and the UK, the

89 (2006) 43 EHRR 16.
90 Ibid [143]–[145].
91 App no. 67724/09 (ECtHR, 11 October 2012).
92 App no. 4239/08 (ECtHR, 13 November 2012).
93 *CN and V* (n96) [77]–[79].
94 *CN v UK* (n97) [69].
95 *CN and V* (n96) [106].
96 *CN and V* (n96) [108].
97 In the UK, section 71 of the Coroner's Act 2009 was introduced; in France, Articles 225-13, 225-14 and 225-15 of the Criminal Code were amended prior to the delivery of the *Siliadin* judgment; and, in Ireland, the Criminal Law (Human Trafficking) (Amendment) Act 2013.
98 Council of Europe Group of Experts on Action against Trafficking in Human Beings, *Report concerning the Implementation of the Council of Europe Convention on Action against Trafficking in Human Beings by Ireland* (26 September 2013), in particular at 58–61; *Report concerning the Implementation of the Council of Europe Convention on Action against Trafficking in Human Beings by the United Kingdom* (12 September 2012), in particular at 78–81.

efficacy of the deterrent provided by a criminal law prohibition where there is no accompanying adequate employment law route to redress for many undocumented migrant workers is questionable. As a result, employers are highly unlikely to be penalised through either criminal or civil proceedings for labour exploitation of undocumented workers. An Article 4 claim based on the argument that the current approach to "illegality" and the enforcement of employment law constitutes a failure to effectively protect individuals from slavery, forced labour or servitude would provide some welcome clarification on the scope of Article 4 and its potential to address access to employment law issues.

Conclusion

Migrant domestic workers face serious obstacles to accessing legal redress for breaches of employment law, caught as they are "between the excesses of immigration regulation on the one hand and employment deregulation on the other".[99] For migrant domestic workers in an irregular situation in Ireland and the UK, these "excesses" mean that access to justice is blocked by operation of law. The cases mentioned in this chapter expose the limitations of applying contract law, grounded in assumptions of capacity and consent, in the context of the employment of migrant domestic workers. For example, in *Hounga v Allen*, Ms Hounga was described as a "willing party" by the Employment Appeals Tribunal,[100] but she was also described by the Court of Appeal as "a young, illiterate person of uncertain age although with a good command of English".[101] While she had sworn an affidavit which she knew to be incorrect and lied to UK immigration officers, the EAT found:

> We do not believe that [Ms Hounga] on her own would have known how to go about changing her name, applying for a passport and visa and obtaining an aeroplane ticket to enable her to journey to the United Kingdom. We have no doubt that the plan was "masterminded" by Mr Edeniyi Aboyade-Cole and the Aboyade-Cole family in Lagos and [Ms Hounga] went along with what was suggested and did what she was told.[102]

To exclude Ms Hounga from taking a race discrimination dismissal claim in these circumstances raises serious questions of agency and consent, questions which arise even in cases in which the Court does not accept that the situation involved (or was very close to) trafficking. While the Supreme Court

99 Anderson (n5) 176.
100 *Hounga* (n46) [37], referring to [23] of the EAT decision.
101 Ibid [34].
102 Ibid [36].

ultimately found in favour of the migrant domestic worker in *Hounga*, the judgment was narrow and certainly did not address these more abstract issues. Its promise may lie in its treatment of public policy arguments, and in its recognition that cases arising from the employment context need not always be automatically excluded solely on the basis that an undocumented worker is involved, but it does not significantly change the law on access to employment protections for undocumented migrant workers. Overall, it is seen from the French example that legislators could make the choice to expressly specify that undocumented workers are protected by the basic principles of employment law, but they have not done so in the UK and Ireland. The Irish Employment Permits (Amendment) Bill 2014 shows that there is unlikely to be any radical rethinking of the normative framework in this regard. Similarly, the limited scope of the Employers' Sanctions Directive shows that the EU is unlikely to intervene further in this sphere.

From a human rights perspective, the Inter-American Court of Human Rights, in its Advisory Opinion on the juridical condition and rights of undocumented migrants,[103] found that the principles of non-discrimination, equality before the law and equal protection before the law require states to respect all workers' human rights once an employment relationship is established, even if the worker is undocumented. For the moment, in the European context, this chapter has shown that the most realistic avenue for a human rights challenge to the *status quo*, in the appropriate case, lies with Article 4 of the ECHR.

103 Advisory Opinion OC 18/03 (17 September 2003).

7 Traditions, Law and Practice: Migrant Domestic Workers in Lebanon

Gulnara Shahinian

Domestic work has been the subject of much research and analysis. Progress in standard setting has been made at both international and domestic levels: labour law coverage at domestic levels has been expanded in many states, and the International Labour Organization (ILO) Convention no. 189 on Decent Work for Domestic Workers has entered into force. Because of the nature of the relationships involved and the place of work (within the family unit) – a guardian of traditions, identity and class – domestic work exhibits many diverse and distinct characteristics, specific to its geographical, historical and cultural location. This diversity, in itself, presents challenges for human rights law reform. This chapter examines the phenomenon of *kafala*, the sponsorship mechanism used by states to regulate the entry, stay, work relationship and return of migrant domestic workers (MDWs). I will argue that the *kafala* system, as currently used, represents the transformation of a tradition of care and protection of the alien, to one of control over migrant workers. The chapter examines, in particular, the impact of *kafala* on the status of MDWs in the Gulf Cooperation Council states and in Lebanon.

The demand for MDWs has increased because of the increasing numbers of women employed outside the home, without the necessary social services structures in place to support the reconciliation of work and family life which includes the care of children and elderly relatives. MDWs can fulfil two goals for employers: continue the traditions of taking good care of elders and siblings; and provide cheaper and better services than are available from the State. For many families, employing an MDW is a sign of financial success and high status.

The *kafala* sponsorship system exists so as to control the entry and presence of aliens, and to ensure that there is someone who is legally responsible for the MDW during her stay, and responsible also for ensuring that the worker departs upon expiration of her contract and visa. In many states, the entry and work of a MDW is under the responsibility of the Ministry of the Interior, not the Ministry of Labour, reflecting a preoccupation with security and immigration control in laws and policies adopted. Debt bondage arising from high recruitment fees paid to employment agencies, insecure migration status and control by traffickers are the factors that enhance vulnerability to servitude for MDWs. In comparison with other forms of slavery, the exploitation of MDWs is difficult to eradicate because it is so deeply entrenched in the global labour markets of sending and receiving countries, and is not yet sufficiently understood. The majority of women migrate voluntarily with the hope of sending remittances home to their families, even if states seek to impose restrictions on recruitment to specific countries of destination. Unfortunately, these women frequently find themselves trapped in situations of slavery and servitude. Even if states have ratified the Palermo Protocol, the protections provided are not extended to MDWs and they are rarely recognized as victims of crime. Additionally, as was stated above, not all domestic workers can qualify under the prohibition of trafficking in human beings, but rather are victims of forced labour or servitude. International law's prohibitions of slavery and forced labour, however, are rarely enforced.

With ILO Convention 189 entering into force, states should now engage in a new process of analyzing law and policy frameworks from the perspective of the protection of human rights, revise their approaches to domestic work by extending labour law coverage and create strong monitoring and enforcement mechanisms. However, in addition to legislative and policy changes, it will be necessary to address deeply entrenched societal attitudes that contribute to widespread discrimination against domestic workers.

'Live-in' domestic work – a human rights concern

In the shadow of global domestic work industry, large numbers of people – mostly women and girls – find their dignity denied. They suffer invisibly in domestic servitude and slavery, contrary to the Universal Declaration of Human Rights (Article 4) and international and regional human rights treaty law. Defined in Article 1 ILO C 189 Convention: "domestic worker means any person engaged in domestic work within an employment relationship"; domestic work "means work performed in or for a household or households". Domestic work constitutes one of the largest yet least visible service industries in the world. The ILO estimates that between 4 and 10 per cent of the employed workforce in developing countries is engaged in domestic work.[1] For industrialized countries, the figure stands at between 1 and 2.5 per cent of total employment. The ILO also estimates that this workforce had grown by more than 19 million since 1995, when the global count of domestic workers was 33.2 million.[2] Increasing demand for domestic work is driven by an expansion in women's employment, without matching policy measures to facilitate the reconciliation of work and family life, and aging

1 ILO, *Decent Work for Domestic Workers*, Report IV(1) (2009), para. 20.
2 ILO, *Domestic Workers Across the World: Global and Regional Statistics and the Extent of Legal Protection* (Geneva: ILO, 2013).

populations coupled with a trend to move towards more home care for the elderly and people with disabilities.

Feminized poverty pushes women and girls into domestic work and makes them vulnerable to exploitation. Women, who often carry the burden of providing for children and for the elderly at home, suffer disproportionately from cuts to welfare programmes and essential public services in a situation of economic crisis and budget cuts. In many countries, the collapse of entire agricultural sectors, often linked to inequitable terms of trade, has also driven women and girls into rural–urban or international migrations. With the supply of cheap, desperate labour outstripping demand, power relationships are often so grossly unequal that the degree of exploitation endured by domestic workers turns on the whims of individual employers, with limited accountability.

Irrespective of the dangers and absence of protection in domestic work, women continue to migrate for domestic work, forced by economic and social pressures, the absence of opportunities in their countries of origin and the wish to create opportunities for themselves and their families. The migration of women for domestic work has rapidly grown and become one of the key factors in the ongoing feminization of migration. An entire industry of migrant domestic work has evolved, driven by a surging demand for domestic work in richer countries, stark global income inequalities and transnational recruitment agencies. Migrants, mainly women from Asia and Africa, are now the largest group of domestic workers in the Middle East and Europe.

Domestic workers are often "physically invisible" to the general public. As in other gendered relationships, domestic work is deliberately made invisible to public scrutiny as it takes place in the private sphere. A "private sphere" is socially constructed, where labour relationships are supposedly beyond state or social control. It is the same thinking that sought to condone domestic violence against women or children as a "private matter", rather than recognizing the crimes that such acts constitute. The domestic worker–employee relationship is frequently not accepted as a contractual relationship between parties with mutual rights and obligations, but rather an informal relationship, with the domestic worker perceived as a "family member", sometimes as an "alien" who is temporarily allowed to "live in" to provide some services, and usually in the context of a master and servant relationship. Depending on the whims of the employer, this can mean very favourable treatment or intolerable encroachment on the personal space and liberties of domestic workers. Research carried out by the ILO[3] shows that only 10 per cent of all domestic workers (or 5.3 million) are covered by general labour legislation to the same extent as other workers. By contrast, more than one-quarter – 29.9 per cent, or some 15.7 million domestic workers – are completely excluded from the scope of national labour legislation.

3 Ibid.

Between these extremes, intermediate regimes exist. Exclusions and partial coverage result in weaker protection for domestic workers in a number of important areas.

Owing to the stated vulnerabilities, domestic workers are often subject to unfair and exploitative labour practices. Some are paid way below minimum wage standards or not at all, while others are confronted with the arbitrary deduction or withholding of wages. Many domestic workers are expected to live with their employers, yet are only offered substandard or degrading living conditions. Live-in workers might be expected to work 16–18 hours a day, be always on call and forego regular rest days and vacations. They frequently face restrictions on their freedom of communication and movement. Physical, emotional and sexual abuse is also common. Because of the criminal and hence clandestine nature of servitude, slavery and forced labour, it is impossible to determine what percentage of domestic workers are actually victims of such crimes. Such crimes have in common that the victim is economically exploited, totally dependent on other individuals and cannot end the relationship at his or her own volition. In cases of slavery, as classically defined by the Slavery, Servitude, Forced Labour and Similar Institutions and Practices Convention of 1926, the perpetrator puts forward a claim of "ownership" to the victim that is enforced by custom, social practice or domestic law, even though it violates international law.[4] In servitude and slavery-like practices, no such claim to formal ownership exists.[5] This does not mean that servitude is a lesser human rights violation: the humiliation, exploitation and suffering can be equally or more intense depending on the nature of the individual case. In the case of domestic servitude and domestic slavery, the exploitation takes place primarily in or around the household of the perpetrators. In many cases, these phenomena go hand in hand with other forms of servitude and slavery. Beyond having to do household chores, for instance, a victim might be forced to work in agriculture, in the market or engage in prostitution. In some countries traditional practices create conditions for enslavement, such as early forced marriages when young girls are forced to be a domestic slave as well as forced into marriage. A precarious visa and immigration status, lack of familiarity with the local context, language and systemic discrimination make MDWs particularly vulnerable to exploitation, abuse and subjugation to slavery-like practices.

In the following sections, I will present some of the situations encountered during missions carried out as part of my mandate as UN Special Rapporteur on Contemporary Forms of Slavery.

4 (Slavery Convention of 1926), 60 L.N.T.S. 253, entered into force 9 March 1927. See also European Court of Human Rights, *Siliadin v. France*, Application No. 73316/01, 26 July 2005, paras. 122 ff.

5 See European Court of Human Rights, *Siliadin v France*, Application No. 73316/01, Judgment of 26 July 2005, paras. 122ff.

Domestic slavery, alongside other forms of slavery, still exists in certain countries of the Sahel region of Western Africa. The phenomenon has such a long history and is so built into the fabric of society that it is accepted as a "vestige" of old slavery, and a consequence of extreme poverty. It has in fact, however, traditional roots in a history of inequality and discrimination within the region. Situations that fall under the definition of slavery can be widely found in certain sectors of society in Mauritania, even though the Government has outlawed and criminalized the practice on three separate occasions.[6] Women and children in particular end up in domestic slavery. They must work from before sunrise to after sunset, caring for the master's children, fetching water, gathering firewood, pounding millet, moving heavy tents and performing other domestic tasks. Besides exploitative living and working conditions and frequent physical and sexual abuse, the specific nature of slavery manifests itself in the fact that the victim and her children are considered to be their master's property and can be rented out, loaned or given as gifts to others. Women are most at risk as they suffer triple discrimination: first as women, second as mothers and third as slaves.

In some countries, traditional practices create conditions for enslavement in domestic work, such as early forced marriages in Madagascar, Niger and Ghana.[7] In a 2008 judgment of the Economic Community of West African States Court of Justice, the Court ordered the Niger Government to pay compensation to a former domestic "slave" sold to her "master" at the age of 12 and made to work for him for almost ten years. Although slavery in Niger is criminalized, national courts did not recognize the plaintiff's right to be free from her "master" and marry another man.[8] Among the instances leading to domestic servitude is debt bondage, also referred to as bonded labour. Article 1 (a) of the 1956 Supplementary Convention on Slavery defines debt bondage as:

> ... the status or condition arising from a pledge by a debtor of his personal services or of those of a person under his control as security for a debt, if the value of those services as reasonably assessed is not applied towards the liquidation of the debt or the length and nature of those services are not respectively limited and defined.

Bonded labour, which has been historically associated with agricultural production and the landless poor, can touch entire families. In addition

6 See *Report of the Special Rapporteur on Contemporary Forms of Slavery, Including Its Causes and Consequences, Gulnara Shahinian Addendum Mission to Mauritania*, UN Doc. A/HRC/15/20/Add.2, 24 August 2010.

7 *Report of the Special Rapporteur on Contemporary Forms of Slavery, Including Its Causes and Consequences, Gulnara Shahinian – Thematic Report on Servile Marriage*, UN Doc. A/HRC/21/41, July 10 2012.

8 Economic Community of West African States, Community Court of Justice, *Hadijatou Mani Koraou v. The Republic of Niger*, Application No. ECW/CCJ/APP/08/08; Judgment No. ECW/CCJ/JUD/06/08 of 27 October 2008.

to the agricultural work performed by men, bonded labour arrangements sometimes extend to women who are forced to serve in the household of the creditor. In some cases, parents are forced to give away one or more of their children to the creditor, who often subjects them to domestic servitude. During my missions I have encountered similar situations while conducting interviews with female-headed households in agricultural communities in Ghana and Madagascar. Through the work of the mandate, I have also received many letters describing situations of bonded labour in Asian countries.

"Neo-bondage" may also emerge in the context of migration for domestic work. MDWs will often assume a considerable debt towards the employer or the agency organizing her recruitment and transport to cover the cost of the air ticket and recruitment fees. The domestic worker is then expected to work off this debt. In many countries, MDWs are not able to change employers as the validity of their visa depends on the initial employer's sponsorship. In addition, they might be blocked from returning to their home country, because employers or recruitment agencies withhold passports or return air tickets. They cannot leave their position before they have worked off their recruitment debt. With salaries often being as low as US$100–300 per month, this means that migrant domestic workers become bonded for long periods to a single employer, making them easily exploitable.[9]

Servitude and other slavery-like practices prohibited by Article 8 of the International Covenant on Civil and Political Rights extend beyond the specific instances recognized by the 1956 Supplementary Convention on Slavery and include a complex of other cases of economic exploitation in which the victim is so dependent on the perpetrator that he or she cannot leave the situation of exploitation. Dependency in this context can derive from a multiplicity of physical, economic, social, cultural, psychological and legal factors. While each factor may by itself not be strong enough to create the severe dependency characterizing servitude, combined, they create a net of dependency factors from which the victim cannot extract herself. Relevant economic factors include advance or deferred payment designed to increase dependency, payment that keeps workers below the poverty level, payment in kind only or prohibitions to freely change employers. Restrictions of domestic workers' human rights to freedom of movement and residence can also be indicators of dependency. In some cases, domestic workers are forced to live with their employers and locked in the house virtually 24 hours a day. This is not only a human rights violation, in itself, but also means that they are isolated, unable to report exploitation to the authorities and incapable of obtaining support from peers, friends or labour union representatives.

Economic and social human rights abuses – for instance, the threat

9 See Anti-Slavery International, "Forced and Bonded Labour in Nepal: Briefing Note" (July 2009).

of withholding food, water or essential medical care where the worker depends on the employer for these goods – can also place the victim in a position where she has no choice but to submit to exploitation. Physical and psychological abuses reinforce dependency and, in extreme cases, become the very cause of domestic servitude (rather than a mere consequence). A domestic worker may, for instance, be subjected to abuse so severe that a psychological dependency on the perpetrator ensues (a phenomenon known as the "battered women syndrome" in the domestic violence context). The victim may be systematically beaten, insulted, humiliated and belittled to force her to submit to excessive working hours, unpaid overtime on rest days, etc. In many countries religion is used as a tool of submission. I met many women who served the employer and his or her family until reaching old age, as they believed that leaving their master would be sinful. These abuses can reinforce other patterns of learned submission based on caste, ethnic or gender discrimination. Sexual violence, ranging from sexual harassment to repeated rape or the threat of trafficking into forced prostitution, is also employed as a tool of subjugation. In a number of countries that I visited, the state authorities had become involuntary accomplices to exploitation and servitude by allowing, or even requiring, employers to restrict the freedom of movement and residence of MDWs or systematically failing to enforce relevant prohibitions on slavery, servitude and forced labour.

Kafala – an extension of slavery status?

Migration provides an opportunity for women from developing countries to find employment abroad and to sustain their families. Many are able to find acceptable conditions to work and help their families by sending remittances. However, a sizable minority of women who emigrate in search of domestic work end up in domestic servitude. MDWs, specifically those who live in with the family of their employer, commonly have a particularly precarious residence status, making them dependent on their employer and hence easy to exploit. A number of countries in Asia and the Middle East have introduced the *kafala* system which seeks to establish control over the migration flows of foreign workers, often in contradiction of obligations accepted by states under international law. The historical and cultural connotations of *kafala* in the Arab world are diverse. Whether rooted in the Bedouin custom of granting strangers temporary protection and care, or practices adopted for the specific purpose of ensuring guardianship of a child, the core common trait is that of providing care and protection to an alien. In its modern manifestation, the core concept of *kafala* – provision of voluntary care and protection to an alien – has been erroneously transformed into an immigration sponsorship system that, through a set of controlling mechanisms, reinforces the vulnerabilities of MDWs and contributes to the revitalization of slavery and servitude.

In modern days, *kafala* is the term used to describe the sponsorship system that operates throughout the Gulf Cooperation Council (GCC) countries of Bahrain, Kuwait, Oman, Qatar, Saudi Arabia and the United Arab Emirates (UAE), and also in the Arab States of Jordan and Lebanon, to regulate the relationship between the *kafeel* (sponsor) and the migrant worker. While this characteristic of the system is no different from many other guest worker programmes operating throughout the world, the uniqueness of the sponsorship system's near total control over workers plays a large role in setting the GCC countries apart from other large labour-importing countries. Slavery has been legally abolished in most parts of the world, and the GCC countries were among those that took this step quite recently, in the 1960s–1970s. Similarly to Mauritania, in the Gulf States, slavery has been abolished in law, in part, because of its inconsistency with the requirements of Islam.

Kafala legally binds the immigration status of migrant workers to an individual employer or sponsor (*kafeel*) for the period of the work contract. Migrant workers under the *kafala* system are provided with only a temporary stay permission and are not eligible for permanent residence status or naturalization, irrespective of the quality of their work or the number of years worked. The right to family reunification is not provided for under *kafala* systems. Governments delegate responsibility for migrants' entry, care, stay and return to a local *kafeel*, creating a hybrid migration management system, jointly managed by the state and employer. The worker must be sponsored by a *kafeel* in order to obtain permission to enter the destination country and remains tied to this *kafeel* throughout their stay. The migrant worker cannot enter the country, transfer employment or leave the country for any reason without obtaining explicit written, notarized permission from the *kafeel*. In his or her turn, the *kafeel* must report to the immigration authorities if the migrant worker leaves their employment and must ensure the worker leaves the country after the contract ends, including paying for the return travel of the migrant worker. Often the *kafeel* exerts further control over the migrant worker by confiscating his or her passport and travel documents, despite legislation in many destination countries that declares this practice illegal.

Thus the core concepts of care and protection and generosity to be provided to the alien have been transformed into a sponsorship law, which allows foreign nationals to remain within a state in exchange for the provision of services. The *kafala* system "establishes" legal "ownership" over the migrant worker, contributing to a revitalization of domestic servitude and slavery. It is important to note that *kafala* is applied only to foreign (alien) migrant workers, thus reinforcing divisions between the local work force and foreign workers. Through its contract mechanisms the law gives the *kafeel* the power of legal "ownership" over the migrant, legally binds the worker to the *kafeel*, denying thus the fundamental rights of the worker, including the right to change or leave the sponsor, social and labour protection, access to justice and free movement, in contradiction of the fundamental human rights enshrined in international law.

Through the legal regulation of immigration status and specific advance payments in the *kafala* system, there is not only a legal assumption of ownership of the employer over the MDW, but also the creation of a psychological sense of ownership, as the employer buys/sponsors the worker. The system is not a progressive evolution in relation to abolition of slavery; rather, it reinforces the concept of "ownership", which is central to slavery and establishes discriminatory practices towards aliens. So the law provides the *kafeel* with all the powers attaching to the rights of ownership over the worker. Indeed, irrespective of the fact that slavery has been abolished in law, this new sponsorship system binds MDWs to the sponsor through legal contract, denies their right to change or leave the sponsor and nullifies their rights, protection and access to justice. MDWs are therefore trapped and, if they try to escape, risk being criminalized as irregular migrants.

Gender stereotyping also shapes expectations relating to domestic work, and has influenced the regulatory shortcomings that we have seen in international and domestic laws. Domestic work is not perceived as "real work". Consequently, those who are employed to perform domestic work are not given due remuneration or recognition for their work, and are frequently excluded from the scope of domestic labour codes. The experiences of domestic workers vary, but discrimination based on nationality, race or skin tone, cultural prejudices, as well as both verbal and physical violence, degrading working and living conditions, and "renting out" to extended family members, are commonplace. Most domestic workers have reported suffering from more than one type of violence during the course of their employment, and many are so traumatized by the experience that it negatively affects their ability to reintegrate into society upon returning home. The *kafala* system binds migrant workers to their local employer in a legal as well as financial dependency, from which they cannot withdraw unilaterally. Domestic workers cannot leave the house or employ of the *kafeel* without his or her permission, and thus without putting their immigration status in jeopardy, and potentially risking arrest and deportation. Within such confines, the system leaves domestic workers highly vulnerable to abuse or exploitation, without providing access to viable recourse or redress.

Lebanon: between opportunity and vulnerability

The case of Alem Dechasa, an Ethiopian MDW in the Lebanon,[10] who took her own life, received widespread attention after an amateur video aired by Lebanese television network LBCI showed a Lebanese man, allegedly her employer, physically assaulting her in front of the Ethiopian Embassy. The

10 See Migrant rights. Advancing migrant rights throughout the Middle East. www.migrant-rights.org/research/hearing-regarding-alem-dechasas-suicide-postponed.

tragic case of Alem Dechasa is not exceptional, or unique; its only uniqueness is in the fact that it became widely known, as now have other recent cases from Kuwait, Libya and Saudi Arabia. New technologies and social media helped to raise knowledge and awareness of these cases and mobilize responses. In other cases, international media and non-governmental organizations (NGOs) were instrumental in mobilizing swift international responses. There are, however, many thousands of other cases in which women MDWs, in particular those who 'live in', find themselves in slavery or slave-like conditions, when their road to employment and dignity turns into a road of violence and humiliation and a road to enslavement.

During the last decade, the situation of MDWs in Lebanon has been the subject of wide media coverage, and a number of important studies conducted by international organizations, international human rights organizations and independent experts have shed light on the conditions of MDWs in Lebanon.[11] Recommendations have been issued by UN human rights treaty bodies and the ILO relating to the elimination of forced labour, and the need to strengthen protection and access to justice for MDWs.[12] In 2012, the Ministry of Labour granted a total of 189,373 work permits, 143,899 of which were to domestic workers (representing more or less 76 per cent of all given work permits). Among these 143,899 permits, 62,448 were granted to Ethiopians, 32,846 to Bangladeshi nationals, 23,574 to Filipinos, 10,468 to Sri Lankans and 5,454 to Nepalese nationals.[13] It should be noted that these statistics do not account for "run-away" workers, who have had to leave their employers (often for reasons of abuse or non-payment of wages), and who, therefore, become irregular migrants, at

11 See, for example, E. Frantz, *Breaking the Isolation: Access to Information and Media Among Migrant Domestic Workers in Jordan and in Lebanon* (Open Society Foundations, February 2014), available at: www.opensocietyfoundations.org/sites/default/files/migrant-workers-information-report-20140223.pdf.

12 In 2005, the UN Committee on Economic, Social and Cultural Rights' General Comment no. 18 on the right to work, reaffirmed the need for State Parties to abolish, forbid and counter all forms of forced labour. It also clarified the need for domestic work to be properly regulated by national legislation so that domestic workers enjoy the same level of protection as other workers. In 2008, the UN Committee on the Elimination of Discrimination Against Women (CEDAW) recommended that Lebanon "speedily enacts the draft law regulating the employment of domestic workers" and supervises its compliance by employment agencies and employers. It also recommended that Lebanon establishes procedures to monitor and safeguard the rights of women domestic workers and adequately prosecute and punish abusive employers. The Committee called upon Lebanon to provide domestic workers with viable avenues of redress against abuse by employers. The Committee further urged the State Party to undertake efforts to ensure that domestic workers are aware of their rights and legal protections and have access to legal aid.

13 See ILO – Caritas Migrant Centre Lebanon *Access to Justice for Migrant Domestic Workers in Lebanon* (Beirut: ILO-Caritas, June 2014) Executive Summary, p.2, fn. 2. The full text of the Report, in French, is available at: www.ilo.org/wcmsp5/groups/public/---arabstates/---ro-beirut/documents/publication/wcms_247034.pdf.

risk of arrest, detention and deportation.[14] Recently, MDWs have begun to arrive in significant numbers from other countries of origin, including Burundi, Ghana, India, Indonesia, Madagascar, Nigeria, Senegal and Vietnam. Migrant workers are stuck between growing poverty in their countries of origin and job opportunities and demand for care workers in Lebanon though in situations of absolute control, violence and denial of rights. Irrespective of the difficulties MDWs encounter, they are motivated to stay in the hope that things will change and they can send remittances or take money back home, thus improving their financial situation and that of their families. Remittances from MDWs are an important source of income for their families and home countries.

The data above demonstrates that the demand for MDWs has increased in Lebanon, as elsewhere. Social services in Lebanon are insufficient, unregulated, expensive and not well managed. Additionally, many Lebanese prefer not to send their elderly relatives to care homes. Lebanese families, therefore, opt to employ a MDW, who is considered to be a lower cost than paying for care by social service institutions or Lebanese national domestic workers. It is also easier for an employer to monitor and manage the work of an MDW. For a majority of Lebanese wealthy and middle-class families, the live-in MDW has become an indispensable part of the household. Even families with a low to middle income have hired MDWs to help them in their households, benefiting from the potential to pay lower wages, and at the same time to ensure compliance with employers' demands, through mechanisms such as the *kafala* sponsorship system.

Kafala in Lebanon

Lebanon took a similar approach to the countries of the GCC, introducing the *kafala* system through a series of Government decrees and regulatory measures. As in other Gulf countries operating the *kafala* system, the residence permits of migrant workers, including domestic workers, are valid only while the workers remain employed by their employers or sponsors.[15] There is no right to change employer, and the dominant policy discourse is one of security or migration management, rather than human rights as such. The nature of the law and the impact on the human rights of domestic workers of the *kafala* system in Lebanon are no different from the system adopted in countries of the GCC and Jordan. The sponsors or employers

14 See Anti-Slavery International, *What is She Worth? An Urgent Call for the Protection of the Rights of Migrant Domestic Workers in Lebanon* (London: Anti-Slavery International, 2012), p.6, cited in Anti-Slavery International, *Into the Unknown: Exploitation of Nepalese Migrant Domestic Workers in Lebanon* (London: Anti-Slavery International, 2014), p.12, fn. 17.

15 See, generally, KAFA (enough) Violence & Exploitation, Policy Paper on Reforming the "Sponsorship System" for Migrant Domestic Workers: Towards an Alternative Governance Scheme in Lebanon (Beirut: KAFA, 2012).

are legally responsible for their employees. In rare cases, MDWs can transfer their permits to another employer but only with the express consent of the former employer. MDWs who "run away" from their employers usually do not possess their identity papers and residency cards (which show their place of work, employer's name and the duration of their visa). An MDW who leaves her employment without permission, for whatever reason, is immediately classified as an irregular migrant and is subject to arrest, administrative detention and deportation. The MDW cannot end her contract unilaterally and is legally tied to her employer.[16]

To date, experience has shown that the *kafala* system is marked by extreme harm to the rights and integrity of domestic workers. MDWs who are found without their passports or who have overstayed their visas are arrested and detained in a General Security detention centre for migrants and refugees. In visiting detention centres, I was able to interview migrant workers who had been detained for more than a year. Theft was the common charge made against domestic workers and many experienced violence in detention centres, as well as detention for extended periods without authorization. A new law codifying penal provisions for trafficking in human beings was adopted in 2011, and has led to prosecutions for the crime of trafficking in forced labour. Delays in the Lebanese criminal justice system, however, continue to pose obstacles to securing effective remedies.[17]

The exemptions for the safeguards of labour law found in other states are present also in Lebanon. MDWs are excluded from the safeguards of the Labour Code, Article 7 of which specifically excludes "domestic servants employed in private households".[18] Prior to 2008, complaints brought by domestic workers to the Labour Arbitration Council were dismissed, as they fell outside of the jurisdiction of the Council, because of the stated exemption in Article 7. In 2009, a decision of the Labour Arbitration Council of Mount-Lebanon found that it had competence to hear a dispute concerning

16 Article 32 of the Act Regulating the Entry and Stay of Foreigners in Lebanon and their Exit from the Country states that criminal sentences for unauthorized entry and stay in Lebanon range from imprisonment for 1–3 months, a fine and/or deportation. 5 Article 17 of the Act Regulating the Entry and Stay of Foreigners in Lebanon and their Exit from the Country stipulates that the State can detain foreigners to establish their identity before they are brought before a court.

17 Human Rights Watch, *Without Protection: How the Lebanese Justice System Fails Migrant Domestic Workers* (2010), available at: www.hrw.org/reports/2010/09/16/without-protection-0#_blank.

18 Article 7 of the Labour Code, Act of 23 September 1946, states: "Are exempted from the present Law: 1) Domestic servants employed in private houses; 2) Agricultural corporations which have no connection with trade or industry and which shall be the object of a special law; 3) Family concerns employing solely members of the family under the management either of the father, the mother or the guardian; 4) Municipal or government services in what concerns the employees and casual wage earners and journeymen, who are not governed by the civil servants regulations. These agents will be the object of a special law."

non-payment of the wages of a domestic worker.[19] Since then, several cases have come before the Labour Arbitration Council concerning domestic workers. These have been confined, however, to disputes concerning non-payment of wages, given the limited jurisdiction afforded to the Councils by the Labour Code. Despite incremental change, access to effective remedies, and to justice, continues to be a significant problem for MDWs in Lebanon, as reported in a major study completed by the ILO and Caritas Migrant Centre, which documents the cases of more than 700 MDWs.[20]

The main document that ties the employee to the employer and legalizes her stay is the contract of employment, where the obligations of both parties are outlined. MDWs generally have to sign contracts with a recruitment agency, pre-departure from their country of origin. The salary, duration of employment, numbers of days off and other terms of work are set out in the contract. However, this first contract, signed in the country of origin, is not recognized in Lebanon, and the domestic worker upon arrival has to sign a second contract, almost always written in Arabic. This usually has more stringent terms and conditions of work, and often compels the MDW to work at a lower monthly salary than originally promised by the agency at home. In January 2009, the Lebanese Ministry of Labour finally introduced a compulsory standard contract that clarifies certain terms and conditions of employment for MDWs.[21] While the contract was considered a step forward in the protection of domestic workers, it it also has major drawbacks and is heavily weighted in favour of the employer. As an example, Article 16 allows an employer to break the contract if the domestic worker "commits a mistake, acts negligently, commits an act of aggression against the employer, or endangers or harms the employer's interest or one of his family members". In such a case, the contract specifies that the domestic worker will have to pay the cost of her own return airfare. It does not set any standard of proof, or define what may constitute a mistake or a negligent act. Article 17 outlines the strictly limited basis on which a MDW can break a contract without incurring a penalty – for example, in cases of violence or sexual harassment. A domestic worker is not allowed to break the contract in the event of other types of mistreatment by her employer, such as food deprivation, verbal abuse, excessive workloads or sexual harassment that does not amount to physical assault. The weakness of the standard contract

19 Labour Arbitration Council of Mount-Lebanon, Petition filed on 10 March 2006, Chandrawathi vs. R.A.Z., Decision No. 261/2008 of 18 March 2008; Labour Arbitration Council of Mount-Lebanon, Petition filed on 20 March 2006, Rizalin Tumaliuan Agub vs. R.Y.H., Decision No. 90/2009 of 27 January 2009.

20 ILO – Caritas Lebanon, *Access to Justice for Migrant Domestic Workers in Lebanon* (ILO – Caritas Migrant Center, June 2014), available at: www.ilo.org/beirut/events/WCMS_247033/lang--en/index.htm.

21 The 'unified contract' was developed by a Lebanese Steering Committee, in cooperation with the ILO and the Office of the High Commissioner for Human Rights. available at: www.ohchr.org/EN/NewsEvents/Pages/UnifiedContractLebanon.aspx.

is further compounded by the failure of the Lebanese authorities to ensure that such contracts are enforced, leaving MDWs, again, outside of the normal protections afforded to workers, and without effective remedies.

Institutional mechanisms to regulate migrant labour

Two government bodies are primarily responsible for the protection of MDWs: the General Security Directorate (which falls under the Ministry of the Interior) and the Ministry of Labour. The General Security Directorate is responsible for controlling the entry, stay and departure of all foreigners, including MDWs in Lebanon, and the Ministry of Labour is responsible for regulating and monitoring the rights of all workers, including migrant workers. The Division for Inspection, Prevention and Safety and the Division for Investigation and Labour Matters investigate all labour law violations. Deficiencies in the institutional structures, delays and complexities in criminal law proceedings and the shifting of responsibility from the State to the individual via the *kafala* regulation mechanism, all contribute to an increasing vulnerability to slavery and to slavery-like violations of the rights of MDWs.[22]

In some instances, the MDW pays the recruitment agency to organize her recruitment or to acquire her visa and transportation to Lebanon. In order to do so, the MDW (and sometimes her family) has to take out huge loans in order to pay the recruitment agency. As a result of her huge personal or family debt, the MDW is under pressure to pay off the loan and is vulnerable to exploitation. Alternatively, the recruitment agency will finance the MDW's expenses and then expect the MDW to work off her debt by deducting money from her salary – sometimes with interest. The wages paid to the MDW are often so low that she finds herself in a situation of debt bondage.[23] MDWs in a debt bondage situation are unable to leave their positions – no matter how abusive – until they pay off the considerable debt they owe to their recruitment agency and/or employer. With salaries for MDWs in Lebanon being as low as US$125 per month, this means that MDWs remain bonded to their employers for a long period of time until their debt is paid off. Additionally, the employer can pay up to US$3,000 to a recruitment agency in order to hire a MDW. Employers regard this sum as an investment and are therefore keen to maximize their investment. Consequently, the employer believes that he or she has a great deal of ownership over the MDW.

22 See Human Rights Watch, *Without Protection: How the Lebanese Justice System Fails Migrant Domestic Workers* (HRW, New York, 2010), available at: www.hrw.org/reports/2010/09/16/without-protection-0# .

23 Article 1 (a) of the 1956 Supplementary Convention on Slavery defines debt bondage as "the status or condition arising from a pledge by a debtor of his personal services or of those of a person under his control as security for a debt, if the value of those services as reasonably assessed is not applied towards the liquidation of the debt or the length and nature of those services are not respectively limited and defined".

Travel restrictions

The inadequacy of the policy framework in countries of origin is matched with an exclusionary set of regulations in Lebanon, increasing even further the risks faced by MDWs. These risks are exacerbated by the imposition of travel bans. The theory behind these restrictive policies is that by making it difficult, if not impossible, for women and girls to migrate, the Government is responding to its obligation to protect its own citizens against abuse and exploitation abroad. Travel bans are not uncommon and many major labour-sending countries have used them to discourage women from travelling to Lebanon for employment as domestic workers. Governments that have imposed travel bans or restrictions include Ethiopia, Madagascar, Nepal and the Philippines. In Madagascar the ban on travel to Lebanon for employment purposes was introduced after the deaths of 17 Malagascan domestic workers in the Lebanon were reported in 2010, leading the Madagascar Government to fly home 86 domestic workers in March 2011. However, it is broadly accepted that travel bans are not effective in preventing domestic workers from migrating abroad, and may in fact create even higher risks as women and other migrant workers are more likely to become dependent on traffickers and smugglers. Indeed, almost two-thirds of MDWs in Lebanon are nationals of countries with full or partial travel bans in place. According to the Lebanese Ministry of Labour's statistics, in 2010, 65 per cent of the MDW permits issued were for nationals of countries that have bans in place, reflecting the ineffectiveness of such measures.[24] Whilst the decision to impose a travel ban is often taken in response to cases of abuse and deaths reported among young women working in the region, such restrictions fall short of addressing the real causes of exploitation and abuse of MDWs and, as many are gender specific, they also violate non-discrimination norms. The Governments of the Philippines and Lebanon have negotiated a Memorandum of Understanding (MOU) and Protocol for MDWs, intended as a step towards lifting the travel restrictions that were previously in place.[25] The MOU and accompanying Protocol, however, have been described by Human Rights Watch as a "band-aid", applicable only to a limited group of MDWs and not addressing the systemic, structural problems in place.[26] There is also a travel ban in place prohibiting Ethiopian women from leaving Ethiopia to travel to Lebanon as

24 www.ohchr.org/EN/Issues/Slavery/SRSlavery/Pages/CountryVisits.aspx. Mission to Lebanon, p.7.

25 See Memorandum of Understanding and Protocol, signed by the Governments of Lebanon and the Philippines, signed 1 February 2012, available at: www.poea.gov.ph/lmi/Bilateral%20Agreements/BLA_PH_Lebanon2012.pdf.

26 See "MOU on Philippine workers won't resolve key problems: rights group" 2 February 2012 (*Daily Star*: *Lebanon News*), available at: www.dailystar.com.lb/News/Lebananon-News/2012/Feb-04/162130-moll-on-philippine-workers-wont-resolve-key-problems-rights-group.ashx ax223HQFPEPrj.

MDWs. Reportedly, women circumvent this restriction by travelling first to Sudan or Yemen, before continuing on to Lebanon.

Societal attitudes: patterns of discrimination

Another important area that requires attention is that of societal attitudes towards MDWs. In many countries I have travelled to, there is a strong disparity between the laws and policies developed by states and societal awareness, acceptance and implementation. In some states the gap is so big that the laws and policies "in the books" have little or no relevance for those living in rural areas, far from metropolitan urban centres.

After the Lebanese civil war of 1975–1990, domestic work became the main source of employment for women migrating to Lebanon. Women from Ethiopia, the Philippines and Sri Lanka were the first to come in search of work. As Sri Lankan nationals soon became the majority of MDWs in Lebanon, the term "Srilankiye" was coined, to refer to a MDW. Domestic work began to be perceived as low-paid, low-status work that could only be performed by migrants. Today, the few Lebanese nationals employed as domestic workers earn four times more than their migrant counterparts, who are seen as second-class citizens. This working pattern stands in contrast to patterns of employment that have developed in other receiving countries (such as Pakistan) where migrant Filipino domestic workers, for example, can command higher wages than their national counterparts.[27]

Racism and discriminatory practices against MDWs are not uncommon. MDWs may often find themselves accused of theft or attempted theft by employers, who use such suspicions to justify imposing restrictions on the movement of the worker. Patterns of discrimination are internalized by both perpetrators and victims, who more or less consciously envisage themselves as "masters" or "servants". While this is most obvious with regard to the enduring patterns of domestic slavery, most domestic workers will be confronted with discrimination of some form.[28] It is important to note that the fact that a worker does not have her freedom of movement restricted does not mean she is not living in servitude or in a situation of forced labour. Many MDWs report restrictions on their communications and associations with family, friends and local communities, entrenching further their experiences of isolation and difficulties in accessing remedies for harms and rights violations endured. Physical restrictions imposed on movement are

27 See A. Shahid, 'Migrant Filipino Domestic Workers in Pakistan: Agency, Rights and the Limits of Law' (Chapter 8 in this volume).

28 See R Jureidini, *Migrant Domestic Workers in Lebanon* (ILO: Beirut, 2001), N. Moukarbel, *Sri Lankan Housemaids in Lebanon: A Case of 'Symbolic Violence' and 'Everyday' Forms of Resistance* (Amsterdam: Amsterdam University Press, 2009).

just one tool, among many, that serve the purpose of creating slavery-like conditions.

Confiscation of passports and identity papers by employers is a common practice, though prohibited by law. Although forced confinement and the withholding of passports are prohibited in the Lebanese penal code, limited information is available on criminal investigations or prosecutions for such crimes in relation to MDWs.

Slavery, practices similar to slavery and servitude are among the worst forms of exploitation that can result from trafficking; the victim's "consent" to such exploitation is immaterial to the criminal nature of the harm endured, and to the State's obligation to prosecute for such crimes.[29]

There have been numerous situations where MDWs in Lebanon received lower salaries than had been agreed, or where salaries were withheld for several months. Agents recruiting MDWs become perpetuators of trafficking when they deliberately deceive MDWs about the conditions of work that they will have to endure, or they engage in illegal practices such as debt bondage in order to exploit MDWs. There have been several cases of recruitment of underage girls for domestic work, despite attempts to restrict the travel of girls aged under 18. Recruitment agencies bear the blame for forging identity papers, and for charging exorbitant fees, which frequently result in debts not only for the girl concerned but also for her family. Where such debts are incurred, girls and women are often reluctant to return home unless they have secured sufficient funds to pay off such debts, and moreover, to replace the assets often disposed of by their family to pay the fees of recruitment agencies.

ILO Convention on Decent Work for Domestic Workers no. 189 and Lebanon

The ILO Convention on Decent Work for Domestic Workers no. 189 entered into force in September 2013. The Convention, in a comprehensive way, sets out the standards and provides for the protection of fundamental principles and rights at work, including: freedom of association and the right to collective bargaining; the elimination of forced or compulsory labour and child labour; and the eradication of employment and occupational discrimination.[30] It requires that domestic workers be protected against all forms of abuse, harassment and violence and that they receive fair terms of employment and decent living conditions. The Convention calls

29 Protocol to Suppress, Punish and Prevent Trafficking in Persons, Especially Women and Children, supplementing the United Nations Convention against Transnational Organized Crime, Article 3.

30 Press Release, International Labour Organization, 100th ILO Annual Conference Decides to Bring an Estimated 53 to 100 Million Domestic Workers Worldwide under Realm of Labour Standards (16 June 2011), available at: www.ilo.org/ilc/ILCSessions/100thSession/media-centre/press-releases/WCMS_157891/lang--en/index.htm.

for ratifying countries to take measures aimed at ensuring the equal treatment of domestic workers compared with workers generally, with respect to hours of work, overtime compensation, periods of daily and weekly rest and annual paid leave. A weekly rest period of at least 24 consecutive hours must be provided. A minimum wage must be set if a minimum wage exists for other workers. The International Labour Organization in its press release described the Domestic Workers Convention as "a breakthrough of great significance", because it is the first time that the ILO has set standards for an occupation in the informal economy, where workers are often excluded from wage and working time legislation and other labour law protections.[31] Similar to other states, Lebanon, if it is to ratify and fully implement the Convention, will have to begin a process of transformation of societal and official attitudes towards MDWs, as well as of the laws and institutional mechanisms required to manage and monitor implementation of the standards set by the Convention.

In recent years, the Lebanese Government has taken some steps to address the vulnerability of MDWs to abuse. These measures include a draft law on domestic workers, development of a standard employment contract for domestic workers and an emergency hotline to the Ministry of Labour. Another instrument to be mentioned is a Code of Conduct developed by the Lebanese Ministry of Labour, the Syndicate of Owners of Recruitment Agencies in Lebanon (SORAL) and Caritas Lebanon's Migrant Centre, in consultation with the Middle East Office of the High Commissioner for Human Rights (OHCHR) and the ILO. The Code of Conduct, a soft-law instrument, was launched in June 2013 and provides guidance to recruiting agencies on promoting and protecting the rights of MDWs. Absent an effective regulatory framework for MDWs in Lebanon, it is a compromise measure that seeks to provide greater safeguards for domestic workers and to induce compliance by recruitment agencies that are often difficult to monitor or to sanction.

Migrant workers greatly contribute to their countries of destination, as well as providing indispensable support to families by undertaking the entire spectrum of care work, from cleaning, cooking, elderly care to child care. There is a strong need to rethink policies towards MDWs, putting their human rights at the centre of States' laws and policies. The government is the guarantor of human rights for all those present within the State, be it permanent citizens or temporary migrant workers. It is essential that migration routes, from countries of origin to destination, are analyzed in full to ensure the elimination of vulnerabilities to violation of human rights of MDWs, from the recruitment stage to employment and to return.

Legislative and policy reforms are necessary to ensure compliance with international human rights and labour standards, and discriminatory mechanisms such as the *kafala* system must be abolished. MDWs must be provided

31 Ibid.

with the same labour protections as other workers, in compliance with the standards set by ILO Convention on Decent Work for Domestic Workers no.189. All forms of slavery, domestic servitude and bonded and forced labour should be criminalized and compensation mechanisms for victims established, to ensure their access to an effective remedy. At national level in Lebanon, there is a need for an overarching framework to bring together all the different actors, policies, laws, procedures and programmes for domestic workers. The National Steering Committee for Domestic Workers needs to be formalized to enable it to effectively coordinate all activities related to MDWs. Irrespective of its legal abolition, slavery in its different forms is a reality in many parts of the world and, according to the ILO, no country is immune to the phenomenon of forced labour. While the introduction and effective implementation of ILO and human rights standards is essential, states need to engage in a systematic educational process to raise awareness of rights to and primacy of standards of equality and non-discrimination. This education is vital to bringing about attitudinal changes and to breaking the invisible chains that condemn MDWs to modern slavery.

8 Migrant Filipino Domestic Workers in Pakistan; Agency, Rights and the Limits of the Law

Ayesha Shahid

Introduction

International labour migration has expanded across the globe creating new migration patterns within countries in the southern hemisphere.[1] Domestic service is one such informal labour sector where international labour migration is taking place. This large-scale transnational labour migration from Southeast Asian nations, in particular, is due to an increased demand for domestic and care workers in the service industries of countries in the northern and southern hemisphere. Domestic service has become one of the key drivers of female labour migration.[2] Hochschild refers to this type of migration as 'care drain', in which women from Third World countries leave their own children in the care of female relatives back home and migrate to care for the children and households of professional women in the West to support their own families.[3] The intimacy that often characterizes the relationship between the employer and the domestic worker makes her seem like a family member – not a worker. This sense of intimacy can be misleading, however, as the relationship between the domestic worker and the employer is characterized by a difference of status, resources and power.[4]

The author is grateful to Prof Shaheen Sardar Ali and Prof Siobhán Mullally for their valuable comments and feedback on the chapter. The author would also like to express special thanks to Prof Ann Stewart for her comments on the first draft of the chapter.

1 Amarjit Kaur, 'Migration Matters in the Asia-Pacific Region: Immigration Frameworks, Knowledge Workers and National Policies' (2007) 9 *International Journal on Multicultural Societies* 135–157; Silki Staab and Kristen Maher, 'The Dual Discourse About Peruvian Domestic Workers in Santiago de Chile: Class, Race and a Nationalist Project' (2006) 48 *Latin American Politics and Societies* 87–116; Nicola Piper, 'Enhancing the Migration Experience: Gendering Political Advocacy and Migrant Labour in Southeast and East Asia' (2007) *International Development Research Centre*, Working Papers on Women's Rights and Citizenship. Social and Economic Policy No. 1.

2 Glenda Labadie-Jackson, 'Reflections on Domestic Work and the Feminization of Migration' (2008–2009) 31 *Campbell Law Review* 67–90.

3 Arlie Russell Hochschild, 'Love and Gold' in Barbara Ehrenreich and Arlie Russell Hochschild (eds) *Global Woman: Nannies, Maids, and Sex Workers in the New Economy* (Granta 2002) 15–30.

4 Bridget Anderson, 'A Very Private Business: Exploring the Demand for Migrant Domestic

According to an estimate given by the International Labour Organization (hereinafter referred to as ILO), domestic work constitutes one of the largest, yet least visible service industries in the world.[5] The increase in female migration and the nature of domestic work constitute a major challenge to the protection of the human and labour rights of domestic workers. As domestic work is performed within the privacy of the home, it is frequently excluded from the scope of labour legislation. Human Rights Watch has stated that almost 30 per cent of the world's domestic workers are employed in countries where they are excluded from national labour laws, including weekly rest days, limits to hours of work, minimum wage coverage and overtime pay. Even when partially covered, domestic workers are often excluded from key protections such as minimum age requirements, maternity leave, social security and occupational health measures.[6]

Historically, performing domestic service for another's household has been an important way of earning a livelihood for women. Affluent families in both developing and developed countries engage both local and migrant women domestic workers. In recent years, Pakistan has become an employment destination for migrant Filipino domestic workers (hereinafter referred to as MFDWs), who are being employed by affluent Pakistani households, despite the presence of a large number of Pakistani female domestic workers available to take such positions. The employment of MFDWs is increasingly a marker of status and affluence, reflecting the racialized and class hierarchies that continue to infuse the sphere of domestic work, both in Pakistan and elsewhere.

Based on a small, exploratory, sample qualitative study of the lived experiences of MFDWs, this chapter addresses the question of whether international human rights and labour standards can provide protection and empowerment

Workers' (2007) 14 *European Journal of Women's Studies* 247; and Bridget Anderson, 'Just Another Job? The Commodification of Domestic Labor' in Barbara Ehrenreich and Arlie Russell Hochschild (eds) *Global Woman: Nannies, Maids, and Sex Workers in the New Economy* (Granta 2002) 104–114.

5 The ILO estimates that between 4 and 10 per cent of the employed workforce in developing countries is engaged in domestic work. For industrialized countries, the figure stands between 1 and 2.5 per cent of total employment. Based on national surveys of 117 countries, this report places the number of both men and women domestic workers above the age of 15 at around 52.6 million. This figure represents around 3.6 per cent of global wage employment. However, experts say that as domestic work is a kind of hidden form of employment and in most countries unregistered, the total number of such workers could be as high as 100 million. Around 83 per cent of these workers are women or girls and many are migrant workers. For instance, women's share of total domestic employment stands at 93.3 per cent in Brazil and 90.7 per cent in Ethiopia. ILO, 'Decent Work for Domestic Workers', *Report IV* (1) (2009), para. 20.

6 Human Rights Watch, 'Claiming Rights: Domestic Workers Movements and Global Advances for Labour Reform' (2012). A Joint Report by the International Domestic Workers' Network and the International Trade Union Confederation and Human Rights Watch. www.hrw.org/sites/default/files/related_material/2013_Global_Domestic Workers.pdf (accessed 25 June 2013).

to MFDWs. Drawing upon the feminist concept of 'women's agency', this chapter examines the extent to which law reforms, drawing upon evolving human rights standards, can support migrant domestic workers' capacity for agency, and more effective implementation of decent work standards.

Agency, resistance and domestic work

In this chapter the feminist concept of 'women's agency'[7] is used to analyze the complexities of domestic work carried out by MFDWs in Pakistan. It is argued that the realization of the right to work under labour rights and human rights standards can accord migrating women greater 'agency', and ensure these standards are effectively implemented. MFDWs have the capacity to use international labour and human rights standards as interpretive tools for demanding justice and enforcement of their rights. Among formal institutions, laws formalize women's rights and provide the framework that defines the environment in which women can exercise agency.

The concept of 'women's agency' is relevant to women's individual well-being and quality of life, and is central to women's capacity to play an active role in shaping institutions, social norms and the well-being of their communities.[8] Naffine considers the legal subject 'woman' as an agent struggling against gender inequality and negotiating women's social relations and identities.[9] Feminist legal scholars, while emphasizing the concept of 'women's agency', consider women's voices, practices and experiences crucial for analysis of the law. Littleton, in her work, argues that 'Feminist jurisprudence must take women's experience as central, and legal categories or doctrines as merely raw material – to cut and paste, stretch, arrange, and sew together to fit that experience.'[10] Cain argues that 'legal scholarship is not feminist unless it is grounded in women's experience'.[11] The concept of 'agency' has also been employed by other feminist scholars to highlight the

7 Agency can be understood as the process through which women and men use their abilities and take advantage of economic opportunities to achieve desired outcomes. The concept of agency reflects an individual's (or group's) ability to make effective choices and to transform those choices into desired outcomes. The concept of women's agency focuses on women's strengths, their resistance and how they strategize in order to cope with their own situations. It stresses the capacity of women to direct their own lives through individual action and choice.

8 Sabina Alkire, 'Concepts and Measures of Agency' in Basu Kaushik and Kanbur Ravi (eds) *Arguments for a Better World: Essays in Honor of Amartya Sen. Vol. I: Ethics, Welfare and Measurement* (Oxford University Press 2009); Naila Kabeer, 'Resources, Agency, Achievements: Reflections on the Measurement of Women's Empowerment' (1999) 30 *Development and Change* 35–64; Amartya Sen, 'Well-Being, Agency and Freedom: The Dewey Lectures 1984' (1985) 82 *Journal of Philosophy* 169–221.

9 Ngaire May Naffine, 'In Praise of Legal Feminism' (2002) 22 *Legal Studies* 71–101.

10 Christine Littleton, 'Book Review: Feminist Jurisprudence: The Difference Method Makes' (1989) 41 *Stanford Law Review* 751–766.

11 Patricia Cain, 'Feminist Legal Scholarship' (1991–1992) 77 *Iowa Law Review* 19–39.

positive aspects of migrant workers' experiences.[12] These agency-centred studies highlight the individual migrant's decision to pursue livelihood opportunities in the global labour market, and foreground the migrant's social and financial gains from international labour migration.

Emphasizing the concept of women's agency does not mean denying the exploitation and abuse that migrant workers face. Migrant domestic workers encounter abuse at the hands of their employers and employment agencies, while the receiving and sending states' laws and policies also discriminate against domestic workers. Various studies have shown that women migrants are often subjected to flagrant abuses of the right to physical integrity, equal protection under the law, fair legal process, freedom of movement and protection against forced labour.[13] Migrant domestic workers are often treated as export–import traded commodities whose labour is reduced and confined to slave-like servitude within the domestic work sector of receiving countries.[14] The term 'precarious worker' is also being used in the literature on low-waged migrants such as domestic workers and those participating in guest-worker-type schemes.[15] The exclusion of domestic workers from protective labour legislation and immigration laws and policies in a number of national settings has been described as enforcing a situation of 'legislative precariousness' for domestic workers.[16]

12 P. Gardiner Barber, 'Agency in Philippine Women's Labour Migration and Provisional Diaspora' (2000) 23 *Women's Studies International Forum* 399–411; Jane Marigold, 'Narratives of Masculinity and Transnational Migration: Filipino Workers in the Middle East' in F. V. Aguilar Jr. (ed.) *Filipinos in Global Migrations: At Home in the World?* (Philippine Migration Research Network 2002); Deirdre McKay, 'Identities in a Culture of Circulation: Performing Selves in Filipina Migration' in K. Robinson (ed.) *Self and Subject in Motion: Southeast Asian and Pacific Cosmopolitans* (Palgrave Macmillan 2007) 190–208.

13 Linda Burnham, Nik Theodore and Barbara Ehrenreich, *Home Economics: The Invisible and Unregulated World of Domestic Work* (National Domestic Workers Alliance Project, New York 2012); Racheal Parreñas, *Servants of Globalization: Women, Migration and Domestic Work* (Stanford University Press 2001); Nicole J. Sayres, *An Analysis of the Situation of Filipino Domestic Workers* (ILO 2005).

14 Bridget Anderson, *Doing the Dirty Work? The Global Politics of Domestic Labour* (Zed Books 2000); Bridget Anderson, 'Mobilizing Migrants, Making Citizens: Migrant Domestic Workers as Political Agents' (2010) 33 *Ethnic and Racial Studies* 60–74; Ann Stewart, *Gender, Law and Justice in a Global Market (Law in Context)* (Cambridge University Press 2011); Christine Chin, *In Service and Servitude: Foreign Female Domestic Workers and the Malaysian 'Modernity' Project* (Columbia University Press 1998); Rina Cohen, 'Women of Color in White Households: Coping Strategies of Live-in Domestic Workers' (1991) 14 *Qualitative Sociology* 197; Rosie Cox, *The Servant Problem: Domestic Employment in a Global Economy* (I.B. Tauris 2006).

15 Laura Fantone, 'Precarious Changes: Gender and Generational Politics in Contemporary Italy' (2007) 87 *Feminist Review* 5–20; Dimitris Papadopoulos, Niamh Stephenson and Vassilis Tsianos, *Escape Routes: Control and Subversion in the 21st Century* (Pluto Press 2008).

16 Bridget Anderson, 'Migration, Immigration Controls, and the Fashioning of Precarious Work' (2010) 24 *Work, Employment and Society* 300–317; Virginia Mantouvalou,

Without doubt the most challenging aspect of domestic work, especially for live-in workers, is the high risk of exposure to workplace physical, mental and sexual abuse. Yet domestic workers have demonstrated that they have the capacity to deal with such situations. Despite all odds and being subjected to discriminatory treatment, migrant domestic workers have been determined in their struggle to support their families and to achieve a better living standard for them. The decision to pursue livelihood opportunities in the global labour market – leaving behind young families for the sake of their better future – their dealings or negotiating skills with their employers, and the altering of gender power relations back home shows the courage, resilience and range of strategies used by domestic workers. Cohen's study of domestic workers in Canada refers to three types of coping strategies present among domestic workers: 1) 'External – mobilizing community resources and ties with people outside the labour situation'; 2) 'Internal – utilizing resources from within work situations'; and 3) 'Cognitive – altering the definition of the situation'.[17] Similarly Silvey, in her study of Indonesian domestic workers in Saudi Arabia, analyzes the transnationalization of women's migration and activism.[18] She looks at the ways in which activist groups in Indonesia construct and mobilize particular 'scale and spaces' in order to pressurize states for regulatory change. Silvey's study highlights how migrant worker organizations in Indonesia have transnationalized their scope by joining advocacy groups, using internet communication networks and international feminist forums to mobilize transnationally.[19] These studies explore the capacity and potential of transnational activism, particularly for migrant domestic workers who may otherwise be isolated in a privatized, domestic sphere.

In this chapter it is argued that listening to the lived experiences of migrant domestic workers dismantles the dominance of the 'passive victim' image, frequently circulating. International legal standards can strengthen the agency of migrant domestic workers, if socio-economic measures are taken to effectively implement such standards. Without being trapped into cultural essentialism and the rhetoric of victimization, this study seeks to contribute to a wider discussion about migrant domestic workers and the role of law reform and human rights activism in securing positive change and decent work standards in practice.

'Human Rights for Precarious Workers: The Legislative Precariousness of Domestic Labour', (2012) 34 *Comparative Labor Law and Policy Journal* 133–166.

17 Cohen, *supra* note 14, 197.

18 Rachel Silvey, 'Consuming the Transnational Family: Indonesian Migrant Domestic Workers to Saudi Arabia', (2006) 6 *Global Networks* 23–40.

19 Ibid., at 28.

The right to work and decent work standards in international law

The right to work is an individual as well as a collective right that guarantees the opportunity to perform dignified work under safe and healthy conditions with fair wages, affording a decent livelihood. It also provides for the right to organize, including the right to form and join trade unions.

At the heart of the concept of human rights is the belief that everyone should be treated equally and with dignity – no matter what their circumstances. In this regard, *universality*, *indivisibility* and *inalienability* are the main principles of human rights regimes along with *equality* and *non-discrimination*, which are fundamental to the right to work. This further includes protection against torture, inhuman or degrading treatment, elimination of slavery or working under slave-like conditions, which means that nobody has the right to 'own' another person or to force them to work under threat of punishment. These principles emphasize that human rights derive from a 'common humanity' and the 'inherent dignity of each human person' rather than from citizenship of a particular country. On the basis of these principles it is argued that human rights apply everywhere and to everyone – including migrants – and they cannot be denied or given up voluntarily. There is no hierarchy of rights and certain types of rights cannot be separated from others. It is further argued that the right to work has to be recognized not merely as a tool in the legal system but as contributing to a more humanized view of the work performed that also emphasizes the worth and dignity of labour.

Various United Nations (UN) and ILO human rights instruments place migration in a human rights context. Under the existing international framework, states are legally responsible for protecting workers from systematic violations of their rights by their employers.[20] The right to equal treatment before the law has been recognized by numerous international

20 A concern about the rights of migrant workers was first voiced in 1972 when the Economic and Social Council, in its resolution 1706 (LIII), expressed alarm at the illegal transportation of labour to some European countries and at the exploitation of workers from some African countries 'in conditions akin to slavery and forced labour'. In the same year, the General Assembly, in its resolution 2920 (XXVII), condemned discrimination against foreign workers and called upon governments to end such practices and to improve reception arrangements for migrant workers. Following a request from the Economic and Social Council in 1973, the Sub-Commission on Prevention of Discrimination and Protection of Minorities adopted a report on the exploitation of labour through illicit and clandestine trafficking in 1976. The report recognized that there were two aspects to the problem, namely illicit and clandestine operations and discriminatory treatment of migrant workers in host states, recommending the formation of a UN convention regarding the rights of migrant workers. This recommendation was echoed at the World Conference to Combat Racism and Racial Discrimination in Geneva in 1978 and in General Assembly resolution 33/163 on measures to improve the situation and ensure the human rights and dignity of all migrant workers.

instruments.[21] Other noticeable provisions include the right to work and free choice of employment (Universal Declaration of Human Rights (UDHR), art. 23(l); International Covenant on Economic, Social and Cultural Rights (ICESCR), art. 6(1)); the right to social security (UDHR, art. 22; ICESCR, art. 9); and the right to freedom of association (UDHR, art. 20(l); ICESCR, art. 8; International Covenant on Civil and Political Rights (ICCPR), art. 22). The International Convention on the Elimination of All Forms of Racial Discrimination (CERD) includes strong language requiring States Parties to prohibit and eliminate racial discrimination in all its forms and to guarantee equality before the law to all without distinction as to 'race, color, or national or ethnic origin'.

However, the inclusion of broad limitation clauses in these major UN treaties allows the space for States Parties to impose restrictions on migrants' entitlement to these rights. The CERD Committee has interpreted these limitation clauses to prohibit their application in a racially discriminatory manner of otherwise permissible distinctions between citizens and non-citizens. At the same time CERD's standards have been interpreted to include prohibitions on gender-specific and gender-differential forms of racial discrimination, making it a very useful tool for women migrant workers.[22]

When compared with the above-mentioned core UN treaties, the ILO offers substantial protection to migrant workers with respect to their economic, social and residence rights. The ILO Declaration on Fundamental Principles and Rights at Work lists eight core ILO conventions which set out universal, non-derogable human rights norms, applicable to all persons regardless of migration status.[23] In its preamble, the ILO Declaration explicitly mentions migrant workers as a group with 'special social needs', requiring 'special attention' in relation to the protection of their fundamental labour rights. The ILO Migration of Employment Convention (No. 143), in art. 8, stipulates that host countries must not restrict a migrant's right to free choice of employment for more than two years; that loss of employment shall not, on its own, imply a loss of residence permit; and that all

21 Convention on the Elimination of all Forms of Discrimination against Women, 18 Dec. 1979, 1249 UN Treaty Series 13. Convention on the Rights of the Child, G.A. Res. 44/25 (Annex), UN General Assembly Official Records, 44th Session, Supp. No. 49, at 166, UN Doc. AIRES/44/49 (1990). Convention Against Torture and Other Cruel, Inhuman or Degrading Treatment or Punishment, G.A. Res. 39/46 (Annex), UN General Assembly Official Records, 39th Session, Supp. No. 51, at 197, UN Doc. A/39/51 (1985). International Convention on the Elimination of All Forms of Racial Discrimination, 4 Jan. 1969, 660 UN Treaty Series 195. Convention Relating to the Status of Refugees, 22 April 1954, 189 UN Treaty Series 150. Protocol Relating to the Status of Refugees, 4 Oct. 1967, 606 UN Treaty Series 267.

22 *General Recommendation* XXV, *Gender-Related Dimensions of Racial Discrimination*, CERD Committee, 56th Session, reprinted in *Compilation of General Comments*, at 214 [hereinafter *General Recommendation XXV*].

23 *International Labour Organization Declaration on Fundamental Principles and Rights at Work*, 18 June 1998, 37 *International Legal Materials* 1233 [hereinafter ILO Declaration].

migrants who have legally resided in the host country 'shall enjoy equality of treatment with nationals in respect in particular of guarantees of security of employment, the provision of alternative employment, relief work and retraining'. Under art. 9, irregular migrant workers should enjoy equality 'in respect of rights arising out of past employment as regards remuneration, social security and other benefits'. Article 10 of ILO Convention (No. 143) widens the scope of the equality guarantee between migrants and nationals of the host state by requiring not only equal treatment but also equality of opportunity in respect of 'employment and occupation, of social security, of trade union and cultural rights and of individual and collective freedoms for persons who as migrant workers or as members of their families are lawfully within its territory'.

The other two most significant international legal instruments that address the rights of migrant workers are the UN International Convention on the Protection of the Rights of All Migrant Workers and Members of Their Families 1990 (hereinafter referred to as CMW) and the ILO Convention on the Decent Work for Domestic Workers (No. 189) and General Recommendation (201) (hereinafter referred to as the Convention). These instruments set out a very comprehensive set of civil, political, economic, social and other rights for migrant workers. Based on more than a decade of negotiations, the UN adopted the CMW in 1990 which sets out a very broad set of rights for migrants, including those living and/or working abroad illegally.[24] The CMW extends fundamental human rights to all migrant workers, both regular and illegal, with additional rights being recognized for regular migrant workers and members of their families. The CMW in particular has become a cornerstone of the rights-based approach to migration advocated by many international organizations and non-governmental organizations (NGOs) concerned with the protection of migrant workers.[25] However, the CMW has certain weaknesses; for example, the ratification level of the CMW is very low, it fails to address the gender-specific problems faced by female migrant workers, and it limits itself to a relatively vague and undifferentiated treatment of foreign domestic workers. It is also criticized for diluting the rights to free choice of employment and to social security as formulated in the ILO conventions.

In 2011, the ILO Governing Body adopted the International Convention for Decent Work for Domestic Workers (No. 189) and Recommendation (No. 201). This Convention sets the first global standards for the estimated 50 to 100 million domestic workers worldwide. For the first time under this Convention domestic workers are recognized as 'workers'. The Convention

24 The UN Convention on Migrant Workers and Their Families comprises 93 articles (compared with 23 articles of ILO Convention 97 and 24 articles of ILO Convention 143).

25 Margaret Satterthwaite, 'Crossing Borders, Claiming Rights: Using Human Rights Law to Empower Women Migrant Workers' (2005) 8 *Yale Human Rights and Development Law Journal* 1–188.

recognizes that domestic work is undervalued and invisible and is mainly carried out by women and girls (Preamble). It defines 'domestic work' as work performed in or for a household, and a 'domestic worker' as any person performing domestic work in an employment relationship (art. 1). This definition results in the exclusion of family members doing unpaid work from the scope of the Convention as well as those who are not in an employment relationship, including agency workers who are viewed as self-employed.[26] There is also a risk that in some jurisdictions, the Convention's use of the language of 'employment relationships' could be interpreted to exclude from its coverage those migrant workers without legal migration status – if their employment contracts are considered to be unenforceable.[27] That is, national jurisprudence varies on the effects of migrant status on the employment relationship, and the new instruments address this matter only indirectly.[28]

The Convention also obligates Member States to take measures to ensure that domestic workers, like workers generally, enjoy fair terms of employment as well as decent working conditions (art. 6), enjoy minimum wage coverage (art. 11), and are paid directly in cash (art. 12). The Convention also requires that members set a minimum age for domestic workers (art. 4), ensure that domestic workers enjoy effective protection against all forms of abuse, harassment and violence (art. 5), have the right to a safe and healthy work environment (art. 13) and to social security protection, especially in respect to maternity (art. 14).

Under the treaty, domestic workers are entitled to protections available to other workers, including weekly days off, limits to hours of work and minimum wage and social security coverage.[29] The purpose of this Convention is to improve the legal status of domestic workers through labour legislation, thus giving them access to a full range of protections and rights linked to decent work, including the right to organize.[30] Both the UN Convention on Migrant Workers and the the ILO Domestic Workers Convention are broadly consistent with existing international labour standards that are applicable to workers generally, and they build on the ILO's position that unless a Convention or Recommendation expressly excludes domestic workers, these workers are included in the international instrument's scope.

The ratification of the Convention is a precondition to protect and promote the rights of all migrant workers; however, the number of states that have ratified the CMW and the ILO Domestic Workers Convention is still

26 Einat Albin and Virginia Mantouvlou, 'The ILO Convention on Domestic Workers: From the Shadows to the Light' (2012) 41 *Industrial Law Journal* 67–78.

27 Adelle Blackett, 'Current Developments: The Decent Work for Domestic Workers Convention and Recommendation' (2011) *American Journal of International Law* 778–794.

28 Ibid., at 787. See also Chapter 4 in this volume.

29 Articles 6, 10 and 13.

30 Article 3, 2 (a).

very low. Nonetheless, states cannot exempt themselves from the duty of providing basic protection as they have ratified other core human rights treaties, and are bound by the Universal Declaration of Human Rights and, more specifically, by its principle of non-discrimination (art. 2). Moreover, it is argued that as other ILO and core UN human rights treaties are applicable to 'workers', they generally apply to all categories of workers. Thus, unless otherwise stated, all ILO Conventions apply to migrant workers, who should not receive differential treatment on the basis that they are not nationals of the countries in which they work.

The Philippines was the second country after Uruguay to ratify the ILO Domestic Workers Convention.[31] Although Pakistan, at the time of writing, has not signed or ratified the Convention, the express will to do so was reflected in June 2011 when all three members from Pakistan voted in favour of the Convention at the International Labour Conference. Moreover, Pakistan is a party to the ILO Discrimination (Employment and Occupation) Convention of 1958 (No. 111) and the ILO Equal Remuneration Convention of 1951 (No. 100). Therefore Pakistan is bound to extend protections available under these two instruments to MFDW; ratification and implementation of the Domestic Workers Convention would complement existing international treaty obligations and open up new opportunities for an integrated approach to human rights protection in all sectors of employment.

General Comments issued by the UN human rights treaty bodies have raised concern on the status of migrant workers. Of particular relevance is the General Comment (No. 15) of the UN Human Rights Committee in which the Committee made clear that there shall be no discrimination between aliens and citizens in the application of the human rights standards contained in the International Covenant on Civil and Political Rights. In August 2004, the Committee on the Elimination of Racial Discrimination also adopted its General Recommendation (No. 30) to eliminate discrimination against non-citizens in relation to working conditions and work requirements, to prevent and redress the serious problems commonly faced by non-citizen workers, in particular by non-citizen domestic workers, including debt bondage, passport retention, illegal confinement, rape and physical assault. The Committee further clarified that 'all individuals are entitled to the enjoyment of labour and employment rights, including migrant workers'. Since there are no express references to either domestic work or domestic workers within the Migrant Workers Convention, the UN Committee on Migrant Workers issued a General Comment in November 2010 to provide guidance to states on how to implement their obligations under the Convention regarding migrant domestic workers.[32] After noting

31 Ten countries have ratified the Domestic Workers Convention: Bolivia, Germany, Guyana, Italy, Mauritius, Nicaragua, Paraguay, Philippines, Uruguay, South Africa.

32 Committee on the Protection of the Rights of All Migrant Workers and Members of Their

that the term 'domestic worker' generally refers to a person who performs work within an employment relationship in or for other people's private homes, whether or not residing in the household, it observes that such workers face 'heightened risk of certain forms of exploitation and abuse'.[33] The Committee also noted that as most domestic workers cannot stay in the country of employment after the termination of their employment relationship, they may be unable to seek remedies if their employers have violated their rights by refusing to pay due compensation or have abused the workers. The Committee also raised the concern that while international treaties regarding human rights law and labour law amply cover migrant workers, many national laws categorically exclude domestic workers 'in ways that contribute to exploitative labour practices and limit avenues for legal redress in cases of violations'.[34]

The UN Committee on the Elimination of Discrimination Against Women issued its General Recommendation No. 26 on Women Migrant Workers in 2009.[35] The General Recommendation identifies the risks faced by women migrant workers throughout the migration cycle – at recruitment stage, pre-departure and in countries of transit, at arrival, during employment and upon return. Moreover, the Office of the High Commissioner for Human Rights and the Special Rapporteur on Contemporary Forms of Slavery, its causes and consequences have also issued reports and recommendations on domestic work.[36]

It is also worth mentioning here the Concluding Observations of the CEDAW Committee on Pakistan's fourth periodic report.[37] The Committee expressed its concern about the job segregation and concentration of women in low-paid and low-skilled jobs and the widening pay gap and lack of legal provisions guaranteeing the principle of equal pay for work of equal value.[38] The Committee in particular raised the issue of non-recognition

Families, *General Comment No. 1 on Migrant Domestic Workers*, UN Doc. CMW/C/12/CRP.2/Rev. 2 (30 Nov. 2010).

33 Ibid., at 9–14.

34 Ibid., at18.

35 For further details see UN Doc. CEDAW/C/2009/WP. I /R (5 Dec. 2008), at http://tbinternet.ohchr.org/_layouts/treatybodyexternal/Download.aspx?symbolno=CEDAW/C/2009/WP.1/R&Lang=en (accessed 25 March 2013).

36 For further details, see UN Human Rights Council, Recommendations of the Forum on Minority Issues at Its Third Session, on Minorities and Effective Participation in Economic Life (14 and 15 December 2010), UN Doc. A/HRC/16/46 (2011); Gulnara Shahinian (Special Rapporteur), *Contemporary Forms of Slavery, Including Its Causes and Consequences*, UN Doc. A/HRC/15/20 (18 June 2010) (this report includes a section entitled 'Domestic Servitude: A Global Human Rights Concern'); see also UN High Commissioner for Human Rights, Rights of Migrant Domestic Workers in Europe, at http://www.europe.ohchr.org/Documents/Publications/Study_Domestic_Migrant_web version.pdf(accessed 15 April 2013).

37 Concluding observations on the fourth periodic report of Pakistan adopted by the Committee at its 54th session CEDAW/C/PAK/Q/4/Add.1.

38 Ibid., at 8.

in the existing labour legislation of women who work in the informal sector (agriculture, domestic and home-based work). The Committee recommended that Pakistan as a State Party to CEDAW should prepare a plan of action for the protection of women working in the informal sector, such as agriculture and domestic work, in line with the Convention, and guarantee women access to social security benefits as well as ratify ILO Convention No. 189 on decent work for domestic workers and amend the relevant domestic legislation accordingly.[39] The UN Country Team to Pakistan also has raised its concern that no legal protection exists for workers in the large informal sector, including agricultural workers and home-based workers. Furthermore, labour inspection is not extended to the informal sector, as a result of which workers suffer with regard to exercising their rights, payment of wages, terms and conditions of work, and cannot access effective remedies at times of disputes.[40] The Philippines, in the interactive response to the Periodical Report submitted by Pakistan on Universal Periodic Review to the Working Group of the Human Rights Council, urged Pakistan to consider ratifying the International Convention on the Protection of the Rights of All Migrant Workers and Their Families as well as the ILO Domestic Workers Convention and the Palermo Protocol on Trafficking in Human Beings.[41]

International human rights standards can enhance 'women's agency', including in the sphere of domestic work, with the ILO Domestic Workers Convention potentially playing an important role in promoting more effective access to remedies for domestic workers, and in requiring states to take more seriously obligations of prevention and protection, so as to safeguard against risks of abuse. Goergen, in her study on Mexican workers, examines international human rights standards and argues that human rights principles safeguarding the right to work, equal employment opportunities and the dignity of labour are aimed at empowering individuals to enable them to assert their own rights more effectively.[42] Similarly, Khan examines whether the Canadian Live-in Caregiver Program pertaining to migrant caregivers and domestic workers is reflective of contemporary international efforts, through the ILO and UN, to ensure equality and effective social protection of migrant workers. These studies show how international standards

39 Ibid., at 8.

40 UN Country Team submission to the Universal Periodic Review on Pakistan, pp. 6 and 7 as discussed in the Office of the High Commissioner for Human Rights (OHCHR) Report. Compilation prepared by the OHCHR in accordance with paragraph 5 of the annex to Human Rights Council resolution 16/2 A/HRC/WG.6/14/PAK/2.

41 Report of the Working Group on the Universal Periodic Review Human Rights Council 22nd session Agenda item 6 Universal Periodic Review A/HRC/22/12.

42 Elizabeth Goergen, 'Women Workers in Mexico: Using the International Human Rights Framework to Achieve Labor Protection' (2008) 39 *Georgetown Journal of International Law* 407–438.

can play a significant role in changing laws and policies of the sending and receiving countries.[43]

Drawing insights from these studies, it can be argued that the range of international labour and human rights standards, now in force, provide a potential site for enhancing women's agency. Further, human rights law can support responses to discrimination and exploitation that do not re-inscribe women as mere 'victims' in need of protection and instead can emphasize women's *de jure* and *de facto* capacity to vindicate rights.

Domestic service sector in Pakistan: challenges to regulation and rights

Domestic service in Pakistan is the single largest informal employment sector in Pakistan, employing both men and women from lower economic backgrounds.[44] It is an unregulated, undervalued and unorganized employment sector.[45] The Fundamental Rights Chapter of the Constitution of Pakistan prohibits slavery and forced labour (art. 11), and safeguards the right to form trade unions (art. 17). Domestic labour legislation, however, largely excludes domestic workers. Only two pieces of legislation specifically include domestic workers within their remit. The Provincial Employees Social Security Ordinance 1965 sets out the employers' responsibility to provide medical care for 'domestic servants' in section 55-A. The Minimum Wages Ordinance of 1961 includes those employed in domestic work within the definition of 'employee'. However, the application of the Ordinance to domestic workers remains unclear, and no further steps have been taken to specify the minimum wages applicable to the domestic work sector; its application in particular to live-in domestic workers is unclear.

A Bill to extend labour protections to domestic workers was introduced in the Senate in 2013, but remains (at the time of writing) pending. The Domestic Workers (Employment Rights) Bill seeks to regulate terms and conditions of work, payment of wages and rest periods, as well as providing access to remedies through a proposed 'dispute resolution committee'. The Domestic Workers (Employment Rights) Bill would cover only the Islamabad Capital Territory (ICT) as labour-related laws are a provincial

43 Sabaa Khan, 'From Labour of Love to Decent Work: Protecting the Human Rights of Migrant Caregivers in Canada', (2009) 24 *Canadian Journal of Law and Society* 23–47.

44 Pakistan's crude labour force participation rate is 32.8 per cent. The total labour force is estimated at 50.79 million in 2008–2009: 78.83 per cent male and 21.17 per cent female. The informal economy accounts for more than 70 per cent of employment in the majority of jobs outside of agriculture. Women are increasingly joining the workforce but often in the informal economy which is dominated by low-paying, poorly protected jobs. In the urban informal sector 67.5 per cent of women work mostly as home-based, casual and domestic workers on low wages. Source: Pakistan Labour Force Survey 2008–2009.

45 Ayesha Shahid, *Silent Voices, Untold Stories: Women Domestic Workers in Pakistan and Their Struggle for Empowerment* (Oxford University Press 2010).

subject under the 18th Constitutional Amendment. The proposal, however, is that each province would follow with their own legislation once the bill passes for the Capital Territory.[46] The ILO, in its Decent Work Country Programme for Pakistan,[47] notes the challenges in implementing labour legislation in Pakistan, and in bringing domestic laws and practice into alignment with international standards. Such challenges are exacerbated in the informal sector of domestic work, where the reach of labour legislation and inspectorate mechanisms is non-existent.

In Pakistan, middle- and upper-class households employ women domestic workers, primarily Pakistani domestic workers. However, over the last 10 to 15 years, Pakistan has become an 'employment destination' for Filipino domestic workers. There has been a shift in the demands of employers in Pakistan, in particular the upper-class, affluent Pakistanis who now prefer to recruit MFDWs over local Pakistani domestic workers.[48] Employing Filipino workers has become a status symbol and a mark of social prestige. There is no doubt that in Pakistan the social, economic and political changes of recent decades have further deepened socio-economic inequalities in Pakistani society. Increased urbanization and faster economic expansion has fuelled significant job creation in the industrial and services sectors. This has led to the growth of the middle classes in Pakistan and an expanded powerful urbanized elite.[49] It is primarily this newly enriched and empowered elite that includes landlords, industrialists, parliamentarians, bankers, foreign diplomats, politicians and high government officials (including the President, and the former and current Prime Minister of Pakistan) who employ MFDWs. There are around 4,000 to 5,000 MFDWs working in Pakistan.[50] MFDWs, in most cases, are employed as domestic workers performing household work, whereas in some cases they are employed only as carers for either an elderly family member, disabled person or a child. MFDWs in Pakistan are live-in workers employed through recruitment agencies or, in some cases, through friends or family members who are already working in Pakistan. When compared with Pakistani domestic workers, MFDWs are well paid, receive

46 See Senate of Pakistan, Press Release, 'Bill Tabled in Senate to Protect Domestic Servants', 20 January 2014.

47 ILO Decent Work Country Programme 2010–2015: Pakistan, available at: www.ilo.org/public/english/bureau/program/dwcp/download/pakistan2010-15.pdf (accessed 1 June 2014).

48 This class comprises of businessmen, landlords, politicians and high-earning professionals, such as doctors, bankers, chief executives of multinationals and high government and military personnel.

49 Pakistan Economic Survey 2011–2012 estimates that there are now 30 to 35 million Pakistanis earning an average of US$10,000 a year.

50 This figure is confirmed by the Philippines Embassy in Pakistan and the Philippines Consulate in Karachi. It includes both documented and undocumented Filipinos in Pakistan. Only 700 to 800 domestic workers are in fact registered with the Philippines Embassy; the remaining numbers are unregistered.

better treatment and have more job security as they are more likely to receive written employment contracts.

In the past two decades the Philippines has sent approximately 1.5 million women migrant workers throughout the Asian region – the majority of them are domestic workers.[51] Taran and Geronimi comment that MFDWs are recognized as the 'invisible engine' of the Philippine economy (maximizing private households' productivity by freeing additional manpower into the labour market at a time when women have increasingly joined the paid workforce).[52] The Philippine Government has always appreciated its overseas workers by considering them as 'heroes and heroines of the nation'. This is not simply a tribute paid by a government to its people, but it is at the same time a way of providing some consolation for the difficulties and hardships these workers face in the absence of proper legal frameworks and mechanisms for their protection.[53]

Remittances from MFDWs constitute a significant source of the country's foreign exchange. Filipinos working abroad send home over US$20 billion per year. The receipt of remittances from MFDWs underpins much of the Philippines' labour export efforts.[54] A situation analysis conducted by the ILO in the Philippines has shown that domestic workers who migrate internationally are drawn from a different pool of labour from those who migrate within the country.[55] Those working overseas tend to come from urban areas, to be more qualified and to have prior work experience in different fields. Indeed, some have qualifications far superior to those required for domestic work. In these circumstances, the higher salaries offered abroad and the opportunity to remit home significant portions of the salaries received weighs in favour of migration for domestic work.[56]

Pakistan has signed an agreement with the Philippines Government to facilitate the recruitment of MFDWs – but domestic workers in Pakistan are not covered by domestic labour legislation or by labour inspection mechanisms. Enforcement and access to remedies, therefore, can often remain illusory, unless the worker can access the protections afforded through a consular office or the Embassy itself. Currently there are approximately 3,000 to 5,000 MFDWs in Pakistan. The majority, however, remain unregistered with the Embassy, and as such are more vulnerable to exploitation given the

51 ILO, 'Decent Work for Domestic Workers', *Report IV* (1) (2009) para. 20.

52 Patrick Taran and Eduardo Geronimi, 'Globalization, Labour and Migration: Protection is Paramount' (2013) International Migration Programme, International Labour Office, Geneva.

53 Ibid., at 8.

54 Denise Spitzer,'Transnational Transitions: Filipino Migrant Workers and Canada's Live-in Caregiver Program', (2011) SEARC Working Papers Series. Southeast Asia Research Centre, City University of Hong Kong,

55 Asha D'Sauza, 'Moving towards Decent Work for Domestic Workers: An Overview of the ILO's Work', ILO Bureau for Gender Equality (Working paper, No. 2/2010) (ILO, 2010) xi, 94.

56 Chin *supra* note 14 and Parreñas *supra* note 13.

limited reach of domestic labour safeguards. Most Filipinos are employed as *Mayordoma*, or head of the household staff, which also includes local female and male domestic workers employed as cooks, cleaners, chauffeurs, gardeners and security guards. The recruitment is usually undertaken by employment agencies and the process takes between six months and a year.[57] Before taking up employment, Filipino workers have to undergo a 15-day pre-departure training programme in the Philippines and attend an orientation seminar. For 350,000 to 400,000 Pakistani rupees, a local agent can ensure that a trained, English-speaking MFDW is legally brought to Pakistan. This amount covers the cost of the work visa, plane ticket and the agency's commission.

In preparing this chapter, field research was conducted through interviews with a group of 20 MFDWs in Karachi, Pakistan, and, separately, with Embassy of the Philippines officials, recruitment agencies and a small sample of employers in Pakistan.

Voices from the field: migrant Filipino domestic workers lived experiences

In the interviews conducted, MFDWs mentioned a number of factors that influence their decision to seek employment in Pakistan, such as poverty, unemployment, the desire to secure a better future for their children and other dependants, and the aspiration to seek better employment opportunities elsewhere, usually in the northern hemisphere. An opportunity to escape an abusive or unhappy intimate relationship was also cited as a reason for choosing emigration, one that was particularly pressing for women from rural communities where divorce and separation remain highly stigmatized. Despite often difficult working conditions in Pakistan, the possibility of returning remittances to families in the Philippines and providing the financial support needed for children's college education was attractive. Although women might be over-qualified for the role of domestic worker, the ability to improve the socio-economic status of families and dependants back home was often cited as a kind of compensation for the choices made. Several women cited a desire to move on from Pakistan, to the USA or Western Europe, building on contacts made and experience gained in the domestic work sector in Pakistan.

Employing migrant domestic workers and, in particular, MFDWs has become a new form of social stratification in urban Pakistan and clearly

57 The recruitment agency forwards domestic workers' CVs to the potential employers. After reviewing the CVs, the employer contacts the agency and informs them of the worker they consider suitable for themselves, then the agency sends the profile of the employer to the worker. If both parties agree, then the employer pays a fee to the agency which then completes all the paperwork and sends it to the worker who will then apply for the visa at the Pakistan Embassy in the Philippines. The initial visa applied for comes under the 'others' category, which is for a period of two years and is a double-entry visa.

reflects the public contestation over the boundaries of class hierarchies. This was reflected in the interviews with employers, one of whom commented: 'We have the means and resources ... we can afford to hire and pay them in dollars so why not enjoy better services.' Another employer, in a comment that points to the rapid commodification of domestic work, said, 'Well if we can buy foreign-made designer clothes and bags and import household goods ... similarly we can get the foreign maids to do our chores.'[58]

The capacity to hire a migrant domestic worker defines an employer's class status where the state elite and the upper-class, in their pursuit of a modern lifestyle, explain a preference for MFDWs against a background of widespread availability of Pakistani women and men to undertake such work.[59] Elsewhere, Williams has referred to an increasing 'discourse of consumerism and the commodification of care', one that may also justify – in the eyes of employers – highly demanding working conditions and expectations.[60] In this regard, Pakistan is no exception.

A significant difference between Pakistani domestic workers and MFDWs is that MFDWs are more likely to receive written employment contracts, a factor that was frequently referred to in interviews as an important safeguard and bargaining tool for domestic workers.[61] However, it was also noted that domestic workers will often accept less than the wages specified in employment contracts as employment opportunities in the Philippines are extremely limited.

Clause 15(h) of the job contract states that an employer must pay 500 rupees per hour for any overtime worked, and a monthly food allowance. Several interviewees reported delays and disputes in securing overtime pay, and even in receiving the agreed monthly food payment, which for many is added to remittances sent home to dependants.

MFDWs are also entitled to one month's annual leave, and to a return air ticket to the Philippines once every two years. Again, interviewees cited disputes with regard to such entitlements, but the ability to draw upon a written contract of employment to support the claim and to make a complaint to the Embassy were important tools in vindicating the rights claimed. One worker commented that she informed her employer:

58 Interview transcripts on file with the author. Sample interviews carried out in Karachi, Pakistan, in 2012–2013.

59 The global move since the 1970s has encouraged open markets and free trade, including not only manufactured goods but also the utilization of the services of migrant workers from developing countries. The affluent class in developed and developing countries depends on the capitalist market for the provision of services by transnational migrant workers.

60 Fiona Williams, 'Trends in Women's Employment, Domestic Service and Female Migration: Changing and Competing Patterns of Solidarity' in Trudie Knijn and Aafke Komter (eds) *Solidarity between the Sexes and Generations: Transformations in Europe* (Edward Elgar 2003) 205–218.

61 These are standard model contracts attested and provided by the Philippines Embassy. A copy of the contract is available on file with the author.

> … in the contract it is written and you cannot refuse my annual leave … but they don't read the contract … when I told them that I will complain in my embassy and to the agent only then they allowed me to avail my leave.

Employers interviewed, despite not always adhering to the terms of a contract, were still very much in favour of written employment contracts. Of particular importance was the requirement to give notice to quit: 'therefore, their chances of disappearing or leaving the job without prior notice are much less as compared to local domestic workers'.

The potential to call upon both the promise of labour rights in a written contract and the additional safeguards potentially offered by consular assistance from an embassy are important. For many migrant domestic workers, such protections remain illusory, however, or may come too late, invoked only as remedies for abuses already endured, but insufficient to safeguard against such abuse or to act as effective preventive mechanisms. In the interviews conducted in undertaking this research, MFDWs shared experiences of harassment at the hands of employers. G, who came to Pakistan 10 years ago, started her first job with a politically influential family in the province of Balochistan. While narrating her experiences she commented that her former employers:

> … treated me as a slave … They made me work from 5 o'clock in the morning till late at night … I was not allowed to cook food for myself and by eating spicy food I got ill … when I told my employer that I was sick she didn't take me to the doctor and gave me some medication herself … I told my employer that I don't want to work with her anymore … on hearing this she became furious and she refused to give me my passport … she told her guards to keep a strict eye on me so that I may not run away … after two months, I managed to call my cousin in Lahore who runs an employment agency … she informed the Philippines Embassy and that is how I was rescued…

Another worker, J, reported sexual abuse by the former employer when his family was away on holiday. The forms of abuse ranged from giving a body massage to forced sex. Upon her resistance, he threatened to fire her and to lodge a false complaint of theft in the police station. As J's passport was with the employer and because of the threats, she was too scared to leave the house. She informed another Filipino, who was working with her employer's friend, and asked her to report the matter to the Philippines Consulate. Upon the Consulate's intervention, she was able to get her passport back and left the job. The employer has now been blacklisted by the Consulate and can no longer hire any MFDW.

As noted, many MFDWs remain unregistered in Pakistan, with limited contacts with embassy or consular services. There is an urgent need for more robust enforcement mechanisms to ensure that employment contracts are upheld by both parties. This can be complemented by other measures, such as a registration campaign by the Philippines Embassy and Consulates. There is a need to undertake a registration process which would help in identifying undocumented workers, with protections against deportation to ensure that such workers are willing to engage with support services. Thailand and Hong Kong have already put in place registration policies and programmes for migrant workers, with some success.[62]

Collective organizing is particularly important for domestic workers, who are often isolated in domestic households. In January 2014, the first ever union of domestic workers was formed in Pakistan, by HomeNet Pakistan – a network of organizations supporting home-based workers – with the support and facilitation of the Pakistan Workers Federation. Domestic workers, drawn primarily from Rawalpindi, came together to form the first collective organization of this kind. Central to their advocacy agenda is legislative reform and effective legislative implementation. Filipino workers have formed a Progressive Filipino Society Pakistan, which is a network of various categories of Filipino employees working in both formal and informal sectors in Pakistan. This organization arranges various activities for Filipinos and also assists if they face problems with their employers. In Karachi at an informal level, MFDWs have formed their own association/network. Social events are organized, particularly around Christian holiday periods, and fund-raising activities are undertaken to support Filipino workers who become unemployed. Importantly, the association also liaises with the Philippines Embassy and supports workers in resolving difficulties relating to employment and immigration status. Collective organizing has been central to domestic workers advocacy globally, including in the development of the ILO Domestic Workers Convention. Trade unions remain weak in Pakistan, both in formal and informal sectors, although the right to freedom of association for all persons is constitutionally protected. The limited effectiveness of unions and of collective organizing reflects both the fragile nature of the state and its institutions, and the rapid and often brutalizing nature of rapid urban and industrial expansion.

62 'Employment Contract for a Domestic Helper Recruited from Outside Hong Kong', Immigration Department of HKSAR, 14 February 2007. In Thailand on 9 November 2012, a new Ministerial Regulation No. 14 (B.E. 2555) was entered into force improving workplace rights for domestic workers in the Kingdom of Thailand. Issued under the Labour Protection Act B.E. 2541 (1998), the Regulation applies to employers employing workers to perform domestic work which does not involve business operations. It aligns several aspects of the legislation with the Domestic Workers Convention, 2011 (No. 189) and Recommendation (No. 201).

Exploring possibilities for labour reform

The nature of domestic work necessitates the need for specific legislation, or clarification as to the scope and applicability of existing legislation, to regulate the relationship between employer and domestic worker. The Philippines Government has taken some measures to prevent abuses and exploitation of domestic workers – including pre-departure orientation seminars, the establishment of a Migrant Workers Loan Guarantee Fund, and the expansion of social protection mechanisms for overseas workers.[63] In 2007, the *Batas Kasambahay*, a Bill for the Protection of Domestic Workers, was introduced during the Thirteenth Congress. Six years later, the Act was enacted into law, as the Act Instituting Policies for the Protection and Welfare of Domestic Workers, 2013.[64] It is a landmark piece of labour and social legislation that extends labour rights, benefits and social protection to an estimated 1.9 million domestic workers in the Philippines. The Act also provides for the protection of domestic workers against abuse, debt bondage and the worst forms of child labour. It sets minimum standards for wages, hours and days of rest, and other benefits for domestic workers. Furthermore, it extends social security and public health insurance to the sector and provides for mechanisms for quick response to abuses and accessible means to redress grievances. The new law improves on the provisions of the Labour Code of the Philippines on Household Helpers and other related social legislation.

In Pakistan, a key challenge is to document and register domestic workers. The National Database and Registration Authority (NADRA) has issued registration forms to the residents of the capital city, Islamabad, on the orders of the Ministry of the Interior to collect data about people employed across the city as domestic workers. The form includes questions related to the employee's nationality, the nature of the work and other personal details. At present, this initiative is limited to the capital city and is unlikely to be expanded nationally for some time. The illegal, or often ambiguous, migration status of many MFDWs is likely to continue to hinder engagement with such initiatives, as the continuing 'deportability' of the worker extends its chilling effect, even in a context of serious risks of abuse.

Pakistan has a commitment under its own constitution, as well as under international human rights treaties, to provide protection to women from

63 For further details, see the Philippines Government's response in its report 'Written Replies by the Government of the Philippines Concerning the List of Issues (CMW/C/PHL/Q/1) Received by the Committee on the Protection of the Rights of All Migrant Workers and Their Families Relating to the Consideration of the Initial Report of the Philippines (CMW/C/PHL/1)' 2009.

64 The Act Instituting Policies for the Protection and Welfare of Domestic Workers (Republic Act 10361), also called the Domestic Workers Act. It was signed into law by President Benigno Simeon Aquino III on 18 January 2013.

all kinds of discrimination and harassment and to ensure dignity of labour.[65] The women-specific articles in the Constitution are generally articulated as a need to protect women, as women are bracketed together with children and other disadvantaged groups of society in need of special protection by the state.[66] As yet, reform has not focused on strengthening the socio-economic rights claims of women workers, with most attention continuing to be focused on gender-based violence and sexual harassment, rather than on payment of wages, security of employment and terms and conditions of work, as such. Against the background of the limited reach of state laws and of enforcement mechanisms, collective organizing and the diplomatic and consular support of embassies and consulates are more likely to yield transformative remedies.

Concluding remarks

Supporting domestic workers in collective organizing, through civil society organizations and trade unions, will be critical to securing further reforms for domestic workers in Pakistan. For migrant domestic workers, particularly MFDWs, registration and regularization of migration status is a necessary step to ensure that domestic workers have effective access to support and protection provided through the embassy and consular services. Where the enforcement of labour standards at domestic level remains weak, and the scope of labour legislation is limited, the advocacy of diplomatic and consular officials will be crucial to migrant domestic workers. The necessity for such advocacy, in the absence of effective domestic safeguards for domestic workers, is already recognized by the Philippines Government and its diplomatic staff in Pakistan and elsewhere. Bilateral negotiations and agreements can serve to fill gaps in rights enforcement. However, the trade-offs between access to employment, a desire to seek better opportunities overseas, and lack of opportunity at home will still push many MFDWs to accept terms and conditions of work that do not meet the standards of decent work. Against this background, the wider move to enhancing the rights of all domestic workers, including through ratification and implementation of the ILO Domestic Workers Convention, will be critical, so that domestic workers can enjoy the full range of human rights entitlements – legal, civil, political, cultural, social and economic.

65 Under Article 25 of the Constitution, everyone has the right to enjoy just and favourable conditions of work both in the private and public sectors. It is the duty of the state to ensure just and humane conditions of work, provide and facilitate employment, as well as develop a social security system which covers infirmity, sickness and unemployment.

66 For details, see Article 34, Article 35, Article 37(e) and Article 27.

Index

For Product Safety Concerns and Information please contact our EU representative GPSR@taylorandfrancis.com Taylor & Francis Verlag GmbH, Kaufingerstraße 24, 80331 München, Germany